African Foreign Policies

African
Foreign
Policies

edited by
Stephen Wright
NORTHERN ARIZONA UNIVERSITY

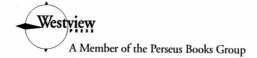

A Member of the Perseus Books Group

Copyright © 1999 by Westview Press, A Member of the Perseus Books Group

Published in 1999 in the United States of America by Westview Press, 5500 Central Avenue, Boulder, Colorado 80301-2877, and in the United Kingdom by Westview Press, 12 Hid's Copse Road, Cumnor Hill, Oxford OX2 9JJ

Library of Congress Cataloging-in-Publication Data
African foreign policies / edited by Stephen Wright.
   p. cm.
  Includes bibliographical references and index.
  ISBN 0-8133-2406-8 (hc). — ISBN 0-8133-2407-6 (pbk.)
  1. Africa, Sub-Saharan—Foreign relations—1960– . I. Wright,
Stephen, 1954– .
DT353.A428 1999
327.67—dc21
                            98-20761
                               CIP

10   9   8   7   6   5   4   3   2

Contents

v

Acronyms

AAA	L'Afrique aide l'Afrique (Africa Aids Africa)
AAPO	All Amhara People's Organization
AASM	African Associate States and Malagasy
ACP	African, Caribbean, and Pacific states
AEC	African Economic Community
AMU	Arab Maghreb Union
ANC	African National Congress
ANDM	Amhara National Democratic Movement
AOF	Afrique Occidentale Française (French West Africa)
APEC	Asia-Pacific Economic Cooperation
ASAS	Association of Southern African States
ASEAN	Association of South East Asian Nations
BAWATA	Baraza Ya Wanawake wa Tanzania
BCEAO	Banque Centrale des États de l'Afrique de l'Ouest
BDF	Botswana Defence Force
BDP	Botswana Democratic Party
CBI	Confederation of British Industry
CCM	Chama cha Mapinduzi
CEAO	Communauté des États d'Afrique de l'Ouest
CFA	Communauté Financière Africaine
CFAF	CFA franc
CILSS	Comité Inter-Etats de Lutte Contre la Sécheresse dans le Sahel (Inter-State Authority in the Fight Against Drought in the Sahel)
CITES	Convention on International Trade in Endangered Species
COMESA	Common Market for East and Southern Africa
COSATU	Congress of South African Trade Unions
DFA	Department of Foreign Affairs
DTI	Department of Trade and Industry
EA	(Department of) External Affairs
EAC	East African Community
ECCAS	Economic Community of Central African States
ECOMOG	ECOWAS Monitoring Group

ECOWAS	Economic Community of West African States
ELF	Eritrean Liberation Front
EPDM	Ethiopian People's Democratic Movement
EPLF	Eritrean People's Liberation Front
EPRDF	Ethiopian People's Revolutionary Democratic Front
EPRP	Ethiopian People's Revolutionary Party
EPZ	export processing zone
ERA	Eritrean Relief Association
ERD	Emergency Relief Desk
ERP	Economic Recovery Program
ESAF	Enhanced Structural Adjustment Facility
ESKOM	Electricity Supply Commission
EU	European Union
FDI	foreign direct investment
FEM	February Eighteen Movement
FERA	February Eighteen Resistance Army
FESTAC	Festival of Black Arts and Culture
FF	French franc
FLIC	financial low-intensity conflict
FLS	Front-Line States
FNLA	National Front for the Liberation of Angola
FNLC	Front Nacional de Liberation du Congo
FORD	Forum for Restoration of Democracy
G77	Group of 77
GATT	General Agreement on Tariffs and Trade
GDP	gross domestic product
GNU	Government of National Unity
HIPC	Highly Indebted Poor Country
HQ	headquarters (staff)
IFI	international financial institution
IGAD	Inter-Governmental Authority on Development
IGO	international governmental organization
IMF	International Monetary Fund
INGO	international nongovernmental organization
IORARC	Indian Ocean Rim Association for Regional Cooperation
IPE	international political economy
ISSC	Inter-State Committee on Security
KADU	Kenya African Democratic Union
KANU	Kenya African National Union
KPU	Kenya People's Union
LNG	liquified natural gas
LPA	Lagos Plan of Action

MFDC	Mouvement des Forces Démocratiques de Casamance (Movement of Casamance Democratic Forces)
MNC	multinational corporation
MNR	Mozambique National Resistance
MOSOP	Movement for the Survival of Ogoni People
MP	member of parliament
MPLA	Popular Movement for the Liberation of Angola
NAFTA	North American Free Trade Agreement
NAM	Nonaligned Movement
NCCR-Mageuzi	National Convention for Construction and Reform
NFD	Northern Frontier District
NGO	nongovernmental organization
NIC	newly industrialized country
NIC	newly industrializing country
NIDL	New International Division of Labor
NIDP	New International Division of Power
NIEO	New International Economic Order
NIIA	Nigerian Institute for International Affairs
NIPSS	Nigerian Institute for Policy and Strategic Studies
NISER	Nigerian Institute for Social and Economic Research
NNPT	Nuclear Non-Proliferation Treaty
NPKF	National Peace-Keeping Force
NPN	National Party of Nigeria
NRA	National Resistance Army
NRM	National Resistance Movement
OAU	Organization of African Unity
OCAM	Organisation Commune Africaine et Mauricienne (Joint African and Malagasy Organization)
OECD	Organization for Economic Cooperation and Development
OIC	Organization of the Islamic Conference
OLF	Oromo Liberation Front
OMVG	Organisation de Mise en Valeur du Fleuve Gambie (Organization for the Development of the Gambia River Valley)
OMVS	Organisation de Mise en Valeur du Fleuve Sénégal (Organization for the Development of the Senegal River Valley)
OP	Office of the President
OPDO	Oromo People's Democratic Organization
OPDS	Organ on Politics, Defence and Security
OPEC	Organization of Petroleum Exporting Countries
OPIC	Overseas Private Investment Corporation

OSCE	Organization for Security and Cooperation in Europe
PAC	Pan-Africanist Congress
PFDJ	People's Front for Democracy and Justice
PIT	Parti de l'Indépendance et du Travail (Independence and Workers Party)
PLO	Palestine Liberation Organization
PRC	People's Republic of China
PRPB	Parti Revolutionaire du Peuples du Benin
PRPD	Parti Revolutionaire du Peuples du Dahomey
PS	Parti Socialist (Socialist Party)
PTA	Preferential Trade Area
RDP	Reconstruction and Development Programme
RENAMO	Mozambique National Resistance Movement
REST	Relief Society of Tigray
RPF	Rwanda Patriotic Front
SA	Republic of South Africa
SACU	Southern African Customs Union
SADC	Southern African Development Community
SADCC	Southern African Development Coordination Conference
SADF	South African Defence Force
SANDF	South African National Defence Force
SAP	structural adjustment program
SPLA	Sudanese People's Liberation Army
SPLA/M	Sudanese People's Liberation Army/Movement
SSA	sub-Saharan Africa
SWAPO	South-West African People's Organization
TAMWA	Tanzania Media Women's Association
TGNP	Tanzania Gender Networking Programme
TPLF	Tigray People's Liberation Front
UDEAO	Union Douanière des États de l'Afrique de l'Ouest
UDI	unilateral declaration of independence
UMOA	Union Monétaire de l'Ouest Africaine
UN	United Nations
UNAVEM	UN Angolan Verification Mission
UNDP	United Nations Development Programme
UNECA	United Nations Economic Commission for Africa
UNEP	UN Environment Programme
UNHRC	UN High Commissioner for Refugees
UNITA	National Union for the Total Independence of Angola
UNOMOZ	United Nations Operation in Mozambique
UNSCR	UN Security Council Resolution
UNSS-Habitat	UN Human Settlement Secretariat

USAID	U.S. Agency for International Development
ZANU	Zimbabwe African National Union
ZANU-PF	ZANU-Patriotic Front
ZAPU	Zimbabwe African People's Union
ZAPU-PF	ZAPU-Patriotic Front
ZIANA/PANA	Zimbabwe Inter-African News Agency/Pan-African News Agency

1

The Changing Context of African Foreign Policies

STEPHEN WRIGHT

It has been four decades since Ghana became the first sub-Saharan African (SSA) state to gain formal independence from colonial rule. There was at this time tremendous anticipation of the role to be played by African states, both within and outside Africa, but during the 1970s and 1980s optimism gave way to pessimism. African states were relegated to peripheral players in the global system and were not particularly constructive in their intra-African relationships. For many, this remains the predominant perception of the continent; however, this volume will show that the late 1990s also offer new challenges and opportunities for African states to reorient their policies in positive and constructive ways.

Over this forty-year period of formal independence, there have been relatively few studies of African foreign policy and even fewer in a comparative vein. Many texts have focused on Africa and the global system, but fewer have focused on the African element of this relationship or on the intra-African dimension to foreign policy.[1] There are some obvious reasons for this deficit: difficulty in collecting information, a disinterest in African studies by many scholars who study foreign policy, and a caution on the part of some African scholars not to move too closely into an area traditionally considered by governments to be beyond the bounds of inquiry.

The foreign policies of African states are today being shaped by rapidly changing international and domestic environments to the extent that it is difficult to isolate purely "foreign" policies. These changes are having both detrimental and positive effects on policy options and are particularly impacting intra-African diplomacy. Indeed, the blurring of bound-

1

aries between domestic and international arenas has been so accentuated that such a distinction hardly exists.

The end of the Cold War has altered superpower and European Union (EU) involvement in Africa, again with mixed implications. Trends within the international political economy (IPE) have increased African marginality within a globalizing economy but have also offered potential flexibility in some policy options. A greater emphasis on IPE explanations of foreign policy exposes the rhetoric of formal policy and points to explanations for the limitations of policy options for most African states in the "new realism" of today.[2]

This volume of essays, then, discusses foreign policy at an important and critical juncture in the continent's development, coincidentally reinforced by the proximity to the new millennium. This introductory chapter identifies elements of continuity and, more important, change in foreign policy. After an initial consideration of traditional approaches to the study of policy, it introduces the current context within which African foreign policies are being framed, highlighting themes taken up in subsequent chapters.

These chapters provide case studies of the foreign policies of eleven SSA states representative of the diversity and complexity of the continent. The final two chapters focus on important thematic questions: the impact of regionalism on individual states' foreign policies and the possible direction for African foreign policies over the next decade.

Traditional Approaches to African Foreign Policy

The use of the term *traditional* is not meant to be derogatory. In this context, the word is used to refer to studies that focused on foreign policies in the early postindependence period or that took an approach that emphasized the state and its formal relations to the outside world, without utilizing more critical explanations that undermined the official, formal policy of the state.[3] Traditional approaches, still undertaken and with some validity today, focus on influences or determinants of policy, objectives, interests of the state, and formal policy toward global actors, as well as on traditional objectives of defense and development.

Much of the literature on African foreign policy before the 1980s could be classified under this heading. The main factors that shaped policy were given as the impact of colonialism, the role of resources, membership of international governmental organizations (IGOs), nonalignment, security and sovereignty, unity against apartheid, economic development, and centralized decisionmaking. It is useful to consider briefly each of these factors to get a more complete grasp of the influences on policy and also because some continue to have a degree of influence on contemporary policy.

Impact of Colonialism

Significant emphasis was rightly placed upon the influence of the outgoing colonial powers on shaping the foreign policy orientations of the newly emergent African states. These influences were all-embracing: political, economic, military, and cultural. For many of the francophone countries, as exemplified by Senegal (Chapter 8), the influence of France was critical in understanding the shaping of policy options. For many anglophone and lusophone countries, the influence was great also, especially among the latter such as Angola (Chapter 2), in pushing countries to challenge the ideological content of the policies of the former colonial power.[4] The early postcolonial role of these former metropoles altered over recent years, though France's influence has remained more consistent over its bloc of former colonies.

Role of Resources

In the early postindependence period, there was considerable optimism that the resource base of Africa—particularly in minerals—would provide a foundation for continental pride and status and would give individual countries the economic capability to project a strong foreign policy within the continent and overseas. This optimism was based on an assumption that these resources would facilitate diversification into other key economic areas and so strengthen policy options further. Ali Mazrui went so far as to predict that by the mid-1990s, Nigeria would "probably be more influential internationally than either Britain or France."[5] Although there are some examples to suggest resources can influence policy options—as with oil diplomacy (for a limited period) in Nigeria (Chapter 7), gold diplomacy in South Africa, or diamond diplomacy in Botswana (Chapter 4)—the resource base of Africa has not brought it significant leverage within the global economy. This is partly because of deteriorating terms of trade and a failure to diversify but also because resources are no longer critical elements of the developing globalized economy.

Coordination Within IGOs

African states placed an emphasis on the active membership of IGOs, such as the United Nations, the Commonwealth, the Nonaligned Movement (NAM), the Organization of African Unity (OAU), and the Group of 77 (G77), as exemplified in most chapters presented here but especially those on Tanzania (Chapter 10) and Zimbabwe (Chapter 11). By pooling energies within such organizations, states were able to project a presence quite beyond what one would expect from their individual capabilities.

With almost one-third of the voting bloc within the UN General Assembly (more when allied to others in the G77), African states had some success in pushing their policy agendas.

However, this presence should be distinguished from real capability. Bloc voting in these IGOs provided an appearance of capability within foreign policy, but the reality was that states had far less influence, as discussed in detail in the study of Nigeria (Chapter 7). The failure to be able to bring economic muscle to bear in North-South deliberations meant that critical decisions were made by others outside the continent.

For most African states, perhaps excluding Tanzania and Zimbabwe as explained in subsequent chapters, the NAM was of marginal utility, and it tended to become a focus of policy attention only at times of summit meetings. The OAU proved more significant in tackling intra-African tensions and helping to formulate regional policies, but even here the organization has struggled to materially impact the policies of individual states, as Olufemi Babarinde points out in Chapter 12.

Nonalignment

Nonalignment proved to be one of the stronger rhetorical policies of states, exemplified by Tanzania (Chapter 10), in an attempt to define some African space in the Cold War conflict.[6] Nonalignment provided some meaning to efforts to find a place for Africa outside the Cold War, but as a policy it was impossible to fully implement, essentially because of economic weakness and "alignment." One foreign policy strategy was to play off the superpowers against each other, but it is arguable whether many states truly had the capability to do that.

There is a strong case to be made that superpower disinterest in most of Africa has been fairly constant since the mid-1960s (with an exception for Angola/Southern Africa and Ethiopia/the Horn[7]). Most states, such as Kenya (Chapter 6), simply became aligned to one or another superpower in terms of foreign aid and military assistance. Tanzania was outspokenly "nonaligned" and "socialist," but in reality it was little of the sort.

Nonalignment today has little traditional relevance in the face of the Russian withdrawal from the continent and the erosion of purely ideological divisions from the global arena, and African states appear to use the term primarily to designate an attempt to steer clear of externally enforced economic restructuring—unfortunately, without much success.

Security and Sovereignty

The desire to maintain secure borders and sovereign control of policy has remained consistent within the continent, though the ability to do so has often been weak and appears to be weakening further. In 1964 states tried to forestall any major revision of borders by agreeing within the OAU to respect those borders existing at independence. These agreements officially held for thirty years, until Eritrea's independence in May 1993 was formally accepted by OAU members (Chapter 5). States officially pursued formal foreign policies as sovereign entities and used their policies toward neighbors to promote their sovereignty, security, and survival—but always with an element of uncertainty as to how successfully such policies could be pursued.

Such strategies were also common in other developing regions. It is interesting to note the relevance to Africa of these comments on the Asian arena: "One is struck by the remarkable tenacity of states as territorial entities. There has not been the large-scale fragmentation, conquest, or fusion of territorial units that many observers had predicted on the basis of the rather artificial nature of many of the colonial boundaries. The durability of ruling elites has also been marked."[8]

Today, the porosity of borders is well documented, and with this and other pressures, many states have a diminished security capability and are unable to police their borders. However, many policymakers couch their policies in the pursuit of traditional notions of state sovereignty, without always recognizing that the real powers of the state to furnish security are limited.

Unity Against Apartheid South Africa

Opposition to apartheid policies carried out in the Republic of South Africa (SA) provided something akin to a reflex unity in African foreign policy, especially within the Front-Line States (FLS) as shown in the case studies of Angola, Botswana, Tanzania, and Zimbabwe in this volume. This consensus on SA helped to maintain African cohesion in organizations such as the UN, the OAU, and the Commonwealth, and it also was effectively used to lobby for economic assistance, particularly by the FLS and within the Southern African Development Coordination Conference (SADCC). On closer inspection, this unity had weaknesses as many states in the region had little choice but to maintain strong trade links with the republic. Despite the ambitions of SADCC to reorient political and economic policy away from SA, overall trade between SADCC countries and SA increased during the organization's existence.

A postapartheid era in South Africa is a most welcome change. However, this change forces an interesting policy predicament in terms of how African states relate politically, economically, and strategically to the new South Africa, by far the most industrialized power in SSA (Chapter 9). For neighboring states, the shift of investment to SA is raising new economic challenges and opportunities for the Southern African Development Community (SADC), whereas the prospects that regional ethnic, linguistic, and religious pressures will mount cannot be totally discounted. As seen in Paul-Henri Bischoff and Roger Southall's chapter on South Africa, there are also questions within that country on how to deal best with its neighbors and Africa as a whole in the postapartheid era.

Economic Development

Within the context of immediate postindependent politics and neocolonial linkages, most states discussed in this volume can be identified as pursuing broadly similar economic development strategies, normally in tune with the wishes of their Western benefactors. Attempts to promote what was defined as "modernization" were widespread, with less resistance than appeared by the 1980s. Such a foreign economic policy often dovetailed with considerations of security (military and economic) and the desire for rapid development, but, as mentioned earlier, it often ran counter to espoused nonalignment policies.

Such strategies became increasingly questioned within Africa when they failed to produce "development." The oil crises of the 1970s led to and were compounded by the emerging debt crises and reschedulings of the 1980s and 1990s and the widespread implementation of structural adjustment programs (SAPs), drawn up by the International Monetary Fund (IMF) and World Bank, that overtly shifted the emphasis of policymaking outside the respective states.

Decisionmaking in Foreign Policy

Traditional approaches to the study of foreign policy focused upon a small, elite group of foreign policy decisionmakers. Many times a president or military head of state was considered the only decisionmaker, with one- or no-party state systems reinforcing the centralization of policy decisionmaking.[9] The difficulty in gathering data has itself reinforced this perception of the policymaking procedure.

More recent approaches, though recognizing that individual leaders still hold considerable sway over policy decisions, have also considered bureaucratic influences on policy, drawing in the role of diplomatic service personnel and various ministries,[10] and have also recognized the existence of economic groups influencing policy outcomes, not least of which those connected to the international financial institutions (IFIs).

Contemporary Influences on African Foreign Policies

It is difficult to point to one single event that has transformed the characteristics of African foreign policies during the 1990s, and it is not easy to provide, with absolute precision and confidence, a year that is a watershed in changing policy procedures. Indeed, after reading the case studies in this volume, one could provocatively argue that foreign policies in the late 1990s display elements of continuity as well as change.

Arguments could be made to justify this continuity. First, Africa has long been a marginal continent, through the slavery and colonial periods, at the periphery of the strengthening global capitalist economy. As Adebayo Adedeji argues, today's marginalization is not new but is significant only as a matter of degree. Adedeji explains his conception of marginalization as "a process of devaluation which results in ever diminishing freedom to act and space to move within the international economic environment."[11]

Second, most African states, as typified in this volume, have never had much capability in their foreign policies, and their role in IGOs, for example, falsely exaggerated their influence. The Cold War played to their advantage because neither superpower wished to embarrass and expose these states' weaknesses for fear of nudging them into the other camp. And third, one could argue that the artificiality of African states, such as those in the Horn of Africa, has always made their borders and sovereignty somewhat suspect. The ability of states, in a classic "realist" sense, to defend themselves and project their influence on neighbors has been ambiguous. So, the weakness of states today is arguably more a matter of continuity than novelty.

Having stated some reservations regarding the concept that the 1990s environment within which policy is made is completely new, I can point to four critical changes within the domestic and international environments, repeatedly raised in subsequent chapters, that offer distinct reference points for African states today. These are the end of the Cold War, the pressures of liberalization and democratization, the changing character of the global economy, and the debate over an "African agenda."

End of the Cold War

Although the end of the Cold War is normally marked by the fall of the Berlin Wall (1989), the unification of Germany (1990), or the disappearance of the USSR (1991), for Africa the end could be said to have come sooner, with the Namibian agreement of 1988. The withdrawal of Cuban troops and the agreement paving the way for Namibian independence signified the end of an era of superpower competition in the continent. With Russia essentially gone from Africa today and the United States displaying disinterest, African states find it difficult to engage these powers and seek concessions from them.[12]

The New International Division of Power (NIDP), as it is often referred to, relegates Africa to marginality in the global security stakes. Liberia,

Ethiopia, and Sierra Leone imploded in the 1990s with only passing direct interest evidenced by the United States. The U.S. debacle in Somalia, combined with the changing domestic political landscape within the United States favoring greater isolationism, has further eroded Washington's direct involvement in Africa.

Such a change presents new opportunities for African states to pursue more autonomous foreign policies, especially within their own subregions, though sometimes still in line with U.S. or European wishes.[13] Potential regional powers, such as Nigeria and South Africa, have more scope to develop stronger regional presences with less fear of outside intervention. Conversely, weaker states have less scope beyond their regions and might become virtual nonplayers even inside their own regions.

Liberalization and Democratization

The global sweep of liberalization, instigating economic reform across Central and Eastern Europe and into China, and the pressures for democratization have had uneven impacts on African states.[14] Many, such as Kenya and Zimbabwe, have struggled to implement reforms, whereas others, such as Nigeria, appear to have failed, possibly temporarily. Where moderate reforms have taken root, as in Benin (Chapter 3) and Senegal (Chapter 8), the framework for foreign policy has been expanded. Parliaments, pressure groups, civil society groups, and nongovernmental organizations (NGOs) have become factors in the foreign policy equation, attempting to shift decisionmaking away from a purely centralized command post (an office of the president). The "quality" of political leadership has also become important. One can begin to talk about multiple (and competing) foreign policies, through which different factions pursue their own goals. In countries where political elites have resisted change, political conditionalities—democracy and human rights—become important levers used by IFIs and Western powers to shape domestic and foreign policies.

Thus far, Britain and France have continued trade relations with their former colonies and have not allowed the failure to democratize in these states to hamper that trade. The French remain patient with Côte d'Ivoire, and the British are tolerant with Kenya and Nigeria. What is evident, however, is that liberalization elsewhere is distracting interest away from Africa. The years since 1990, for example, have witnessed disinvestment by British and French companies in Africa and greater attention paid by EU members to opportunities in Central and Eastern Europe. Failure to democratize, though serious in itself, is not the key factor in weakening African ties to Europe: Rather, problems in providing stability and liberalization tend to be shaping the parameters for foreign economic policy.

The Global Economy

In the absence of the Cold War or another serious security threat, issues within the global economy appear to be moving to center stage. The inter-related developments of regionalization and globalization of markets are facilitated by the role of multinational corporations (MNCs). In a high-tech world, with increasingly global finance and banking, with information technology expanding rapidly, and with talk of a shrinking globe and an "end of geography,"[15] pessimists fear that Africa could become increasingly irrelevant, let alone marginal.

A thorny problem to deal with is a simple one: Where exactly does Africa fit or compete within the evolving global structure and the New International Division of Labor (NIDL)? How can Africa's foreign economic policies maximize potential and overcome dependency and under-development? Is it through the traditional route of the EU and Lomé Convention or through a radical departure toward more self-reliant policies? How can African policies be relevant in a continent arguably lacking any newly industrialized country (NIC) and where low levels of technology and productivity are the norm? How can Africa influence the North-South dialogue, which appears to be less about a Southern agenda for a more just economic order and more about a Northern agenda of privatization, competitiveness, and market adjustment?[16]

Again, the inference for Africa, drawn in many of these chapters, is that it is a marginal player in the global economy, pushed and shoved by the whims of industrial powers, MNCs, and IFIs. Such a conclusion again reinforces an emphasis on the need for more localized/regionalized foreign policy actions and aspirations for most African states, partly indicated by the fresh impetus for regional organizations, cooperation, and peacekeeping. This area of policy is consistently brought up in subsequent chapters.

Debate over an African Agenda

Though somewhat simplified, it is possible to argue that African states' foreign policies were pursued with some commonality of objectives in the early postindependence period. Admittedly, there were different levels of commitment, but there was basic agreement over such formal policies as nonalignment, opposition to apartheid, anticolonialism, and the goal of "modernization"/economic development.

Such common ground appears to have receded in the post–Cold War era, as a "vision" or common agenda for Africa is more hotly contested. States discussed in this volume display a diversity of strategies and objectives. This is especially evident in the debates on IMF/World Bank SAPs and arguments to promote a more self-reliant, alternative path to devel-

opment inimical to IMF/World Bank proscription. Other foreign policy
agendas are also disputed: What role should regional organizations play?
What is the future for the OAU or the African Economic Community
(AEC)? How much support should there be for an African "champion,"
such as South Africa (or Nigeria)? How much effort should be invested in
maintaining the territorial status quo in the continent?

Pan-Africanism and *continentalism* are terms gaining new currency in
Africa out of an urgency to deal with the political, economic, and social
crises facing the continent. Although the devil is in the detail in opera-
tionalizing these terms, there is a growing sense that Africa needs to respond collectively and *as a region* if it is to thrive in the coming years.

Reframing African Foreign Policies

Given the changing context within which African foreign policies are generated, this volume attempts to reframe some of the questions scholars
ask about these policies. This requires them not only to refine and redefine traditional approaches but also to find new methods of considering
foreign policies. In this context, the following sections provide an
overview of the critical questions of foreign policy and offer guidance to
issues raised in subsequent chapters.

Changing Capacity of the State

A persuasive argument is that the African state's capacity to exert influence beyond its borders is declining and that this is leading to greater
caution in considering policy potential. In some countries, such as Liberia
and Somalia, the state seems to have virtually disappeared; in others,
such as Rwanda and pre-1997 Zaire, it is nonfunctioning. Such developments raise novel questions for scholars of foreign policy. Who is making
policy? And is there actually a foreign policy to be studied? The collapse
of the middle class within many African states also raises new questions
about in whose name foreign policy is pursued. It is difficult to decide
whether there is a "national" element present on which the term *national
interest* can be pegged.

But the death of the state in Africa may be somewhat exaggerated. The
symbols of office remain, the diplomatic recognition is intact, and formal
relations with neighbors are maintained. Even if the state itself is in decline, the craving for power remains constant for civilian and military
elites alike. Clearly each state is at a different level of capacity and/or crisis, and individual country case studies, such as those offered in this volume, are needed to throw light on the relative position of each.

Capacity of African Economies

Traditional approaches to the study of African foreign policies assume some degree of latitude and leverage in the external environment, based on trade and economic potential, especially when linked to the advantageous environment of the Cold War and nonalignment. Probably this economic capacity was exaggerated, as African states have had little economic power base to speak of since independence. Certainly today most scholars would agree, as they do in this volume, that the economic bases for successful foreign policy orientations are weak.

Globalization trends within the international economy have altered the character of North-South economic relationships, providing a more complex and uneven environment than that envisioned even at the start of the 1990s. Driven by competition and profit, MNCs have restructured operations on global bases, in which some states or enclaves within states in the South have benefited—but unfortunately not in Africa. One of the key elements of globalization is the search for cheap labor, but African states have been unable to convert this potential to their advantage. How can African states develop the export niche advantages that are so important in today's global economy? How can there be an increase in productivity, considered one of the main elements of "moving up" in the global economy?[17] How can African states move away from commodity dependence to capital-intensive development—if this is indeed a goal? How are policymakers in such countries as Botswana, Nigeria, or South Africa addressing these issues?

What are the strengths of African economies that can be brought to bear on foreign policy? This is difficult to envision. For a country such as Nigeria, the "oil weapon" so often pointed to as the resource base for foreign policy no longer exists, if it ever did. The ability to hold back exports is not a policy likely to win many converts, and that approach is simply not practicable because states need to maintain international confidence in their economies and retain resources to pay off debt.

Perhaps states can play off foreign competitors against one another, as they did the superpowers during the Cold War, in the newly privatized markets of Africa, thereby extracting the best deal for their resources. But how does Africa become competitive? Overseas aid flows to SSA have been steadily declining and are unlikely to provide greater revenues in the near future. The United Nations Economic Commission for Africa (UNECA) estimates that $148 billion has been lost to the continent in capital flight, and this would be a potential source of investment to tap into if the required political and social climate can be developed. Unfortunately, the Uruguay General Agreement on Tariffs and Trade (GATT) is expected to impoverish further the African continent, the only "losers" in the global agreement.[18]

The World Bank leads the chorus calling on African states to promote export diversification to bolster their economies, in hopes they can imitate the gains made by the Asian miracle states. But the bank admitted that such imitation is unlikely: "These countries tend to have the lowest GDP [gross domestic product] growth, the highest incidence of poverty and the fastest growing populations in the developing world. Their low levels of human and physical capital will probably prevent them from replicating the success of the East Asian or Latin American commodity exporters."[19]

Thus, few states are likely to be competitive, leaving tantalizing questions of the "why Asia and not Africa?" category, as well as more serious headaches for those attempting to shape foreign economic policy agendas.[20] Even South Africa, by far the most industrialized state in Africa, is probably not competitive at a global level and has not been able to attract the degree of international investment originally thought possible. The countries of the SADC region in 1995 only attracted $90 million each on average in foreign investment, a far cry from the $7 billion for Singapore. Talk of South Africa being Africa's first NIC is premature, as its qualified membership in the Lomé Convention in April 1997 partially indicates; besides certain pockets of economic strength, the economy overall is relatively weak by NIC standards. Ideas of other states aspiring to this status or being elevated to membership in the Organization for Economic Cooperation and Development (OECD), as, for example, Mexico has been, are implausible.

Globalization is already creating a deepening divide between the rich and poor in the world, and SSA is the net loser, with the continent expecting to increase its share of the world's poor to 32 percent by 2000. And as James Mittelman concludes: "Globalization debars the bulk of Africa from gaining access to world society's productive processes. For the countries of Africa, the greatest challenge is to demarginalise when national options are severely constrained by the forces of globalization."[21]

It would be fair to conclude, then, that African foreign economic policies would best be focused on enlightened self-interest at the regional level, but even here there are difficult problems to overcome, part political and part economic. Official intraregional trade remains low: For both the Economic Community of West African States (ECOWAS) and SADC, it is less than 5 percent of total trade. The extroverted nature of African economies continues to emphasize South-North linkages, even though there are tremendous flows of unofficial trade that need to be capitalized on (see Chapter 3 on Benin). Talk of creating common markets and currency zones within these regions should move toward implementation, but leaders must deal with the ambiguity of official and nonofficial trade sectors, highlighting again a novelty of the African foreign policy arena. Plans for an AEC by 2025 could have far-ranging implications for economic policy, but at present they are still in their infancy, even though the AEC was officially inaugurated in June 1997.

Changing Security Perspectives

Porous, artificial borders have always provided interesting dynamics for foreign policy in promoting territorial security, but today there appear to be different challenges to face, as the end of the Cold War has not resolved Africa's security concerns but simply altered them.[22] It could be not so much the enemy outside as the perceived enemy within that provokes the strongest security pressures—survival of the regime rather than territorial inviolability. In some states, autocratic personal rule in the "shadow state" has undermined the traditional view of the state and foreign policy and has contributed at times to a breakdown or distortion of patron-client relations and bureaucratic structures. Alternative centers of power, displayed as warlordism or less militaristic forms of dissent, have appeared across the continent from Somalia to Rwanda to Sierra Leone,[23] raising new questions about security and "formal" foreign policy.

Partial democratization also may unleash internal destabilization that undermines domestic security and aggravates ethnic tensions, as is argued in Kenya and Nigeria. Sometimes these problems are deepened by ethnic affiliations beyond the boundaries of the state. Tracking the security concerns of Angola (Chapter 2), Liberia, Somalia, or Sudan provides far from traditional conceptions of foreign policy. Declining state power combined with increasing ethnicity-cum-democratization points the way to other scenarios similar to Ethiopia/Eritrea (Chapter 5), where the state can no longer maintain itself.

The traditional reliance on outside powers—Belgium, France, the UK, the United States, the USSR—to intervene in security considerations has been replaced by an assumption that they will not. Will this lead to less or more insecurity in Africa? Africa appears to pose little strategic threat to anyone outside of the continent. It is a nonnuclear continent (after South Africa's supposed unilateral dismantling), and African states seem to be uninvolved in the proliferation of chemical and biological weapons. Under what conditions could we anticipate external involvement in African security issues?[24] If events in Liberia or Rwanda did not provoke external involvement, what will?

This strategic marginality provides new opportunities for states to coordinate nonaggression pacts or regional peacekeeping arrangements, such as the ECOWAS Monitoring Group (ECOMOG) in West Africa and the Organ on Politics, Defence and Security (OPDS) in Southern Africa, or a grander African high command within the OAU, as has been discussed for years.[25] It also allows for greater mediation efforts by leaders, such as those

made by Daniel arap Moi in Chad and Uganda in the 1980s and Nelson
Mandela in Angola in the 1990s, to name just two examples. The potential
vacuum caused by superpower withdrawal also allows militarily stronger
states to flex their muscles in more activist foreign policies within their regions. The possibility of the South African military operating in such a capacity within the region raises many interesting issues, not least of all for
neighboring states, but this appears to be an element of U.S. and Western
policy toward the region.[26] But are African armies, individually or collectively, strong enough to impose peace on unruly neighbors? Certainly the
costs (both economic and social) of continuing conflict in Africa are well
known, as evidenced by the accounts of Angola (Chapter 2) and
Ethiopia/Eritrea (Chapter 5) and by our knowledge of other wars and civil
conflicts in the continent.[27] The increasing use of boy and girl soldiers in
civil conflicts also has serious detrimental effects on all aspects of society.

But overall, the opportunity for peacekeeping in Africa by Africans is a
very positive development in the changing security environment and one
that raises new questions for foreign and security policy implementation
and coordination.

There are also novel security concerns, such as those related to AIDS
and other viruses, regional water supplies, famine and food, rapid urbanization, land mines, and the environment.[28] Environmental degradation
will increasingly lead to greater migration and the creation of refugees
and will place more strain on African societies. This is an area where
African policymakers have been beginning to seek common ground and
solutions, though much needs to be done. The environment could also become an area of foreign policy cooperation among African states in their
relationship with the North, thereby revitalizing NAM and/or G77 structures.[29] The impact of a global ban on land mines would be tremendous in
Africa, especially in the Southern African region, and would have significant repercussions for continental policy and warfare.

Democratization and Civil Society

The growing significance of civil society in many states is leading to new
influences on foreign policy machineries. The decline (or more accurately
in some cases, the repackaging) of authoritarian leaders (Moi? Jerry Rawlings?) has given nongovernmental organizations,[30] women's groups, religious groups, trade unions, and student groups a greater opportunity to
have input into decisionmaking processes, in what Christopher Clapham
has called the "privatization of diplomacy."[31] The occasionally watchful
eye of Western governments and their political conditionalities may also
have a constraining influence on recalcitrant leaders, and governance conditionalities became increasingly important during 1997 in agencies such as

the United Nations Development Programme (UNDP) and UNECA. The failure to democratize, as in Nigeria or the former Zaire, brings greater attention and warns us about continuing authoritarianism.[32]

The military success of Laurent Kabila in the Democratic Republic of the Congo may point, somewhat ironically, to a changed perspective of good governance in Africa held by neighboring states. The UN secretary-general, Kofi Annan, used the OAU summit in June 1997 to hammer home the importance of respect for human rights and the economic implications of falling behind such standards.[33] Nigeria's bombardment of Sierra Leone at the same time to restore democracy was full of irony, yet it also helped to support a principle of the need for greater democracy in the continent. Legitimate government and reinvigorated public institutions are now widely recognized as key elements in building viable political economies, a message that South Africa is relaying to the rest of the continent.

These changes require scholars to reconsider decisionmaking mechanisms in African states. The simplification of the head-of-state-as-decisionmaker approach, though it has residual validity, needs to be broadened to take account of these other groups, as many of the subsequent chapters do. Increasing factionalism—an early product of partial democratization—often leads to competing foreign policy agendas within states as well as between states. Religious influences, as seen in Senegal (Chapter 8), can become significant in influencing policy. And "public opinion" is becoming something to note in policy formulation in various states, though it is often difficult to pinpoint because it involves many diverse groups: prodemocracy groups, liberation fighters, and newspaper editors, to name a few. The role of gender is also increasingly working its way onto foreign policy agendas, most recently recognized by SADC's Gender Declaration at its summit meeting in September 1997.

Interesting developments occur, too, when democracies and nondemocracies become neighbors. As they attempt to deal with each other inside regional organizations, novel questions about foreign policies arise. The case studies of Angola and Benin provide some assessments of these problems, as do all the chapters relating to the Southern African region. As Paul Ntungwe Ndue points out: "Democratic regimes are frail and cannot long survive in a hostile environment. In Africa, the regional spread of pluralism could help to strengthen them by rescuing them from dangerous isolation. Political pluralism may be consolidated all the more easily when it extends across several adjacent states."[34]

Regionalism and Regional Powers

Though regionalism is by no means new, changes in the African political economy have brought to the forefront the likely centrality of regional organizations in the future viability of the continent.[35] The record of these groupings, such as ECOWAS, SADC, and the Common Market for East and Southern Africa (COMESA), has been poor to date in developing regional agendas, foreign policies, and identities. The fluctuating record of the East African Community (EAC) is discussed in both the Kenya and Tanzania chapters, and SADC is discussed in all the chapters relating to Southern Africa.

This patchy record is more marked in contrast to a booming cross-border (illegal) trade that reveals elements of cooperation not found at official levels. How can Africa take advantage of this dynamic, energetic, yet illegal trade? The continuing reorganization of groupings—SADCC changing to SADC, the Preferential Trade Area (PTA) to COMESA, FLS to the Association of Southern African States (ASAS) to OPDS—points to efforts to reform and revitalize, but positive results are still needed. Does the decline of superpower involvement leave open the prospect of increasingly active regional entities? Will we see national foreign policies coordinated more at the regional level? Will we see the emergence of regional "hegemons," such as Nigeria, Kenya, or South Africa, exerting influence over these regions and organizations? And is regionalization the best way for African political economies to withstand the intense pressures of globalization?

Such questions, of course, integrally link political and economic considerations. Lessons from the EU indicate a possibly difficult struggle to have states relinquish their sovereignty. But the cooperation of European states, just like cooperation in groupings such as the Association of South East Asian Nations (ASEAN), the Asia-Pacific Economic Cooperation (APEC), and the North American Free Trade Agreement (NAFTA), demands that African states also organize themselves into productive and competitive regional groupings. The marginality and in some cases collapse of African states might lead to a greater impetus for change in promoting sound regional policies. But regional leadership by a "hegemonic" power appears potentially dangerous, as subsequent chapters show, partly because of residual national jealousies and hostilities within the respective regions.

Nevertheless, regionalism probably provides the most realistic alternative for African states, as authors conclude in this volume. As Timothy Shaw has pointed out elsewhere:

> This new economic and strategic conjuncture—the NIDL now joined by the NIDP—provides an alternative, indeed compelling, occasion for redirecting foreign policy away from global chimeras and towards "new" regionalisms. Such reorientation would, for example, reinforce OAU and ECA inclinations and precedents from *Lagos Plan* and *African Alternative Framework* to *African Economic Community*—but would also serve to recognise informal economies and encourage informal polities: civil societies at a regional level.[36]

External Influences on Policy

I have already argued that espousing nonalignment as a key foreign policy platform for states did not undermine the important influence of Western nations or IFIs in African policies. Today, the focus of foreign policy has shifted somewhat from an emphasis on country relationships to the all-pervasive influence of IFIs, notably the IMF and World Bank, with additional pressures brought to bear by the debt agencies of the London and Paris Clubs. Economic policy has evolved from "low politics" to "high politics," and subsequent chapters highlight how important domestic debates on foreign policy have shifted from the political arena to the economic arena—to finance ministries and central banks.

Half of the continent is under World Bank SAPs, which significantly impact indigenous policy initiatives and add an element of "realism" that was not always present before; SAPs have serious implications for traditional notions of sovereignty, and they limit "independent" policy implementation. African states have had to fight to retain the capacity to pursue foreign economic policies of their own choosing, and the majority are now implementing mixed market economies—with promising results, so the World Bank claims,[37] though most authors in this volume are less confident. As Susan George has pointed out, IFIs use debt and SAPs as weapons in their relations with African states, leading to what she calls FLIC—financial low-intensity conflict.[38] Proposals for an African "containment" strategy to keep these IFIs at bay gather support, though actual policy coordination and implementation is again difficult to envision.

The full impact of SAPs is beyond the scope of this introductory chapter, but a continuing role for the IFIs in African decisionmaking is very likely, unless radical policy options favoring self-reliance and inward-looking policies are pursued. The World Bank, in its *1997 World Development Report*, emphasized the importance of reinvigorating the state and state institutions in African development, a policy long overdue in the eyes of many observers. But as an indication of the endemic problems of long-term debt and the weakness of states, the bank also began a new debt relief program for Highly Indebted Poor Countries (HIPCs), of which Uganda became the first recipient in April 1997.

A final area of discussion here is the future relationship between the EU and Africa through the Lomé Convention. The EU's green paper issued in November 1996 laid out broad parameters for discussion in the lead-up to negotiations due to begin in late 1998 for Lomé V.[39] The changing character of European relations with Africa and in particular the downplaying of French roles in the continent[40] leave many thinking that there might not be a Lomé V (see Chapter 12). Again, this is an area of intense interest for foreign economic policies and one that will have a wide impact on many aspects of African society. But it is possible that the lack of African diplomatic clout in Brussels will prove detrimental to Africa's political and economic interests. As Glenn Brigaldino has argued, "Without a well-organized and articulate political constituency for stronger cooperation with Sub-Saharan Africa within the EU, further marginalization of Africa can be expected."[41]

Continentalism(?)

There is an urgent need to find common areas of interest upon which policy cooperation can coalesce. Nonalignment and antiapartheid have each, in the past, offered a common focus for foreign policy, but today there is little concrete to draw together disparate states. What could be the bases for a common regional foreign policy? Is it possible for the OAU to gain the center ground of African continental policy? Can regions historically torn apart by conflicts, such as Southern Africa and the Horn, find areas of common policy? Can the bitterness of partners within East Africa be overcome in a revived regional community? What would be the costs for Africa if states continued to pursue purely independent foreign policies, if that is even possible?

The importance and problems of the OAU are well known:

> The OAU has experienced more failures than successes, but it remains a focal point for collective initiatives and for conflict management. The attempt to construct solidarity at the continental level is not a sentimental illusion but rather a reasoned response to Africa's dependent position in the global economic system. African leaders are conscious of the utility of cooperation at the same time that they have found cooperation difficult to achieve in practice.[42]

An emerging set of foreign policy issues seems to require such continental cooperation, partly because they transcend traditional state boundaries. Such "new" foreign policy issues as narcotics, poaching, viruses, illegal trade, and the environment all require cross-border cooperation. The movement toward greater South-South linkages can perhaps be achieved on a state-to-state basis, but such linkages appear far more meaningful when handled on a region-to-region basis. Closer ties to Asian economies, pursued aggressively by such states as Botswana (Chapter 4) and Kenya (Chapter 6), need to be pushed further (as does an understanding of the reasons for the Asian "miracle" economies). But how can African policies toward Asia, the Middle East, or Latin America be coordinated? And what can we learn of African foreign policies by studying the efforts at cooperation in those other areas?

Conclusion

This introductory chapter has begun to formulate some of the interesting questions that are raised within the chapters of this volume. Traditional approaches to foreign policy, though still occasionally throwing useful light on issues, need to be reconfigured by new sets of research questions that address the continent in the changed global and regional environments of the late 1990s. It is evident that many problems are afflicting the continent and that their continuance could see Africa completely and perhaps permanently marginalized from the global political economy and society. The challenges raised by issues and questions discussed in this volume, then, are not simply academic but go to the heart of how the future of the continent is to be shaped.

Overall, successful democratization appears to be the key to the continent's survival. From that should flow more measured foreign policies, more equitable domestic societies, more capable political leaderships, and, it is hoped, more productive and diversified economies. Without strengthening the economic base of African societies, foreign policies will be severely limited, perhaps extending just to neighboring states—though admittedly, that result would have some merit. Regional cooperation seems to be an essential step for African states to take whether or not the continent remains attached to global society.

NOTES

1. Some useful texts throwing light on these issues are Timothy M. Shaw and Julius Emeka Okolo (eds.), *The Political Economy of Foreign Policy in ECOWAS* (New York: St. Martin's, 1994); Adebayo Adedeji (ed.), *Africa Within the World: Beyond Dispossession and Dependence* (London: Zed Press, 1993); Ralph I. Onwuka and Timothy M. Shaw (eds.), *Africa in World Politics: Into the 1990s* (New York: St. Martin's, 1989); Olatunde J.C.B. Ojo, D. K. Orwa, and C.M.B. Utete, *African International Relations* (Harlow, England: Longman, 1985); Timothy M. Shaw and Olajide Aluko (eds.), *The Political Economy of African Foreign Policy* (Aldershot, England: Gower, 1984); and Olajide Aluko (ed.), *The Foreign Policies of African States* (London: Hodder and Stoughton, 1977).

For an overall review of the field of foreign policy analysis, see Valerie M. Hudson, "Foreign Policy Analysis Yesterday, Today, and Tomorrow," *Mershon International Studies Review*, 39(2), 1995, pp. 209–238.

2. For interesting comparative studies of other regions, see Bahgat Korany and Ali E. Hillal Dessouki (eds.), *The Foreign Policies of Arab States* (Boulder: Westview Press, 1991), and David Wurfel and Bruce Burton (eds.), *The Political Economy of Foreign Policy in Southeast Asia* (New York: St. Martin's, 1990).

3. See Vernon McKay (ed.), *African Diplomacy: Studies in the Determinants of Foreign Policy* (New York: Praeger, 1966). For a general overview of more traditional

policy, see Stephen Wright, "The Foreign Policy of Africa," in Roy C. Macridis (ed.), *Foreign Policy in World Politics* (Englewood Cliffs, N.J.: Prentice-Hall, 1992), pp. 330–356.

4. It is interesting to read Immanuel Wallerstein's views written during the early postindependence period; see Immanuel Wallerstein, *Africa: The Politics of Independence* (New York: Vantage, 1961).

5. Ali A. Mazrui, *Africa's International Relations: The Diplomacy of Dependency and Change* (London: Heinemann, 1977), p. 2.

6. See David Kimche, *The Afro-Asian Movement: Ideology and Foreign Policy of the Third World* (Jerusalem: Israel University Press, 1973), pp. 238–249.

7. Zaki Laïdi, *The Superpowers and Africa: The Constraints of a Rivalry, 1960–1990* (Chicago: University of Chicago Press, 1990).

8. Charles E. Morrison and Astri Suhrke, *Strategies of Survival: The Foreign Policy Dilemmas of Smaller Asian States* (New York: St. Martin's, 1978), p. 289.

9. Robert Jackson and Carl G. Rosberg, *Personal Rule in Africa: Prince, Autocrat, Prophet, Tyrant* (Berkeley and Los Angeles: University of California Press, 1982).

10. Bahgat Korany (ed.), *How Foreign Policy Decisions Are Made in the Third World: A Comparative Analysis* (Boulder: Westview Press, 1986). Also, Bahgat Korany, "Analyzing Third-World Foreign Policies: A Critique and a Reordered Research Agenda," in Wurfel and Burton (eds.), *The Political Economy of Foreign Policy in Southeast Asia*, pp. 21–37. For a specific country study, see Ibrahim A. Gambari, *Theory and Reality in Foreign Policy Making: Nigeria After the Second Republic* (Atlantic Highlands, N.J.: Humanities, 1989). For an earlier comparative text that attempted to address these issues, see Christopher Clapham (ed.), *Foreign Policy Making in Developing States* (Farnborough, England: Saxon House, 1977).

11. Adebayo Adedeji, "Marginalisation and Marginality: Context, Issues and Viewpoints," in Adedeji (ed.), *Africa Within the World*, p. 8.

12. Michael Clough, *U.S. Policy Towards Africa and the End of the Cold War* (New York: Council on Foreign Relations, 1992). See also Peter Schraeder, "Trends in the United States Africa Policies After the End of the Cold War," *Journal of the Third World Spectrum*, 1(2), 1994, pp. 1–16.

13. Such prospects are also being considered in other regions. See, for example, James C. Hsiung (ed.), *Asia Pacific in the New World Politics* (Boulder: Lynne Rienner, 1993).

14. See USAID, *Economic Reform in Africa's New Era of Political Liberalization* (Washington, D.C.: USAID, 1993).

15. Richard O'Brien, *Global Financial Integration: The End of Geography* (New York: Council on Foreign Relations/RIIA, 1992). For one view of the changing global economy, see John M. Stopford and Susan Strange, *Rival States, Rival Firms: Competition for World Market Shares* (Cambridge: Cambridge University Press, 1991).

16. Claude Ake, "The New World Order: A View from Africa," in Hans-Henrik Holm and Georg Sørensen (eds.), *Whose World Order? Uneven Globalization and the End of the Cold War* (Boulder: Westview Press, 1995), pp. 1–17.

17. Gary Gereffi, "The Elusive Last Lap in the Quest for Developed-Country Status," in James H. Mittelman (ed.), *Globalization: Critical Reflections* (Boulder: Lynne Rienner, 1996), pp. 53–81.

18. Overseas Development Institute (London), Briefing Paper 3, May 1995.

19. *Global Economic Progress and the Developing Countries, 1994* (Washington, D.C.: World Bank, 1994), p. 4.

20. A recent book by the OECD explores many of these issues; see Jean-Claude Berthélemy (ed.), *Whither African Economies?* (Paris: OECD, 1995). The UN World Institute for Development Economics Research (WIDER) has been engaged through 1997–1998 on such a project, under the leadership of Gerald Helleiner.

21. James H. Mittelman, "The Dynamics of Globalization," in Mittelman, *Globalization*, p. 18.

22. Sheryl J. Brown and Kimber M. Schraub (eds.), *Resolving Third World Conflict: Challenges for a New Era* (Washington, D.C.: U.S. Institute for Peace, 1993).

23. William Reno, "Privatizing War in Sierra Leone," *Current History*, 96(610), May 1997, pp. 227–230; also William Reno, *Corruption and State Politics in Sierra Leone* (Cambridge: Cambridge University Press, 1995).

24. An earlier study of Africa focused on such crises, though it seems unlikely that such a book could be written today. See Gerald J. Bender, James S. Coleman, and Richard L. Sklar, *African Crisis Areas and U.S. Foreign Policy* (Berkeley and Los Angeles: University of California Press, 1985).

25. Ali Mazrui, "Africa in Search of Self-Pacification," *African Affairs*, 93, 1994, pp. 39–42.

26. Chris Landsberg, "The Western Powers, South Africa and Africa: Burden Sharing, Burden Shift, and Spheres of Influence," paper presented at a conference entitled "Africa, France, and the United States," in Bordeaux, May 1997; for interesting ideas on security, see Peter Vale, "Securing Southern Africa," *The Courier* (Brussels), 153, September-October 1995, pp. 66–67.

27. Paul Collier, "Civil War and the Economics of the Peace Dividend," Working Paper Series 95–8, Centre for the Study of African Economies, Oxford, 1995.

28. See Anders Hjort af Ornäs and M. A. Mohamed Salih (eds.), *Ecology and Politics: Environmental Stress and Security in Africa* (Uppsala, Sweden: Scandinavian Institute of African Studies, 1989); Stephen Wright, "Africa: Environmental Problems," in Robert Paehlke (ed.), *Conservation and Environmentalism: An Encyclopedia* (New York: Garland, 1995), pp. 8–11.

29. Marc Williams, "Re-articulating the Third World Coalition: The Role of the Environmental Agenda," *Third World Quarterly*, 14(1), 1993, pp. 7–29.

30. Eve Sandberg (ed.), *The Changing Politics of Non-Governmental Organizations and African States* (Westport, Conn.: Praeger, 1994). Also see Julius Nyang'oro, "Reflections on the State, Democracy and NGOs in Africa," in Larry A. Swatuk and Timothy M. Shaw (eds.), *The South at the End of the Twentieth Century* (London: Macmillan, 1994), pp. 130–137.

31. Christopher Clapham, *Africa and the International System: The Politics of State Survival* (Cambridge: Cambridge University Press, 1996); also Patrick Chabal, "Democracy and Daily Life in Black Africa," *International Affairs*, 70(1), 1994, pp. 83–91.

32. Samuel M. Makinda, "Democracy and Multi-Party Politics in Africa," *Journal of Modern African Studies*, 34(4), 1996, pp. 555–573; Larry Diamond, "Promoting Democracy in Africa: U.S. and International Policies in Transition," in John W.

Harbeson and Donald Rothchild (eds.), *Africa in World Politics: Post–Cold War Challenges* (Boulder: Westview Press, 1995), pp. 250–277.

33. *Africa Recovery*, 11(1), July 1997, p. 3.

34. Paul Ntungwe Ndue, "Africa's Turn Towards Pluralism," *Journal of Democracy*, 5, 1994, p. 54.

35. See Guy Martin, "African Regional Cooperation and Integration: Achievements, Problems and Prospects," in Ann Seidman and Frederick Anang (eds.), *Twenty-First-Century Africa: Towards a New Vision of Self-Sustainable Development* (Trenton, N.J.: Africa World Press, 1992), pp. 69–99. For an interesting general discussion of some of these issues, see Peter Robson, "The New Regionalism and Developing Countries," *Journal of Common Market Studies*, 31(3), 1993, pp. 329–348. Also see Andrew Hurrell, "Explaining the Resurgence of Regionalism in World Politics," *Review of International Studies*, 21(4), October 1995, pp. 331–358.

36. Timothy M. Shaw, "The South in the 'New World (Dis)Order': Towards a Political Economy of Third World Foreign Policy in the 1990s," *Third World Quarterly*, 15(1), 1994, p. 21.

37. Edward V.K. Jaycox, *The Challenges of African Development* (Washington, D.C.: World Bank, 1992). For interesting case studies of negotiations in Nigeria and Zaire, see Thomas J. Biersteker (ed.), *Dealing with Debt: International Financial Negotiations and Adjustment Bargaining* (Boulder: Westview Press, 1993). For a more introspective (and humorous) view of World Bank efforts, see Robert Klitgaard, *Tropical Gangsters* (New York: Basic Books, 1990).

38. Susan George, "Uses and Abuses of African Debt," in Adedeji (ed.), *Africa Within the World*, pp. 59–72.

39. *The Courier* (Brussels), 162, March-April 1997, pp. 7–31.

40. Peter J. Schraeder, "France and the Great Game in Africa," *Current History*, 96(610), May 1997, pp. 206–211; also Oladeji O. Ojo (ed.), *Africa and Europe: The Changing Economic Relationship* (London: Zed, with the African Development Bank, 1996); also Stefan Brune, Joachim Betz, and Winrich Kuhne (eds.), *Africa and Europe: Relations of Two Continents in Transition* (Hamburg: Lit, 1994).

41. Glenn Brigaldino, "African-European Relations at the Turning Point," *Africa Today*, 44(1), 1997, p. 54. See also Gordon Crawford, "Whither Lomé? The Mid-Term Review and the Decline of Partnership," *Journal of Modern African Studies*, 34(3), 1996, pp. 503–518.

42. Naomi Chazan, Robert Mortimer, John Ravenhill, and Donald Rothchild, *Politics and Society in Contemporary Africa* (Boulder: Lynne Rienner, 1992), pp. 323–324.

2

Angola: The Foreign Policy of a Decaying State

ASSIS MALAQUIAS

Angola's experience since achieving independence from Portugal in 1975 has been particularly painful even by postcolonial African standards. Numerous, concurrent, and multifaceted crises have brought the state to the verge of internal collapse and international irrelevance. This chapter focuses on how a particularly weak African state, unable to exercise authority within its own borders let alone project influence abroad, used diplomacy to engage important regional and international actors in the search for solutions to domestic problems and thus, ultimately, ensure its survival.

Like most African countries in the mid-1970s, Angola expected to achieve a measure of relevance in international relations by playing one superpower off against the other and pursuing nonalignment as the main pillar of foreign policy (for similar stances, see Chapters 10 and 11 on Tanzania and Zimbabwe). However, in the wake of the chaos that surrounded the nation's transition to independence, survival became the overriding consideration of the new regime. The initial vision of a foreign policy solidly grounded on the principles of nonalignment had to be quickly abandoned in the late 1970s in favor of a more pro-Soviet posture.

With this foreign policy shift the governing Popular Movement for the Liberation of Angola (MPLA) hoped to better prepare Angola to withstand major threats from both within and without its borders, since the regime's main domestic rivals, the National Union for the Total Independence of Angola (UNITA) and the National Front for the Liberation of Angola (FNLA), had important backers regionally and internationally.[1]

The lines separating domestic and regional problems were often blurred, and, in the context of the Cold War, internal matters such as the presence of Soviet and Cuban troops on Angolan soil became an international concern. Thus, this interplay of domestic/regional/international contexts, on the one hand, and the political/military/economic factors, on the other, is crucial to understanding Angola's foreign policy.

Domestic Environment

At the domestic level, civil war and economic mismanagement have seriously weakened the Angolan state. The postcolonial state in Angola never really had the capacity or competence to exercise authority beyond the capital city and provincial capitals. International nongovernment organizations (INGOs)—such as the International Committee of the Red Cross, Care International, Medicins Sans Frontières, Oxfam, and Save the Children—and, more recently, the United Nations have been carrying out most tasks commonly associated with the state, especially in rural areas affected by war. The rudimentary national bureaucracy functions on a quasi-voluntary basis partly because the state is not able to provide full remuneration to its employees. Consequently, bureaucrats resort to extorting bribes and/or joining the informal sector to survive. The collapse of key sectors such as health care, education, transport and communications, and banking has accompanied the breakdown of the rule of law. More than three decades of war have turned Angola into an extremely militarized and violent society, and it is within this domestic context that the Angolan state has carried out its foreign policy.

Angola's foreign policy can be best understood in relation to the MPLA regime's own strategies of survival since gaining power. Unlike its counterparts in the other former Portuguese colonies, MPLA never had the time to consolidate its rule. In fact, its window of opportunity lasted only three years, from independence in 1975 until the second invasion of Zaire in 1978.[2] However, even during this period, with internal opponents in disarray, there were serious domestic problems that weakened MPLA's hold on power. At the political level, the governing party had little support outside Luanda as most of the population in the north and south still supported FNLA and UNITA, respectively. Also, the new regime did not have the administrative capacity to fill the void left by departing colonial administrators.

This mass departure of the settler community hastened the breakdown of the Angolan economy. Portuguese settlers abandoned thousands of farms and enterprises and took with them "every asset they could transport."[3] Thus, between 1974 and 1976, "every sector of the economy experienced sharp output declines (ranging up to 100 percent)."[4] Without government authority, especially in the countryside, and given the severity of the economic problems, increasing numbers of people were resorting to criminal activities, which created a situation approaching anarchy in many parts of the country.

Agostinho Neto believed that the consolidation of the MPLA regime in Angola could not be achieved unless the new state's territorial security was assured through the establishment of good relations with neighboring countries.[5] Some of these, notably South Africa and Zaire, still exhibited hostile intentions and provided support and sanctuary for UNITA and FNLA.

Angola's arduous birth as a sovereign state had a profound and lasting effect on the MPLA leadership.[6] However, the various factions composing the governing party had different interpretations of the tragic events surrounding independence, which, in turn, prejudiced subsequent foreign policy options. For many influential leaders, including Lucio Lara, Iko Carreira, and Paulo Jorge,[7] these events could only be interpreted from a Cold War perspective. They perceived the actions of Zaire and South Africa in the context of a much wider and sinister Western "imperialist" conspiracy to establish a form of neocolonial domination in Angola. This hard-line faction argued for the establishment of very close relations with socialist countries, especially the Soviet Union and Cuba, to counter Western "neocolonialist" tendencies.

Neto did not fully endorse the ideological interpretations propounded by the hard-liners. For him, both Zaire and South Africa were acting on behalf of the United States to fill a potentially destabilizing vacuum in the region created by Portugal's precipitous departure. Neto believed that the preservation of the nascent state's territorial integrity ultimately depended on its ability to establish good relations with neighboring states. Cold War dynamics, important as they were at the time, could be properly managed through membership in international organizations such as the UN, OAU, and especially the NAM.

Unlike some more doctrinaire members of the MPLA leadership, Neto wanted to limit the extent of Angola's cooperation with the USSR once the internal threat posed by UNITA and FNLA was eliminated. The MPLA inserted into the new constitution a clause prohibiting the establishment of foreign bases on Angolan soil and continued to welcome foreign oil and diamond companies to exploit the country's vast natural resources. But, as the following sections show, this pragmatic, nonaligned posture did not produce the anticipated foreign policy outcomes. Attempts to make peace with Zaire and South Africa were unsuccessful, and these neighboring countries continued to interfere in Angola's domestic affairs on the side of UNITA.

Regional Environment

No Success with Mobutu's Zaire

As a first step to normalizing relations with Zaire, Neto was prepared to expel the Zairian secessionist forces from Angola in return for a similar measure from Mobutu Sese Seko regarding FNLA. The Zairian president kept his promise to close all FNLA bases in Zaire, expel its leaders, and severely curtail the activities of its sympathizers remaining in Zaire. Neto, however, was not able to deliver. Instead, members of the more radical faction of MPLA—many of whom had fought against invading Zairian troops attempting to prevent MPLA's coming to power in 1975—frustrated Neto's plans by unleashing the Zairian rebels on two occasions, in 1977 and 1978, to carry out major military incursions into Zaire from Angola. Mobutu felt betrayed and held Neto personally responsible.

In retrospect, although the invasions of Zaire exposed Mobutu's vulnerability, the negative repercussions for Angola were much greater. Mobutu's allies, including the United States, France, Belgium, and Morocco, promptly came to his rescue and quickly pushed the invading forces back to Angola. However, the MPLA would suffer the consequences for many years because those invasions provided Mobutu and his Western allies with a convenient excuse for continuing intervention in Angola. Within a Cold War context, Angola's actions—whether with or without Cuban and Soviet consent—were seen as an attempt to expand the USSR's sphere of influence in Southern and Central Africa. Predictably, the United States and its allies responded with massive military support for Mobutu, and Western intelligence services accelerated efforts to provide training and weapons to UNITA. Thus, in 1978, a large number of UNITA military officers were sent to Morocco for various types of military training while many more were trained in Zaire. Most of the equipment used during the Western operation to rescue Mobutu and in subsequent joint military maneuvers was handed over to UNITA. This Western-Zairian-UNITA connection seriously weakened the new Angolan state and constituted a major threat to its territorial security, exactly opposite to the policy outcome Neto had envisioned. For example, during the 1980s, the United States supplied UNITA through the Kamina air base in southern Zaire. This base also served as a convenient transit port for UNITA's $.5 billion per year diamond smuggling operations.[8]

In the 1990s, after being abandoned by its main Cold War supporters—the United States and South Africa—UNITA continued the mutually beneficial relationship it had forged with Mobutu's Zaire since the late 1970s. Thus, reports that "close relatives and aides of Zairian President Mobutu Sese Seko have been smuggling hundreds of tons of weapons to former rebels in Angola for huge profits" came as no surprise to most attentive observers.[9] It is also not surprising that Angola retaliated by putting between 1,000 and 2,000 Zairian exiles at the disposal of Laurent Kabila's Alliance of Democratic Forces for the Liberation of Congo-Zaire, which successfully toppled Mobutu's regime in 1997.[10]

The failure to deal successfully with Mobutu's Zaire and thereby enhance rather than diminish Angola's security highlights a serious deficiency in this state's foreign policy: the lack of focus. The provision of open support and sanctuary to Zairian rebels, particularly in the late 1970s, a time when Angola desperately needed friendly relations with Zaire, was not an adequate policy option. This peculiar propensity to choose less than optimal foreign policy options would characterize Angola's relations with other states in the region, including South Africa.

Neto's Failed Overtures to South Africa

Angola's early policy toward South Africa was just as disastrous as other diplomatic forays in the region, partly due to Neto's initial misreading of how the apartheid regime perceived the end of Portuguese colonialism and the subsequent independence of Angola and Mozambique. Neto mistakenly believed that South Africa would eventually come to accept and deal with the new Marxist states without antagonism. Therefore, he was initially willing to appease South Africa to preserve territorial integrity and solve mounting political, economic, and military problems at home.

But Neto's overtures to South Africa were not successful because the collapse of the colonial regime in Portugal and the consequent geostrategic changes in Southern Africa led to an immediate hardening of Afrikaner positions and policies in attempts to preserve apartheid. South Africa's main response to the momentous changes in the region in the mid-1970s came in the form of the so-called total strategy, a desperate set of policies aimed at ensuring the survival of the regime through a combination of reform and repression.

The main proponents of the total strategy argued that the source of instability and conflict, both inside South Africa and in the region, was neither apartheid nor colonialism but external intervention. Therefore, it was necessary to ensure that neighboring states refrained from actively supporting the armed liberation struggle for South Africa and Namibia and that no "communist" power gained a foothold in the region. Thus, South Africa further expanded its security and military apparatus to both suppress opposition at home and destabilize the region. Angola became identified as South Africa's principal enemy in the region due to its ideological orientation, economic potential, and the fact that it was the main South-West African People's Organization (SWAPO) sanctuary and an important

African National Congress (ANC) base. South Africa used two main instruments to threaten Angola's territorial integrity: (1) frequent, well-planned military invasions deep into Angolan territory, and (2) the instrumentalization of UNITA as a proxy in its regional destabilization policies. (See Chapters 9 and 11 for further discussions of the South African role.)

This strategy resulted in tremendous devastation both in human lives lost and infrastructure destroyed. Between 1975 and 1989, South Africa mounted yearly large-scale military invasions of Angola. South Africa also successfully transformed UNITA into a proxy army to execute the apartheid's destabilization strategy within Angola. Although virtually destroyed by MPLA and Cuban troops in 1975 and 1976, UNITA was reorganized into a powerful military force by 1979. While MPLA government and Cuban troops were preoccupied with building massive defensive systems to deter South African military aggression, UNITA was already beginning to move northward from its bases in the southeast to consolidate new positions in central Angola along the Benguela Railway. This was particularly important for the implementation of South Africa's strategy, since UNITA's military actions effectively rendered the vital railway—one of the region's major transportation links to the Atlantic Ocean—inoperable. UNITA would also seriously disrupt the government's attempts to jump-start agricultural production in the central highlands, Angola's traditional breadbasket. Even more important for the long-term survival prospects of the MPLA regime, UNITA was planning military operations farther north, with the objective of disrupting both oil and diamond exploration—the government's main sources of foreign revenues.[11]

When Neto met his untimely and mysterious death in a Moscow hospital in September 1979, a combination of domestic and international factors were threatening the viability of the new and fragile Angolan state: The departure of the settler community and subsequent mismanagement had driven the economy to ruin; the civil war had paralyzed an already weak state, rendering it inoperative inasmuch as its reach and authority outside the capital and a handful of major cities was decreasing rapidly, resulting in its incapacity to provide security to citizens; the state's authority was being further challenged by UNITA's rule over a large portion of the country with a working political-military apparatus and organized economy, even if primitive; and the legislative process had become irrelevant, since laws could not be implemented due to lack of state authority. Moreover, Angola's foreign policy was in disarray. Neto's main foreign policy objective of making peace with neighboring states to preserve territorial integrity had failed, thereby compounding the domestic crisis.

The magnitude of this multifaceted, multilayered crisis had reached such alarming proportions that when José Eduardo dos Santos succeeded Neto, he was given little chance of securing the regime's survival beyond several months. However, dos Santos would survive beyond all expectations. What factors ensured the survival of the MPLA regime given its domestic problems and growing international isolation?

The Imperative of Regime Survival

José Eduardo dos Santos's early attempts to solve the multiple crises facing Angola at the end of the 1970s were met with considerable resistance at home because he lacked sufficient political clout, even within his own party. He was not the MPLA's first choice to succeed Neto. Veterans of the fourteen-year war against the colonial regime were not ready to accept a thirty-seven-year-old president whose participation in the liberation struggle had been minor.[12] Consequently, the new president's main focus during the crucial first years of his administration revolved around creating a strong domestic political base and establishing his command over the military.

At the international level, dos Santos abandoned nonalignment in favor of closer ties with the USSR and Cuba, due to a quickly deteriorating domestic situation. Unlike his predecessor, dos Santos was prepared to give greater latitude to the Soviets in determining the main guidelines of the new state's domestic and foreign policy. Previously frustrated with Neto's flirtation with nonalignment, the USSR welcomed this new foreign policy orientation because Angola provided an important base in Southern Africa from which to affect change during a period of great instability caused by both regional and Cold War dynamics. The USSR was particularly interested in influencing events in South Africa, the richest and most developed state in the subcontinent, and thus fulfill its self-proclaimed role as the vanguard of Third World liberation movements and oversee the implementation of the Soviet model of political, economic, and social development.

Cuba also agreed to provide additional support for dos Santos. Despite its own serious domestic and international problems, Cuba was willing to provide various types of assistance to Angola and other Third World countries to further its own foreign policy objectives, primarily including an assertion of its leadership in the NAM.[13] However, given their own problems and limitations, neither the USSR nor Cuba could solve the MPLA's domestic problems. In particular, they could not help solve Angola's economic problems or prevent UNITA from becoming a growing threat with Zairian, South African, and U.S. assistance.

The International Environment

Surviving Constructive Engagement and the Reagan Doctrine

Unlike the USSR, the United States had been interested and involved in Southern Africa prior to the collapse of the Portuguese colonial regime.

The United States, like other Western countries, has historically maintained a presence in Southern Africa to safeguard its access to the region's vast deposits of minerals. During the Cold War, the containment of the perceived Soviet expansionist threat in the region provided the rationale for additional involvement.[14]

However, the U.S. involvement in Angola has been problematic due to Washington's intervention on the side of FNLA and UNITA during the chaotic transition to independence, its withholding of diplomatic recognition to the MPLA regime, and its continuing support for UNITA. Consequently, U.S.-Angolan relations never moved past mutually beneficial commercial interests, notably with U.S. companies' exploration of the vast Angolan oil fields. Although this commercial relationship, initiated during the colonial period, continued uninterrupted when the MPLA assumed power, the United States preferred not to deal with the MPLA government at a political level until it held democratic elections in Angola. It was assumed in Washington that free and fair elections would bring UNITA to power, since this party's main base of support was among Angola's largest ethnolinguistic group, the Ovimbundu.

Beginning in the early 1980s, the United States under Ronald Reagan pursued a clear and unambiguous policy to overthrow the MPLA and force other regimes in the region to undertake fundamental political transformations. To this end, two major U.S. policy initiatives, "constructive engagement" and the "Reagan Doctrine," were actively promoted. Constructive engagement was the policy devised by the Reagan administration to "help foster a climate conducive to compromise and accommodation in both Southern and South Africa."[15] This policy emerged from the belief that Southern Africa's problems were fundamentally intertwined and that solutions could only be found if this basic interdependence was recognized. Thus, the need to change the attitudes of the main players in this search for solutions to regional problems provided the primary official rationale for constructive engagement. However, given the Cold War logic prevailing at the time, this policy initiative became the main U.S. foreign policy instrument to force an end to "Soviet-Cuban adventurism"[16] in the region.

If constructive engagement had a primarily politico-diplomatic tone, the more global Reagan Doctrine had a manifest strategic and military rationale. It was conceived as "a full-blown, global campaign" for providing overt U.S. support for anticommunist guerrilla movements around the world.[17] Chester Crocker explained the "logic" of this doctrine in these terms: "Soviet imperial expansion had created imperial vulnerabilities that could be exploited at low cost. It was much more expensive and challenging to sustain an incumbent government than to back a rebel movement. By providing tangible as well as moral support for anti-Communist insurgents, the United States could raise the price of the Soviet's Third World empire."[18]

The Reagan Doctrine had an almost immediate impact on the Angolan civil war since UNITA became a major recipient of sophisticated U.S. weaponry, including Stinger antiaircraft missiles that for the first time upset the air supremacy enjoyed by the MPLA government. This doctrine further emboldened the apartheid regime, leading it to intervene even more aggressively in Angola on the side of UNITA. Consequently, all major military offensives mounted by the MPLA/Cuban/Soviet forces to dislodge the Angolan rebels from their bases in southern Angola ended in failure. For example, massive U.S. and South African Defence Force (SADF) assistance was crucial in saving UNITA in 1988 from advancing MPLA and crack Cuban units during the battle for Cuito-Cuanavale, in what has been described as one of the fiercest conventional battles on African soil.[19]

International Solutions for Domestic Problems

Military Stalemate: First Step to Peace?

The battle for Cuito-Cuanavale proved to Cuba and South Africa—both small, subimperial interventionist states—that protracted military engagements would result in an unbearable loss of lives. Consequently, both countries accepted the inevitability of a negotiated framework for regional peace involving both the withdrawal of Cuban troops from Angola and the implementation of UN Security Council Resolution (UNSCR) 435/78 regarding Namibia's independence.[20]

It can be argued, therefore, that the military stalemate on the ground hastened the cease-fire accord reached between the governments of Angola, Cuba, and South Africa on 8 August 1988 and the historic agreement by these same governments on 22 December in New York, providing for the phased withdrawal of 50,000 Cuban troops from Angola over a period of twenty-seven months in return for the implementation of the UN plan for Namibia's independence.

Both accords marked the culmination of eight years of mediating efforts by the United States, and they were heralded as a major diplomatic coup for the Reagan administration. The agreements eased Namibia's transition to independence but did little to speed up the resolution of the civil war in Angola itself, partly because they did not involve UNITA.

The talks leading to the signing of the accords were conducted along two tracks. Track 1 involved negotiations regarding the removal of Cuban troops from Angola in return for South African withdrawal from Namibia and independence for the latter. Track 2 entailed consultations aimed at achieving national reconciliation between MPLA and UNITA. Both tracks were supposed to be pursued simultaneously. However, since the parties to the negotiation had previously agreed that the question of national reconciliation for Angola was an internal matter, no pressure was put on either the MPLA government or UNITA to settle their differences within the framework of the negotiations. In any event, the Reagan administration was convinced that once Cuban troops withdrew entirely, reconciliation between the Angolan government and UNITA would naturally follow. According to a senior U.S. official involved in the negotiations, "Military solutions have been tried many times and have failed. What this agreement does is address the international question of foreign troops. That should encourage the parties to explore internal solutions."[21]

African leaders were also pushing for a negotiated settlement that would bring together the two warring factions in some form of coalition or national government, as in Zimbabwe and Namibia. President Mobutu of Zaire, for example, was quoted as saying that "many African countries are calling with all their might for national reconciliation in Angola."[22] The presidents of Congo and Gabon also suggested this option to dos Santos. Nigeria, an important player in African affairs, was ready to "pass on the lesson of [its] own civil war, for speedy reconciliation and reconstruction"[23] and suggested that "a lot of African countries would buy the idea of a resolution once the foreign forces decamp."[24]

Track 2 led nowhere because the Angolan government at the time was not prepared to end the war through political means since this would require a framework for power sharing with UNITA. Two months before the signing of the regional peace agreement, dos Santos declared that an internal peace process in Angola would not entail the sharing of power with UNITA. For the MPLA, negotiations with UNITA would be contrary to the constitutional principles of the "people's republic." Dos Santos argued that "the Angolan state is a one-party state and so the acceptance of such a political organization [UNITA] is out of the question."[25] Instead, he suggested that his government would seek "national harmonization" through a policy of clemency and reintegration of UNITA members into Angolan society that would eventually lead to an end of the civil war. As the president explained, "The idea is to bring all Angolans together under the same anthem and flag, under the same state."[26]

Dos Santos and his government were planning to address the possibility of ending the civil war only after a regional peace accord was signed. Thus, Angola's main diplomatic efforts were directed at ensuring that the New York Accords were fully implemented. The MPLA government believed that, even without Cuban support, its armed forces could crush the rebels once SADF withdrew from Namibia. In the words of an Angolan government spokesperson, "If we resolve this problem with South Africa, the internal peace process will move very quickly and neither negotiations nor any other kind of agreement with UNITA will be necessary."[27] This "problem with South Africa" was finally settled by diplomatic means with the signing of the Brazzaville Protocol by Angola, Cuba, and South Africa, calling for the withdrawal of Cuban troops from Angola and the implementation of the UN plan for Namibia's independence. The Brazzaville Protocol also committed South Africa to halting all support for UNITA. Without this crucial support, Jonas Savimbi's organization appeared vulnerable. It would have to rely almost exclusively on U.S. patronage channeled through neighboring Zaire. However, the Angolan government did not fully appreciate the extent of the U.S. commitment to supporting UNITA.

With a regional peace plan in place, the MPLA was convinced that UNITA would "cease to exist in a year" through a combination of political and military operations.[28] This approach to internal conflict resolution was seriously flawed since it gravely underestimated UNITA's own political and military strengths and resources, both internal and external. Even before the signing of the Brazzaville Protocol and the New York Accords, Savimbi rejected the government's approach for ending the civil war through harmonization and clemency, declaring prophetically and ominously that "there will be no peace in Angola without UNITA."[29]

Although Savimbi constantly affirmed his desire for peace and reconciliation, he was hesitant about embracing a peace process that excluded his organization. He preferred direct talks with the MPLA government as a first step toward creating a transitional government of national unity to pave the way for internationally supervised, multiparty elections. However, despite Savimbi's conciliatory overtures, there were early signs that he was not completely reneging on his long-standing quest to seize power by any means. He often suggested that he had a messianic mission to rule: "I spent thirty years of my adult life fighting for freedom and dignity of the black man in this country. If the Cubans want to stay, I will fight on and I will win. If the Cubans leave and there is no negotiation with the MPLA, we win. If the Cubans leave and we have elections, we win."[30]

Savimbi was leaving no viable political alternatives open for himself or his organization, and he conceived of no other possibility than outright victory. This predisposition was not suitable to a constructive political process, as would later become abundantly clear.

Savimbi appeared confident about his chances of victory because the MPLA government's diplomatic efforts—especially regarding peace with South Africa—had not succeeded in isolating UNITA. In fact, South Africa's role as UNITA's main backer was simply taken over by the United States. In his first foreign policy commitment, President-Elect George Bush sent a letter to Savimbi with assurances of continued U.S.

military and diplomatic support until the Angolan government agreed to reach a political settlement with UNITA.[31] Since peace with South Africa did not result in the outcome expected by the MPLA government, dos Santos had few policy options other than a return to diplomacy to end the civil war.

Engaging African States: Gbadolite and Harare

South Africa's withdrawal from Angola in the late 1980s represented a hollow victory for the MPLA regime in the sense that it did not alter significantly the stalemate with UNITA on the ground. It also came at a time of major international changes, which included the disengagement by the USSR from international commitments due to its own internal crisis and "new thinking" in foreign policy, which in turn affected Cuba.

These profound changes at the international level forced dos Santos to seek peace for Angola within a regional framework. To this end, he invited eight African heads of state to Luanda on 16 May 1989 to discuss ways to end the war.[32] The framework for peace that emerged from this summit envisioned "national reconciliation" for the first time and suggested the possibility of direct dialogue between the warring parties. As a result of this summit, dos Santos and Savimbi met for the first time on 22 June 1989 in Gbadolite, Zaire, at a special summit of African heads of state convened by President Mobutu. Both Angolan leaders declared publicly their mutual desire to end the conflict and begin the critical dialogue that would eventually lead to national reconciliation.

The Gbadolite summit, however, ended in failure because the participants had different interpretations of what they had agreed to at the meeting. The final communiqué stated that all the parties had reached agreement on three points: (1) the mutual desire to end the war and effect national reconciliation; (2) the proclamation of a cease-fire effective 24 June 1989; and (3) the establishment of a mixed UNITA-MPLA commission under the mediation of President Mobutu to negotiate the political future of Angola.[33]

However, this directly contradicted President Mousa Traore's version of events. Traore, as acting OAU president, claimed that the leaders gathered at Gbadolite had discussed and agreed on six points: (1) an end to armed opposition, (2) security for Savimbi and his followers, (3) the voluntary and temporary withdrawal of Savimbi, (4) the granting of a post to Savimbi, (5) the integration of UNITA elements, and (6) the conditions for their integration.[34]

UNITA categorically rejected this interpretation. The rebels' version of events was closer to that expressed in the final communiqué and was corroborated by the summit's host, President Mobutu, who asserted that the agreement included "nothing about exile" for Savimbi.[35] Amid diverging interpretations of what was pledged in Gbadolite, dos Santos returned to Luanda seriously weakened politically. Hard-liners within his regime used the Gbadolite fiasco as an indication of the futility of diplomatic efforts to end the conflict. They took advantage of dos Santos's temporary weakness to launch a major military offensive against one of UNITA's most important bases at Mavinga on 18 August 1989. Again, this offensive ended in failure due to South African and U.S. assistance.

Against the background of military conflict and public acrimony, a follow-up summit of African leaders took place in Harare on 22 August 1989. Savimbi was not invited to participate partly because President Robert Mugabe, given his alliance with dos Santos in the Angolan conflict, was not willing to give the rebel leader the benefit of the doubt, as Mobutu had been. The Harare summit's final communiqué revisited Gbadolite and asserted that three additional principles, previously undisclosed, had been agreed upon at the earlier summit: (1) respect for the constitution and laws of the People's Republic of Angola, (2) integration of UNITA into existing MPLA institutions, and (3)acceptance of Jonas Savimbi's temporary and voluntary exile.[36]

African diplomatic efforts to end the civil war in Angola seemed just as incoherent as the MPLA's efforts over the previous decade. African leaders also misinterpreted the Angolan situation in the sense that they failed to grasp the crux of the matter—that Savimbi was not likely to abandon his lifelong quest for personal power and a dominant position for his party in Angolan politics.

U.S.-Soviet Cooperation: Peace at Last?

The next major opportunity to resolve the civil war occurred as an outcome of the new post–Cold War relationship between the United States and the USSR, with behind-the-scenes diplomacy involving various regional and global actors. The decision by the superpowers to press the MPLA government and UNITA to begin direct talks on national reconciliation came at a meeting between former U.S. secretary of state James Baker and his Soviet counterpart, Eduard Shevardnadze, while both attended Namibia's independence ceremonies in March 1990. Namibia itself had gained independence partly because of earlier U.S.-Soviet efforts to bring about an agreement ending SADF cross-border invasions into Angola in return for Cuban troop withdrawal. For both the United States and the USSR, at the end of the Cold War, Angola could provide a good opportunity to repeat the collaboration that hastened Namibia's independence. Moreover, the U.S. government promised diplomatic recognition for Angola once free and democratic elections were held.

Another positive external factor was Portugal's willingness to become involved again in helping its former colony settle the turmoil that followed the granting of independence. Several factors—including Portugal's ability to communicate with both sides, a desire for a higher diplomatic profile, a sense of guilt for abruptly leaving Angola without preparing a peaceful transition, and a yearning to regain a business foothold in the former colony—contributed to thrusting Portugal back on the diplomatic center stage in attempts to sort out the legacy of settler colonial rule in Angola.

On 25 April 1990, the Angolan government announced that it would enter direct talks with UNITA, mediated by the Portuguese government, to "find the path to national reconciliation in Angola."[37] However, friction and confrontation characterized these talks, reflective of much of the relationship between the two sides. The seemingly intractable barriers separating the warring factions were set aside only due to direct U.S. and Soviet intervention. In a coordinated diplomatic offensive, Baker and Shevardnadze called Savimbi and Pedro de Castro Van Dunem to Washington, where both were told that no additional military and financial aid would be forthcoming to continue the war.

The United States and the USSR strengthened their collaborative engagement in the peace process and, along with Portugal, formulated the main documents for negotiations between the MPLA government and UNITA. These documents covered five basic political principles and technical-military issues: (1) Angola would become a democratic and multiparty nation; (2) the international community would guarantee a ceasefire; (3) there would be free and fair elections in Angola, verified by the international community; (4) the signing of a cease-fire would be preceded by an accord on the date for free and fair elections; and (5) all military assistance from abroad would stop once a cease-fire accord was signed.[38]

These principles formed the basis for the Bicesse Peace Accord signed in Portugal on 31 May 1991 by dos Santos and Savimbi. In principle, this accord appeared solid, but like the ones before, it was doomed from the beginning because UNITA perceived it as another attempt by the MPLA regime to prolong its hold on power. Although both the MPLA government and UNITA participated in the implementation of the Bicesse Peace Accord, it amounted to no more than a tragic exercise in make-believe intended to satisfy the demands of the international community, particularly the United States. Predictably, once the internationally supervised process resulted in UNITA's defeat at the polls, Savimbi removed his generals from the embryonic unified army and sent them back to war.

The MPLA regime was able to withstand the postelectoral crisis of 1992 partly because the international community remained engaged in the complex Angolan situation even after UNITA unilaterally abandoned the peace process. This continuing engagement, the result of the international community's reluctance to abandon Angola at a particularly critical time, eventually persuaded UNITA to return to the negotiating table in 1993. Exploratory talks were held in Addis Ababa before peace talks resumed in Lusaka under UN mediation.[39] After more than a year of negotiations, both parties signed a power-sharing agreement commonly referred to as the Lusaka Protocol.[40] Yet, as they were signing this document establishing a new framework for peace, government troops were overrunning UNITA from most of the areas it had captured in 1992, including the rebels' headquarters at Huambo. This prompted UNITA's General Eugenio Manuvakola to issue a threat:

> We believe that the government is not interested in the [peace] accord. I think that the government does not believe in UN mediation. It believes neither in the UN presence nor in UNITA. It believes in a military solution. If the government wants to follow the military option, we seriously need to think about a military option, as well. I would like to say that, so far, we have been waging a conventional war to defend cities and towns, which is not our specialty. Our specialty is a bush war. That is our war. We think that we are not on a path of weakness, but a path of strength. We can adapt ourselves to the new situation quickly, and we will see whether Angola will have peace or war for a few more years.[41]

Will the Lusaka Protocol fail like all other previous attempts to bring peace to Angola? Although Savimbi publicly embraced dos Santos in Lusaka on 6 May 1995 and promised to "cooperate in the consolidation of peace," he has not returned to Luanda, and his party is yet to contribute cadres for the government of national reconciliation that should have been formed after the Lusaka agreement. More than three years after the signing of the latest peace accord, the inability to agree on the composition of a government of national unity—especially Savimbi's role in it—masks deep-seated and persistent disagreements between MPLA and UNITA. The Angolan rebels seem to be keeping all their options open, including the possibility of returning to war if the current peace process fails.

Further clouding the prospects for peace in Angola is the fact that, even though the UN Angolan Verification Mission (UNAVEM III) has the human and material resources that previous missions lacked,[42] the implementation of the Lusaka agreement is facing serious difficulties, especially in the confinement of UNITA soldiers to designated areas. Given these problems on the ground and the UN's own financial afflictions, there is considerable pressure in New York to bring UNAVEM III to a close with or without peace in Angola.

Conclusion

A combination of important factors affecting the domestic, regional, and international environments have profoundly and negatively affected Angola's capacity to implement an effective foreign policy since 1975. Although the end of the Cold War offered new opportunities, particularly through the engagement of the international community in the various attempts to reach a peaceful solution to the civil war, Angola's unresolved domestic problems will continue to have a negative influence on the state's ability to carry out its functions at home, let alone its capacity to play an important role abroad.

At the regional level, Angola's diplomatic efforts have yielded meager results. The MPLA regime paid a high price for its assistance to Zairian rebels. This was used as a convenient excuse for giving massive Western and Zairian support to UNITA for more than two decades. Angola's relations with the other major player in the region, South Africa, have also been highly problematic, even after the demise of apartheid. Much to the MPLA's resentment and frustration, the ANC—to which Angola provided considerable help, suffering heavy consequences in turn—has not provided the type of diplomatic support Angola was anticipating once South Africa was liberated from apartheid. The South African government has been reluctant to publicly take sides in Angola; instead, President Nelson Mandela has preferred the role of a facilitator of peace and dialogue between dos Santos and Savimbi. (This is part of Mandela's wider African peace strategy; see Chapter 9.) He has gone as far as inviting Savimbi to South Africa for discussions on ways to settle UNITA's differences with MPLA. This token of diplomatic legitimacy given to Savimbi by Africa's greatest statesman is not what MPLA had expected in return for helping ANC during its darkest hours in the struggle against apartheid, of which Savimbi was a favorite son.

At the international level, although President dos Santos has once again changed Angola's foreign policy orientation—this time seeking greater proximity with the United States to conform with new post–Cold War realities—few positive outcomes can be expected in the foreseeable future. The United States is expected to continue focusing on oil as the basis for its relationship with Angola. Current and future U.S. administrations are also expected to continue prodding Angola down the path of economic reform via international financial institutions such as the IMF and the World Bank. Political liberalization, a more problematic prospect, is likely to receive less attention once current international efforts expire.

In the final analysis, even in the unlikely event that UNITA concedes military defeat and accepts a secondary role in a new, still MPLA-dominated political system, Angola will have to concentrate all efforts to reestablish the basic domestic prerequisites for a relevant foreign policy: a stable and all-inclusive political system with a wider space and greater role for civil society, the reestablishment of the rule of law, economic development based on diversification, and the accountable use of oil and diamond revenues.

Peace may finally enable Angola to fully exploit its natural resources. However, the development of this vast potential alone will not assure relevance within the new international division of labor and power as Botswana (Chapter 4) and Nigeria (Chapter 7)—to take the two examples most relevant for Angola—have demonstrated. Relevance within the present global economy depends not so much on a country's natural resource base. Rather, it emanates from a country's ability to participate and compete in the high-tech and information-driven international economy.

The human and material losses incurred during Angola's civil war will continue to affect the viability of the state for decades to come. Therefore, Angola's foreign policy must be redesigned as a tool to help the state reconstitute itself as a first step to an eventual and relevant participation in the global economy. For Angola, this process of reconstitution can best be achieved through greater diplomatic and economic involvement at the regional level. In particular, Angola must learn from the experience of other countries in the region—such as South Africa, Zimbabwe, Namibia, and even Mozambique—that are also attempting to overcome the legacy of many years of internal conflict.

NOTES

1. UNITA and FNLA had also participated in the fourteen-year liberation war against Portuguese colonial rule but lost out to the MPLA in a violent power struggle that preceded Angola's transition to independence in 1975. South Africa and the United States supported UNITA; FNLA was backed by Zaire and also the United States. The MPLA was supported by the former Soviet Union and Cuba.

2. The two invasions of Zaire from Angolan soil, in 1977 and 1978, were carried out by the Front Nacional de Liberation du Congo (FNLC). This separatist movement, based in the former province of Katanga (present-day Shaba), was created by Moises Tshombe in the mid-1960s. Many of its members fled to Angola when the objective of secession from Zaire did not materialize. They were subsequently used by the Portuguese colonial authorities in counterinsurgency operations against the nationalist movements in Angola. The FNLC, now under the leadership of Nathaniel Mbumba, sided with the MPLA in the early stages of the civil war in Angola.

3. World Bank, *Angola: An Introductory Economic Review* (Washington, D.C.: World Bank, 1991), p. 6.

4. Ibid.

5. Neto was the leader of the MPLA and Angola's president from 1975 to 1979.

6. When the Portuguese colonial administration hastily devolved power to Angolans on 11 November 1975, the country was immersed in a full-scale civil war and had been invaded by two neighboring countries: Zaire and South Africa. FNLA, supported by regular units of the Zairian army and a motley assortment of mercenaries, had advanced to within a few miles of Luanda, the capital city. In an equally threatening move, South African forces invaded from their bases in occupied Namibia in a desperate attempt to place Savimbi in power before Portugal officially granted independence.

7. All three are mulatto, or mixed-raced, Angolans; they represented the party's hard-line element.

8. This figure was given to me by a high-ranking Angolan government official, who requested anonymity.

9. *Washington Post*, 21 March 1997, p. A01.

10. *Washington Post*, 16 March 1997, p. A27.

11. UNITA wanted to shorten the regime's life by disrupting its main sources of foreign exchange—the oil and diamond industries—even if this conflicted with Western economic interests.

12. Dos Santos was born in Luanda on 28 August 1942. He joined the MPLA in 1961 and was awarded a scholarship to study petroleum engineering in the former Soviet Union. Upon graduating in 1969, he stayed in the USSR to study military communications. He returned to Angola just before the collapse of the colonial regime to head the MPLA's Foreign Affairs Department. He was named minister of foreign affairs in Agostinho Neto's first cabinet. He was subsequently named first deputy prime minister and minister of planning before Neto's death in 1979.

13. S. Neil Macfarlane, "Soviet-Angolan Relations, 1975–90," in George W. Breslauer (ed.), *Soviet Policy in Africa* (Berkeley: University of California Press, 1992), p. 87.

14. Oye Ogunbadejo, *The International Politics of Africa's Strategic Minerals* (Westport, Conn.: Greenwood Press, 1985), p. 3.

15. Chester Crocker, *High Noon in Southern Africa: Making Peace in a Rough Neighborhood* (New York: W. W. Norton, 1992), p. 75.

16. Ibid., p. 77.

17. Ibid., p. 290.

18. Ibid., p. 292.

19. Horace Campbel, "The Military Defeat of South Africans in Angola," *Monthly Review*, 40(11), April 1989, p. 1.

20. Crocker, *High Noon in Southern Africa*, pp. 506–511.

21. *Washington Post*, 14 December 1988, p. A1.

22. *New York Times*, 19 September 1988, p. A3.

23. Nigeria's former foreign minister, Major General Ike Nwachuku, quoted in the *New York Times*, 2 November 1988, p. A27.

24. *New York Times*, 19 September 1988, p. A3.

25. *Reuters*, 1 October 1988.

26. Ibid.

27. *Reuters*, 23 November 1988.

28. Luis Neto Kiambata, former Angolan ambassador in Zambia, quoted by *Reuters*, 11 December 1988.

29. *Reuters*, 11 December 1988.

30. *Washington Post*, 20 November 1988.

31. *Washington Post*, 12 January 1989, p. A1.

32. The presidents of Congo, Gabon, Mozambique, Sao Tome e Principe, Zaire, Zambia, and Zimbabwe attended this summit.

33. The text of the Gbadolite Declaration was broadcast on Radio Nacional de Angola on 23 June 1989.

34. Mousa Traore, interview with Radiodiffusion-Television Malienne, 23 June 1989.

35. *Washington Post*, 25 June 1989, p. A21.

36. Text of communiqué, quoted by the Zimbabwe Inter-African News Agency/Pan-African News Agency (ZIANA/PANA), 22 August 1989.

37. Pedro de Castro Van Dunem, Angola's minister of foreign affairs, *Associated Press*, 25 April 1990.

38. Radio Nacional de Angola, 23 January 1991.

39. The United States, Russia, and Portugal participated in the talks as observers.

40. Under the terms of the Lusaka Protocol, signed on 22 November 1994, UNITA would be awarded four ministerial portfolios, seven state secretary posts, six ambassadorial positions, three provincial governorships, five deputy-governorships, thirty district administrator positions, and thirty-five deputy district administrator positions.

41. Eugenio Manuvakola, UNITA's general secretary, FBIS-AFR–94–223, 18 November 1994, p. 24.

42. UNAVEM III was created in February 1995 to enforce the Lusaka Protocol. Previous UN missions in Angola, UNAVEM I and II, were responsible for the verification of the Cuban troop withdrawal and the 1991–1992 peace process.

SELECT BIBLIOGRAPHY

Beaudet, Pierre, Daniel dos Santos, and Brian Wood. "Angola in the New Regional Order," in Nancy Thede and Pierre Beaudet (eds.), *A Post-Apartheid Southern Africa?* (New York: St. Martin's Press, 1993), pp. 118–141.

Bender, Gerald J. "Peacemaking in Southern Africa: The Luanda-Pretoria Tug of War," *Third World Quarterly*, 11, January 1989, pp. 15–30.

Bridgland, Fred. *The War for Africa: Twelve Months That Transformed a Continent* (Gibraltar: Ashanti, 1990).

Campbel, Horace. "The Military Defeat of South Africans in Angola," *Monthly Review*, 40(11), April 1989.

Crocker, Chester. *High Noon in Southern Africa: Making Peace in a Rough Neighborhood* (New York: W. W. Norton, 1992).

Hoper, Jim. "UNITA Guerrillas Attack with Impunity," *International Defense Review*, 22, June 1989, pp. 747–749.

Kempton, Daniel R. *Soviet Strategy Toward Southern Africa: The Liberation Movement Connection* (New York: Praeger, 1989).

Macfarlane, S. Neil. "Soviet-Angolan Relations, 1975–90," in George W. Breslauer (ed.), *Soviet Policy in Africa* (Berkeley: University of California, 1992).

McFaul, Michael. "Rethinking the Reagan Doctrine in Angola," *International Security*, 14, Winter 1989, pp. 99–135.

Ogunbadejo, Oye. *The International Politics of Africa's Strategic Minerals* (Westport, Conn.: Greenwood Press, 1985).

World Bank. *Angola: An Introductory Economic Review* (Washington, D.C.: World Bank, 1990).

3

The Flea on Nigeria's Back: The Foreign Policy of Benin

JOHN R. HEILBRUNN

Benin is a francophone country on the west coast of Africa that by any measurement is small: Approximately 5 million people inhabit a territory roughly the size of Pennsylvania. Most Beninois work in agriculture, and reportedly they earned an average annual per capita income of $420 in 1992.[1] In order of importance, the country's principal exports include cotton, palm products, and tropical fruits. A tiny offshore oil field near the Nigerian border provides the government with some additional foreign earnings.

The territory that we know today as Benin originally comprised three kingdoms that France conquered in the 1890s and then assembled into a colony called Dahomey.[2] French colonial administrators enforced a rather tense truce among the peoples of these three kingdoms. This truce ended in the 1950s with the introduction of political parties that formed almost exclusively along ethnoregional lines. After independence, Dahomey rapidly acquired notoriety not only for its dynamic and intelligent population but also for its chronic political instability. A vocal urban population and a historical resentment of foreign domination created a fortuitous environment for political opportunists who plotted against ruling governments and fomented coups d'état. The country's remarkable intelligentsia made constant demands on successive governments to end political dependence on France during Dahomey's first twelve years of independence. Their criticisms of French political domination were echoed in the calls of the Dahomean commercial class that resented French control of Dahomey's economy. Finally, Dahomey's political class was compelled with disturbing regularity to pursue a foreign policy that consisted of little more than asking France for financial assistance to meet bud-

getary shortfalls. These three groups constituted the major domestic influences on foreign policy.

This chapter argues that Benin's foreign policy has undergone a subtle
change from a dependent relationship on France to a complex foreign
policy that emphasizes the peaceful resolution of regional problems. This
shift suggests a recognition of the deleterious impact regional instability
has on every economy. The shift became especially apparent after Benin's
successful transition to democracy in 1991. The evolution in foreign policy from a colonial relationship to a complex, multi-issue orientation reflects the increasing interlinkage of West African states. Benin's foreign
policy recognized that regional issues have grown in salience since the
late 1980s. To explain this crucial development in issue linkage, the chapter will first discuss how small states such as Benin formulate their foreign policies. Then Benin's postindependence history will be divided
chronologically to analyze changes in its foreign policy. The years 1974 to
1984 were a critical period in which Benin adopted a policy based on a
Marxist ideology and sought an alliance with the Soviet bloc. A second
period is 1985 to 1990, when the Marxist-Leninist regime ceased to provide any public goods, including a coherent foreign policy, and finally
collapsed. The chapter will end with an analysis of Benin's foreign policy
after 1990, when a government with political institutions characterized by
democracy actively engaged in regional diplomacy.

Foreign Policy Formulation

Small states operate in foreign policy environments marked by interdependence and vulnerability. Because their domestic economies produce
only part of their needs, these states rely upon imported goods not available in their domestic markets. Whereas small European states' domestic
niches permit policy adjustments to cope with fluctuations in the international economy, their counterparts in the developing world lack the flexibility needed to adjust prices to changes in their terms of trade.[3] Robert H.
Bates has recently noted how both dependency and neoclassical trade
theory would assume that small African states are "price takers" that lack
autonomy in their foreign policy decisions. Bates points to the highly exposed position of small African economies in regard to variations in
world markets.

Francophone African states are particularly vulnerable to external
shocks over which they have no control. One explanation for this is that
francophone African states have very limited control over a currency that
is pegged to the French franc. At the end of colonialism, France provided
its former colonies guarantees of monetary stability through membership
in the Communauté Financière Africaine (CFA). The CFA franc has been a

crucial pillar of Franco-African postcolonial economic structures. Before 1993, the Bank of France would directly exchange banknotes at a parity of 50 CFA francs (CFAF) to 1 French franc (FF). In January 1994, finance ministers from France and all francophone African states met with representatives of the World Bank and the International Monetary Fund to discuss the value of the CFA franc. The product of their meeting was a halving of the CFA franc, making the parity 100 CFAF to 1 FF. The devaluation unsettled African politics, and popular opinion blamed France for a disregard of the resulting dislocations.[4] Most important, however, the devaluation signaled a dramatic shift in Franco-Africa relations.

A second shock resulted from the long-term decline in commodities prices. A significant number of francophone African countries export primary commodities overwhelmingly to France. Conversely, small African states depend on France for their manufactured imports. The extent of political-economic links is manifest in preferential trade agreements that keep African markets open to French business. African politicians accord French companies special access to markets and a competitive edge over investors from other countries.[5] In return, France provides investment credit, development assistance, and guarantees of military protection in international conflicts. (For a discussion of similar issues in Senegal, see Chapter 8.)

Jean-François Bayart has suggested that francophone African states lack a foreign policy autonomous of French wishes.[6] Various reports asserted that the 1994 devaluation was foisted on the Africans as a fait accompli, thus lending support to notions that African small states are foreign policy takers.[7] Indeed, since signing the Abidjan Doctrine in September 1993, France has required African governments to reach an accommodation with the Bretton Woods IFIs before soliciting bilateral aid.[8] The Abidjan Doctrine has effectively fulfilled Paul Collier's prediction that these IFIs would become "agencies of restraint" imposing fiscal discipline on otherwise recalcitrant African governments, as had the colonial state.[9]

Reality, however, is far more complex, and any given regime's foreign policy reflects a dynamic interaction of domestic interests, economic exigencies, and international pressures. Robert Putnam has convincingly argued that an "adequate account of domestic determinants of foreign policy and international relations must stress *politics*: parties, social classes, interest groups (both economic and non-economic), legislators, and even public opinion and elections, not simply executive officials and institutional arrangements."[10] However, he has added a crucial third actor when he notes that "it is wrong to assume that the executive is unified in its views."[11]

Foreign investors have paid little attention to the few resources Benin offers, preferring instead the huge and chaotic Nigerian market of 100 million people, Cameroon's entrepreneurial dynamism, or Côte d'Ivoire's tightly managed opportunities. French economic concerns active in much of Africa are relatively inactive in Benin, leaving the country in relative economic isolation. An effect of this isolation has been a rhetorical battle between Beninese intellectuals and the French government. Indeed, the foreign policy of Matieu Kérékou's government reflected his efforts to subdue increasing pressures from these intellectuals while trying to avoid any threats to French largesse. Benin's foreign policy was therefore a response to competing interests manifest in foreign pressures, domestic coalitions in society, and factions within the regime. Kérékou's appointments to the Ministry of Foreign Affairs demonstrated shifting coalitions within the regime according to whoever was in Kérékou's favor or whatever ideas were particularly compelling at the time.[12] The justification for ideological policies was often derived from fashionable ideas in the international arena and reflected what Peter Gourevitch has called the "second image reversed."[13] Benin seemed to flop from position to position, as its needs often conflicted with the debates occurring in its society.

Foreign Policy Under Marxism-Leninism, 1974–1990

Instability was Dahomey's hallmark after independence. It was a consequence of constant poverty, budgetary shortages, and ethnoregional conflicts that caused social cleavages. In preindependence elections, a remarkably unified north would vote for a single candidate, while the numerically larger yet divided south split its vote between two candidates. Interregional competition and the invidious comparisons, so poignant in ethnic conflicts, aggravated ethnoregional competition.[14] Perhaps, as Dov Ronen has argued, the source of Dahomey's tragic instability was the absence of a single strong leader able to lead the country to independence and endow its government with legitimacy.[15] Political parties formed on a regional basis, and politicians plotted to destabilize their rivals' governments.

In the 1960s, the military emerged as a potent political actor willing to topple civilian governments when threatened.[16] In time, cliques formed around particular officers in the army as politicians descended into open conflicts that failed to resolve the country's repressive poverty. Although the instability transformed the army into one of the few stable institutions in Dahomean society, military officers behaved much as the politicians did. In time, social conflicts insinuated themselves into the military, and Dahomey suffered coups and countercoups that perplexed any attempts to develop the country. Between 1963 and 1972, the country experienced six coups and multiple constitutions. Without stability, the government of any given day could not formulate a coherent foreign policy beyond seeking French assistance.

In 1972, soldiers toppled a civilian government in Dahomey's sixth military coup. The coup's leader, Major Mathieu Kérékou, pandered to a vitriolic and shrill Left. Ronen has speculated that the coup was a preemptive strike by senior officers to prevent radical junior officers from taking power.[17] However, many of these junior officers entered the Kérékou government. Their leadership debated policies in the language of *tier-mondisme* (Third World radicalism), currently in fashion among French intellectuals. The regime's ideologues had received their training in France during the late 1960s: They condemned French domination of Dahomey and called for a Marxist-Leninist, socialist orientation and a nonaligned foreign policy stance. Their ascension to power was evident in the October 1974 announcement that "on this day we solemnly proclaim that a society in which the good life is provided must be a socialist society. We therefore declare that the only historic and just path for the Dahomean people irreversibly leads to a Dahomean revolution. . . . The philosophical foundation on which we must build our revolution is Marxism-Leninism."[18]

The declaration signaled a series of nationalizations, strict regulations on profits, and the creation of a new political party, the Parti Revolutionaire du Peuples du Dahomey (PRPD), later named the Parti Revolutionaire du Peuples du Benin (PRPB). With guidance from East German advisers, the Kérékou regime established party cells in workplaces and agricultural communities. In 1975, Kérékou gave the new socialist country a new name: the People's Republic of Benin.

Although Kérékou had rhetorically adopted Marxist-Leninist principles and criticized the "imperialist" French government, he still needed substantial bilateral assistance. Benin retained its membership in the various arrangements that France had established for francophone Africa. The Communauté des États d'Afrique de l'Ouest (CEAO), the Communauté Financière Africaine, the Union Monétaire de l'Ouest Africaine (UMOA), the Banque Centrale des États de l'Afrique de l'Ouest (BCEAO), the Organisation Commune Africaine et Mauricienne (OCAM), and the Union Douanière des États de l'Afrique de l'Ouest (UDEAO) all ensured France economic predominance in West Africa after the dismantling of its colonial empire.[19]

In 1975, Beninese diplomats actively participated in negotiations that resulted in the Economic Community of West African States. From all appearances, Benin had chosen a foreign policy of nonaligned pragmatism colored by Marxist-Leninist rhetoric. Benin's government carefully adhered to its postcolonial treaty agreements with France, while declaring itself a member of the international socialist community.

Foreign Policy, 1974–1984

With a self-designation as a Marxist-Leninist society, Benin joined Congo-Brazzaville as one of two communist francophone African states.[20] Of course, in neither country could an ideological pronouncement end the multitude of links with France. The Congolese regime received critical income through its contracts with the French oil conglomerate Elf-Aquitaine, which had rights to manage the exploitation of offshore oil fields. By contrast, Benin possessed small offshore petroleum reserves and practically no natural resources. Although Kérékou signed a contract with the Norwegian oil company Saga, the People's Republic of Benin remained dependent on French aid. Hence, it is critical to understand the domestic and international sources of Benin's ideological shift as expressed in its foreign policy.

One possible explanation is that Kérékou was simply realigning with a new, more generous patron in the Soviet Union. Between 1974 and 1976, Benin vocally supported the nonaligned movement. The Charte de la Diplomatie Nouvelle of 16 May 1976 defined Benin's diplomatic orientation as "anti-French, anti-American, and pro-Romanian."[21] Considering the stingy nature of Soviet aid, the declaration of Marxism-Leninism could hardly have been because the Soviets would help Benin develop. Assistance from the Soviet bloc was paltry: "The most important recipients were Ethiopia with 57.9 percent, Mozambique 13.8 percent, Egypt 6.6 percent, Madagascar 4.2 percent, Congo 2.6 percent, Angola 2.8 percent, and Tunisia 2.1 percent. The remainder, taken individually, received under 2.0 percent of disbursements. Most received nothing."[22] Kérékou had effectively aligned Benin with a declining Soviet Union that was financially unable to provide even basic development assistance.

Most probably the ideological shift satisfied radical members of the regime who advocated delinkage and nonalignment, concepts popular among intellectuals in Africa and the developing world during the early 1970s. Benin has a long intellectual tradition that earned the country a reputation as the "Latin Quarter" of francophone Africa. In the 1960s, the Dahomean intelligentsia condemned the links with France as neocolonialism. Stagnation, poverty, and cultural domination of knowledge were cited as evidence of continuing French exploitation. Africa's intellectuals justified an ideological movement against the "regimes" France established to maintain the norms and principles embodied in its two administrative zones, Afrique Occidentale Française and Afrique Equitoriale Française, on the basis of this evidence.[23] Some individuals expressed their nationalist sentiments in calls for an "Africanization" of the economy; others demanded nonalignment or outright delinkage from the capitalist world economy. Dependency theory influenced Dahomey's intelligentsia with its ideas that only after delinkage from the capitalist world economy could any development occur in Africa.[24] Notions of the "development of underdevelopment" informed Benin's foreign policy rhetoric between 1972 and 1990.

The extent to which this ideological allegiance was genuine depended largely on the individual and time. Without question, different factions in the Kérékou regime pursued a foreign policy based on Leninist principles that criticized the expansionist principles of imperialism. It was equally plausible, however, that others used theoretical constructs to reject French pressures to relinquish rule. Still others used the ideology to justify a seizure of private property. Whatever the ideological perspective, Kérékou's regime balanced a complex mixture of diverse interests.

During Kérékou's early rule, a more radical fringe pushed for a centrally planned economy and a "socialist society." In December 1974, a decree nationalized all banks and consolidated industries into public enterprises under the direction of Kérékou's inner circle. These actions fundamentally shook Franco-Beninese relations. As one French observer bitterly noted:

> It is impossible not to make a comparison with the methods [of nationalizations] employed by Togo [Benin's western neighbor]. When General Eyadéma nationalized Cotomib, he made no ideological pronouncements. He reimbursed all investors, retained personnel hired under treaties of technical assistance. . . . The Dahomean strategy showed none of this efficiency. . . . One must question in whose interests all the stocks in stores were seized and how these stocks, which will soon be gone, will be replenished without significant assurances provided to banking establishments of support forthcoming from the Dahomean economy.[25]

Disputes over reimbursements for French investors soured relations between Benin and France for years to come. Benin's isolation worsened when French negotiators were confronted by shrill accusations of neocolonialism and exploitation in response to their demands to be reimbursed for seized and expropriated property.

Although Kérékou received repeated warnings about squandering French goodwill, his regime continued to condemn neocolonialist imperialism in international forums. In 1976, the Commission des Relations Extérieures du Comité Central issued an official pronouncement defining Benin's foreign policy. Its official position was that

> until October 26, 1972, Benin had been pillaged, exploited, and humiliated by international imperialism that ruled by creating havoc throughout Benin. It is clear that for twelve years Beninese diplomacy was nothing more than an appendix of the imperialist powers. Benin's external policies were only instruments in the imperialists' hands to weave their intrigues and plots against the Beninese people and their social and economic development.[26]

Under a cloud of increasingly radical declarations, a chill spread over Franco-Beninese relations. This freeze continued until 1984 when Kérékou initiated what Roger Jouffrey has called *"le pragmatisme béninois"* (Beninese pragmatism), perhaps reflecting a recognition that Benin's economy had regressed in the ten years of Marxism-Leninism.[27]

Benin's experiment with communism failed. Some have argued that "the regime in Benin was not a 'marxist regime,'" preferring instead to call the political system "Laxism-Beninism."[28] A further argument is that "despite its self-description as a marxist regime, complete with constitution, ruling party (PRPB) and appropriate vocabulary, the People's Republic of Benin is better seen as having been a variant on a common African system: centralised-bureaucratic rule."[29] By 1986, however, Benin's government had fragmented into disarticulated organizations in bankrupt ministries competing for tiny allotments of revenues to be stolen by corrupt officials.

In an important regard, Kérékou survived in power because he decentralized rule. A core within the regime never seriously threatened the centers of traditional authority in the country's three regions. Even the antifeudal campaigns of the mid-1970s barely touched the foundations of traditional authority at the village level. In this sense, the government's self-designation as a Marxist-Leninist regime quieted radical nationalist groups while leaving most Beninois alone in their daily pursuits. It is critical to recognize, however, that Kérékou presided over a military dictatorship that imprisoned anyone deemed a threat to its security. Despite its authoritarianism, the regime never attained the levels of institutionalized repression characteristic of Mobutu's Zaire or Gnassingbé Eyadéma's Togo. Although Amnesty International and other human rights organizations noted minor violations, primarily in Cotonou's main prison, the *relatively* benign regime gained limited credibility in its criticisms of France, the United States, and other Western governments. Radical rhetoric legitimated the regime and was a source of pride for the Beninese and perhaps allowed them to feel less marginal.

During the 1970s, the regime pursued a more activist foreign policy than had characterized its predecessors. In July 1976, Kérékou visited numerous socialist states to establish diplomatic ties and solicit development assistance. Obvious similarities between his voyages to Moscow, Beijing, and other socialist capitals and the annual trips routinely made by Dahomey's presidents to Paris were carefully ignored. In spite of its overtures to Eastern bloc governments, the Benin government remained profoundly dependent on France for fiscal assistance. While the government's one hand tested the limits of French patience by rhetorical condemnations, its other was begging for revenue transfers to enable its survival.

In early 1976, Benin took its rotation to a seat in the United Nations Security Council. In this capacity, Benin cosponsored a resolution to impose an embargo on South Africa, nominated Angola for membership in the UN, condemned Israel for the Entebbe raid to free hostages, and roundly criticized any developing country that aligned with the West.[30] The Kérékou regime signed treaties of cooperation with China, North Korea, Romania, and the USSR. Although Giscard d'Estaing's government grew increasingly perplexed by Kérékou's condemnations, France continued to provide substantial amounts of bilateral assistance. When France even increased its military aid to Benin in 1976, it appeared that the Kérékou regime was effectively walking the line between offending French patrons and defusing domestic opposition.

This balancing ended after the infamous French mercenary Bob Denard led an ill-fated invasion in 1977. On 16 January, a plane landed at the Cotonou airport, and a number of mercenaries drove into the city. After several hours, the Beninese militia awoke from its torpor and chased them back to the airport. This invasion might well have been forgotten except for Benin's position on the Security Council. A series of hearings disclosed the details of Denard's invasion, and Benin condemned "the cowardly and barbarous aggression committed by the imperialists and their mercenaries against the People's Republic of Benin."[31] An official report accused France, Gabon, Morocco, Togo, Côte d'Ivoire, and Senegal of trying to "set up a puppet government in the pay of French imperialism."[32]

Relations between France and Benin perceptibly chilled, and an angered d'Estaing government recalled its ambassador and left the post vacant for over a year.[33] France suspended numerous projects and cut its bilateral assistance. In response to French diplomatic protests, Benin's leaders accused the French of neocolonialism and imperialism. Meanwhile, they signed a treaty of cooperation to permit Soviet aircraft to refuel in Cotonou en route to Angola. This treaty elicited diplomatic protests and veiled threats from Washington. Relations with France and the United States deteriorated; both nations downgraded their diplomatic missions and withdrew practically all bilateral aid.

Franco-Beninese relations were in limbo for a protracted period until May 1981 when François Mitterrand was elected president. In September 1981, Kérékou visited France despite strong domestic opposition to renewed relations, especially among radical factions in the politburo. Individuals who advocated alliance with China and North Korea still held positions of influence, and Benin's foreign policies reflected their ideological biases. However, an expulsion of illegal migrants from Nigeria in 1983, high international interest rates, an overvalued dollar, and two successive devaluations of the French franc began to reveal economic weaknesses that resulted from rampant official corruption in the Kérékou government. The prices for primary commodities declined in 1985, Benin's economy declined even further, and the government grew desperate for funds.

The Flea on Nigeria's Back

As long as the neighboring Nigerian market provided considerable profits, merchants would find a way to engage in the clandestine cross-border trade. Indeed, trade relations were built upon extremely complex historical, cultural, and political links. Since long before colonial rule, merchants in the subregion had engaged in a thriving trade among villages and cities.[34] After independence, Benin has continued to export food and luxury goods to a hungry Nigerian market and received gasoline and manufactured products in return.[35] Merchants who smuggled goods into Nigeria acquired relative fortunes independently of the formal sector market. This trade provided import duties the state desperately needed. However, notions that Benin had evolved into an entrepôt state ignore the fact that the Beninese government has long received a major portion of its revenues from import and export duties.[36] Declining state revenues diminished the government's capacity to provide public services. Roads, schools, hospitals, and other projects and entities that received government allocations suffered. Meanwhile, a thriving informal sector, aggravated by corruption in the customs offices, led to a dismal collection of import duties. Benin's informal sector contributed to increased corruption and tax evasion, with the simple outcome of a miserably poor government and a collapsing infrastructure.

The sources of this informal trade were tied to the relative economic stability attained from the high volume of imports that arrived at Cotonou's port. The oil boom had produced an extraordinary wealth in Nigeria, and its population demanded food, cars, and otherwise unavailable and often illegal luxury goods. Large quantities of champagne, liquors, cigarettes, and cloth entered Cotonou's port before making the overland journey to markets in Lagos, Ibadan, Ilorin, and other Nigerian cities. (For a Nigerian perspective on these issues, see Chapter 7.) Beninese customs officers, police, and merchants profited from this illicit trade. The gains from smuggling reached both the top and bottom of Benin's political economy. For everyone from low-level teachers to high-level officials, participation in the cross-border trade softened the economic fall and slowed the growing rate of poverty in Beninese society. Private accumulation of wealth afforded the Kérékou regime a great deal of flexibility in its chronically late payment of salaries. However, this yielded an unstable situation: The impact of border closures revealed structural weaknesses in the Beninese economy and extreme poverty in its society. People who depended on trade and bribes or provided services for the illicit commerce lost all income while the borders remained closed. These people were economically paralyzed by border closures in 1984, 1986, and other times.

Kérékou's desperate attempts to attract capital reflected a stunted formal economy that provided few revenues. Among the first targets for expropriation of capital were foreign investors, followed by domestic entrepreneurs. When the regime had tried to regulate profits, many Beninese merchants simply exited from the formal economy and entered a thriving clandestine trade.[37] The Nigerian Second Republic's fall on New Year's

Eve in 1983 slowed this clandestine trade. General Muhammadu Buhari, the coup's leader, closed Nigeria's borders and jailed smugglers as economic saboteurs. Obviously, not all traders lost their share of the huge Nigerian market; the biggest merchants continued to pay bribes large enough to ensure the stability of their shipments. However, for the small-scale smugglers, the elasticity of what they could pay in bribes rapidly exceeded their earnings; many dropped out of the trade or, worse, were incarcerated as economic saboteurs. For a very short period after 1984, cross-border trade between Nigeria and Benin was the domain of large-scale smugglers capable of paying bribes and moving shipments large enough to merit the payments.

Closed borders could hardly stem the clandestine trade for an extended time.[38] An overall equilibrium point, meaning the point at which extortion discouraged trade, probably affected only the poorest merchants who engaged in periodic markets. A small number of wealthy Beninese traders continued to smuggle goods into Nigeria. However, trade in petroleum products was far too profitable to remain slack for long; smugglers from both sides of the border resumed activities within a short time.[39] The border closure and subsequent restrictions on commerce may well have increased the costs of smuggling and eroded the trade regime that had informally evolved between Nigeria and Benin. A politicization of international borders enriched officials who captured rents available from clandestine trade; the border itself had become a source of income.[40] Hence, these individuals pressured the regime to protect their access to the rents available at international borders.

The depth of the economic depression that began in 1985 had a far more negative impact on trade than the border closures. Indeed, economic depression and corrupt officials made the various cooperative ventures between Benin and Nigeria unprofitable. Treaties with Nigeria provided for a jointly funded cement factory in Onigbolo, and both countries invested with the Lonhro Corporation to build a sugar refinery in Savé. It was hoped that these projects would integrate Nigerian and Beninese markets more closely and diminish the hugely profitable informal sector. Conversely, the Nigerian government hoped that the cement plant and sugar refinery would supply its domestic market. Unfortunately, these projects failed to produce cement or sugar for sale in domestic or international markets.

Economic depression undercut the security of corrupt officials who suddenly found they needed their salaries. Even as domestic groups exerted some pressure on the regime to enhance trade, Marxist ideologues in the politburo confounded Kérékou's ability to seek foreign assistance. Indeed, different factions within the state vied to keep an ideological orthodoxy in line with Moscow or Beijing. At the same time, Benin's merchants vainly sought to keep open their access to Nigeria's market. Commerce therefore constituted a fundamental concern for one important group, even as nonalignment and allegiance to socialist orthodoxy informed another. Nonetheless, economic realities slowly eroded the position of Benin's ideological elite and eventually compelled Kérékou to adopt a pragmatic foreign policy stance.

Desperation and Economic Collapse: Foreign Policy, 1984–1990

After 1984, Kérékou solicited the intervention of France and the multilateral institutions while keeping up his ideological pronouncements. The Mitterrand government put graduated pressure on Kérékou to reach an accommodation with the IFIs for balance-of-payments equilibrium. However, domestic opposition within the politburo prevented Kérékou from seriously approaching the IMF until 1987. By that time, the government had expended practically every effort to find funding from other sources.

Desperation for financial assistance increasingly motivated Benin's foreign policy in the mid-1980s. Alliance with the Soviet bloc had brought no discernible development; infrastructure in Benin had so deteriorated that dilapidated roads, hospitals, and schools were common; civil servants regularly received their salaries late; and a parallel economy far overshadowed formal sector commerce. Even the minor offshore oil field contributed practically nothing to the GDP; reportedly, corrupt officials siphoned off the earnings before they ever entered the treasury. Ten years of Kérékou's regime had left the economy in utter shambles.

The urgency of Kérékou's situation was obvious from his clumsy attempts to raise revenues. In 1982, he fired Simon Ogouma as his minister of foreign affairs. Ogouma had been a member of the most radical faction in Kérékou's regime and promoted relations with China and North Korea. Tiamiou Adjibade replaced Ogouma; he launched a policy to open toward the West, particularly the United States. Adjibade also approached Libya and other Arab states to establish diplomatic relations. Libya responded positively: In 1983, Ma'ammar Gadhafi's government opened an embassy in Cotonou and began providing aid to build mosques, establish Islamic educational centers, fund scholarships, and support minor military cooperation. Rumors circulating in Cotonou during that time suggested that Kérékou had converted to Islam as a condition for this assistance.

For this meager assistance, Libyan president Gadhafi demanded strict reciprocity. Benin was thus drawn into the Chadian conflict and sent troops to fight on the side of rebel leader Goukonni Weddeyi. Planes from Tripoli transited via Cotonou and carried troops and supplies for Libya's various excursions in sub-Saharan Africa. By 1987, a large Libyan embassy was allegedly stockpiling weapons in Benin and running a number of programs from Cotonou. In May 1988, a *New York Times* article reported that U.S. officials had openly accused the Kérékou regime of permitting Libyan terrorists to operate out of Benin.[41] Although Kérékou denied the accusations, threats of serious retaliation shook the regime. Shortly after the article appeared, Kérékou expelled the Libyan ambassador and closed the embassy in Cotonou.

A second incident occurred in 1985 when Pan Ocean Oil (also called Panoco), a Swiss-based company, took over the contract from Saga of Norway to manage Benin's offshore wells.[42] Panoco had promised to invest $2 billion in construction of an air base, an oil refinery, irrigation facilities, and other development projects in Benin. However, it rapidly became apparent that Panoco had little intention of completing any projects. Norwegian investigators learned that Panoco had only been established in March 1985, shortly before tendering the unusual bid for the Semé fields.[43] Almost immediately after Panoco assumed management of the fields, production fell. The final straw came when Panoco failed to provide the World Bank and European Investment Bank with financial statements. Both institutions had loaned money to build the platforms, and they demanded that Kérékou suspend the contract.[44] Subsequent unconfirmed allegations suggested that Panoco may have been a front organization for European underworld figures seeking quick profits in Africa. Kérékou's failure to raise funds pushed the regime to the edge of bankruptcy.

In January 1988, Kérékou signed a contract with Sesco Ltd., a Gibraltar-based company, to accept between 1 and 5 million tons of toxic waste over ten years at $2.50 a ton.[45] Construction of the dump quickly began, and the operation lasted for six months until the European Environmental Agency released details of the contract. Particularly controversial was the decision to situate the toxic wastes at a site near Abomey. Representatives from Abomey raised such an outcry that Kérékou was forced to rescind the contract. Worse yet, this incident brought Kérékou's intentions toward Benin increasingly into question. By June 1988, the state tottered on bankruptcy, and Kérékou lacked popular support.

Kérékou seriously began negotiations with the IMF and the World Bank for a structural adjustment program in early 1987. Kérékou announced a series of subsidy cuts to comply with IMF conditions. These cuts primarily affected urban workers and students.[46] Domestic coalitions formed among the "losers" of the austerity programs, particularly students, labor, and civil servants, to oppose structural adjustment. Within weeks of the announcement, two coup attempts occurred, shaking an increasingly isolated Kérékou regime. Despite this rocky beginning, Benin had to offset severe budgetary shortfalls by obtaining loans from the IMF and accepting its conditionalities.[47] These measures drove apart many of the coalitions that had supported Kérékou, and his isolated regime faced an increasingly hostile populace.

In reality, Kérékou had no choice; the situation in Benin was nothing short of desperate. As an economist from the World Bank has noted, "Between 1985 and 1987, a period of government incapacity, real GDP fell. ... Revenues declined to below 12 percent of GDP, compared with some 15 percent earlier. The government drew down its deposits in the banking system to finance the deficit. ... By the end of 1987, it was some 70 billion CFA francs in domestic arrears."[48]

To many in Cotonou, Kérékou's acceptance of the SAP meant that he had simply replaced French neocolonialism with the cold, technocratic prescriptions of the World Bank and IMF. For the corrupt members of his regime, an accord with the IFIs meant that their unfettered access to state revenues was soon ending. The pace of corruption actually increased until November 1988, when Benin's three state-owned banks crashed. The banking crash precipitated an economic collapse as commerce was paralyzed by a lack of credit and the government was unable to pay its civil servants. Practically all Beninese recognized that the fiscal austerity required by the SAP was preferable to economic collapse. Political exigencies were then to remove Kérékou and his corrupt regime from power.

Surrounded by sycophants and venal politicians, Kérékou lurched from one fiscal crisis to another until the economy collapsed in 1989. The ease with which Kérékou had taken power did not prepare him for the difficult task of relinquishing office. In 1990, a national conference, based on several other assemblies in Beninese history, transferred power from the president's office to the newly created Office of the Prime Minister.[49] This conference was the first in francophone Africa, and it provided a model for the region. At its conclusion, Nicéphore Soglo, a technocrat trained at the prestigious French Ecole Nationale d'Administration, was elected prime minister. In March 1991, Soglo defeated Kérékou in presidential elections and became Benin's new leader.

The National Conference and Democracy: A New Foreign Policy, 1990–1995

As a wave of democracy swept across Eastern Europe and Latin America in 1989, an appreciative audience in Benin demanded democratic reform of the government.[50] Benin's domestic and foreign policies changed as the country gained prominence as a solitary African case of peaceful democratic transition. Benin went from being an outcast state to being an exporter of democratic institutions and an adviser to countries seeking to effect a transition to democracy. Benin's success with a national conference elicited considerable international attention and approval. The United States enthusiastically endorsed the outcome and pledged millions of dollars in development assistance for Benin. Unfortunately, experiences in Gabon, Togo, Congo, and other francophone countries showed that reform through a national conference was problematic. The difficulties inherent in transferring institutions between societies were at times impossible to overcome.

Benin's transition had become a model extolled by Western powers. Robert Dossou, one of the principal architects of Benin's conference, began advising opposition groups in Togo, Congo-Brazzaville, and Niger on how to organize similar assemblies. The new status it gained in making a successful democratic transition made Benin eligible to receive crucially needed funds from Western governments and multilateral institutions. Soglo took to the pulpit as an advocate of national conferences to effect democratic reform. He successfully renewed formal relations with Western governments and traveled to France, Germany, Canada, and the United States to procure bilateral aid. Along with this aid came an increase in foreign and domestic investment that enabled Benin to experience relatively high levels of economic growth.

However, regional events were evolving rapidly, and the newly elected government had to fashion a foreign policy that went beyond soliciting development assistance. The civil war in Liberia was slowly absorbing more resources and disturbing the regional economy. Soglo undoubtedly recognized that as long as the conflict continued, foreign investors would view West Africa as a region fraught with problems. An inability to quell the conflict suggested that the regional peacekeeping force (ECOMOG) had itself become a belligerent, and the conflict had become a quagmire. Meanwhile, refugees had fled to Sierra Leone and Côte d'Ivoire and destabilized the political economies of those two countries.

Soglo's regional standing increased markedly in July 1992, when he was elected to head ECOWAS. He immediately started working on elevating awareness of the Liberian conflict in the international community beyond Africa. Soglo called on the UN to mediate an end to the conflict. His inaugural speech at the annual summit of ECOWAS heads of state proposed a new course for conflict resolution in Africa. He declared that "it is an African responsibility to resolve African problems,"[51] and he emphasized that supranationality had to replace the seemingly inviolable tenets of sovereignty and nonintervention that were embodied in the defense protocols of treaties establishing ECOWAS and the Organization of African Unity. It was clear to Soglo that supranationality was critical "to reinforce cooperation and integration in the subregion." It would justify the use of an intervention force such as the one operating in Liberia. A treaty signed at the summit's conclusion revised the 1975 ECOWAS treaty's provisions of nonintervention. The new agreement also legitimated the use of regional peacekeeping forces in regional conflicts. (See

Chapter 12 for a broader discussion of regional peacekeeping and policy initiatives.)

Success at ECOWAS hardly eased Soglo's attempts to mediate the Togolese crisis. Togo's president, General Eyadéma, blamed Benin's transition for an emboldened opposition that had emerged in 1991. He therefore took pains to destabilize his eastern neighbor, most probably in the hopes that Benin's disgruntled army would overthrow the newly elected democratic government. In late 1992, Pascal Tawes, an officer in Kérékou's presidential guard, agitated disgruntled officers to participate in a coup. When the revolt failed, Tawes fled across the border to Togo. From reports, he went directly to Eyadéma's residence in northern Togo, where the president received him and then arranged for his transport to Ouagadougou.[52] The Tawes affair aggravated Togo-Benin relations as evidence surfaced that Eyadéma or someone in his regime had furnished Tawes with arms and money. Indeed, rumors circulated in Cotonou that Eyadéma had paid various agents provocateurs to provoke the violence that occurred during the 1991 presidential elections in northern Benin.

Tensions between Benin and Togo increased as the successful transition in Benin became a model for Togo's reform movement. The Soglo government was increasingly concerned with instability in neighboring Togo after its 1991 national conference. Although Eyadéma had been willing to permit the conference, he patently refused to cede power, and Togo entered a period of extreme unrest.[53] Any attempt to remove Eyadéma from office threatened an army that he had composed almost exclusively from members of his own northern ethnic group.[54] In January 1993, reports from Lomé alleged that the Togolese army had killed a large civilian population in city wards known to oppose the president. What in 1992 had been a trickle of refugees became a flood in 1993; over 145,000 Togolese refugees fled to Benin, and another 250,000 escaped to Ghana. The crisis thereafter moved rapidly to the top of Soglo's foreign policy agenda, for a huge refugee population seriously taxed Benin's vulnerable economy.

The crisis in Togo increased subregional tensions, especially between Eyadéma and the Ghanaian President Jerry Rawlings. Border closures, accusations, and counteraccusations disrupted trade and damaged the region's prospects for attracting foreign investment. The immediacy of these problems prompted Soglo to seek some means to resolve the crisis. Benin's foreign minister, Robert Dossou, announced a regional initiative to resolve the Togo-Ghana crisis in 1994. His initiative de-emphasized Benin's democratic success to avoid giving Eyadéma further reason to tamper with Benin's retired army.[55] However, only French disapproval appeared to have an impact on Eyadéma's domestic policy.

Benin's intervention in the Togo crisis attested to its return to the francophone fold. Further evidence is clear from the joint military exercises

France held in southwestern Benin. Although the immediate objective was to show a French regional presence in light of increasing tensions between Nigeria and Cameroon, choosing Benin demonstrated the country's reinsertion into the francophone community. France was clearly expressing its concerns about the Nigerian military actions in the Bekpassi peninsula. Nigeria expressed disquiet about the exercises, and Togo remained silent.[56] The choice of holding the exercises in Benin underlined its position as "a flea on Nigeria's back."

Relations with Nigeria have consistently occupied a primary position in Benin's foreign policy. After 1990, the thriving cross-border trade fueled a vast informal network of merchants and the political appointees in both countries who protected their illicit interests. Both governments lost revenues that would normally have accrued from duties and export taxes. However, the 1994 devaluation of the CFA franc had a greater impact on this commerce than border closures or attempts at increased policing. The devaluation, combined with a decision to increase gasoline prices in Nigeria, led to a marked decline in informal trade. Still, Cotonou's port receives considerable portage transiting to Burkina Faso, Niger, and Nigeria, largely due to continued instability in Togo. The depth of Benin-Nigerian-Togo trade networks suggests that cooperative trends within regional politics will increase in importance for each country's foreign policy.

The Second Kérékou Presidency and Foreign Policy

In March 1996, a rehabilitated Mathieu Kérékou defeated Nicéphore Soglo to again become the president of Benin. Kérékou effectively assembled a coalition government to defeat Soglo. He immediately appointed Adrien Houngbedji, a successful attorney and leader of a major political faction, as his prime minister. However, neither Kérékou nor Houngbedji had much latitude for autonomous actions in their foreign policy, given Benin's dependence on foreign aid. Under Soglo, the country had moved closer to France, the United States, and especially the IFIs. In July 1996, Benin increased its reliance on multilateral institutions by signing an SAP, which allowed the release of bilateral funds from Japan, France, and the United States. After signing the SAP, Benin received an Enhanced Structural Adjustment Facility (ESAF) from the IMF as part of an effort to keep the economy functioning.[57] Crucial benefits accrued from this willingness to comply with the multilateral agencies: Bilateral aid flows increased, and the Beninese economy grew at a relatively stable rate of 6 percent between 1991 and 1996.

Relations with the United States and France have improved as Benin has become a showcase for democracy in Africa. Propaganda from U.S. government–funded organizations heralded its constitution as having an

"American-style separation of power."[58] The accuracy—or rather, inaccuracy—of this assertion was irrelevant to the propaganda value of stating that Benin had seemingly succeeded to democratize after adopting U.S. political institutions. As the country increased in symbolic importance, its receipts of foreign aid jumped as well. However, although its economic circumstances improved, the government lost autonomy in foreign policy beyond compliance with demands emanating from Washington and Paris. This loss of autonomy spilled over into the private sector, as is well evidenced by the signing of a contract that permitted Tarpon Benin, a subsidiary of the Bettis Group from Dallas, Texas, to begin explorations for offshore oil reserves.[59]

Reliance on foreign aid demonstrated that Beninese foreign policy has resumed its dependence on external sources of revenue for basic operating funds. The major change has been the emergence of a combination of countries and multilateral institutions that have replaced French political-economic dominance. First, the IFIs have moved into a position of great influence in Beninese politics. At the États Généraux and national conferences that Soglo and Kérékou held to debate major policy initiatives, representatives of the World Bank and the IMF figured prominently among the invited guests. The European Union has become a major contributor to Beninese development, as evidenced by its influence in elections and privatization programs. This shift from reliance on bilateral assistance to multilateral concessionary loans is consistent with experiences across Africa. Improved relations with the United States and France have been critical to Benin's foreign policy. Western governments have extolled the Beninese experience as a model for democracy in Africa. Unfortunately, the U.S. Agency for International Development (USAID) and the French Ministère de la Coopération found that the exportation of Benin's experience failed to take root in other francophone African societies. Finally, French businesses have increased their investment in Benin, and their presence in Cotonou has visibly grown. Although Benin has experienced certain difficulties in consolidating democracy, the French have continued to counsel Kérékou and provide bilateral assistance. It was no coincidence that immediately upon taking power, Kérékou visited President Jacques Chirac to discuss bilateral relations, including French development assistance.

Conclusion

Foreign policy reflects compromises and conflicts among three sets of actors: domestic coalitions, factions internal to the state, and international actors. Policies may demonstrate the ascendance of one or another faction. In Benin, coalitions within the state limited the regime's ability to decide foreign policy autonomously. Again, membership in these factions resulted from how the government balanced domestic pressures. At one extreme, the country was a foreign "policy taker"; its regime had to accept the prescriptions dictated by Paris. This situation reflected the regime's dependence on the previous metropole's largesse. However, international actors, particularly regional interests, assumed greater importance as economic decline became a serious crisis in 1990.

Throughout its first twenty-five years of independence, Benin engaged in a dialogue with France, but a subtle change occurred between 1974 and 1984 wherein the importance of regional politics pushed aside the colony-metropole relationship. A forced repatriation of refugees in 1983 demonstrated the potentially unsettling effects of regional incidents. Although the cause of the event was internal Nigerian politics, the ramifications were decidedly regional. A later repatriation in 1985 reinforced the importance of regional politics. A recession that followed the commodities market collapse devastated Benin's economy. Again the primacy of regional events clearly demonstrated the vulnerability of Benin's political economy. This lesson was obvious to Nicéphore Soglo, who advanced an activist foreign policy after he took office in 1991.

Soglo showed an understanding that an unstable West Africa means that regional economic development will be retarded. Instability repels foreign investment, a critical component of development. Moreover, instability prevents policy planning. West African states have always been highly interdependent; upheaval in one generally affects others. Linkages have increased since the end of colonialism as trade has grown between anglophone and francophone African states. In part, this increase in commerce is a consequence of ECOWAS, but equally important has been the explosion of population and accompanying markets.

By 1996, Benin entered a new phase of political development. A critical maturity had entered its foreign policy, demonstrating a recognition that regional politics were primary. Soglo had propelled Benin into a new age in which relations with France are now important but no longer primary. Kérékou has built upon the developments achieved by the Soglo administration and deepened Benin's relations with the World Bank and the IMF. Regional interdependence may lead to greater economic and perhaps even political integration among West African countries. Benin may evolve into a leader for such an evolution.

Notes

1. World Bank, *World Development Report, 1995* (New York: Oxford University Press, 1995).

2. In November 1975, Dahomey became the People's Republic of Benin. It changed its name again in 1990 to the Republic of Benin.

3. Peter J. Katzenstein, *Small States in World Markets: Industrial Policy in Europe* (Ithaca: Cornell University Press, 1985), pp. 39–79.

4. M.-P. S., "Incompréhension et amertume: Les relations entre l'Afrique et la France," *Le Monde*, 20 January 1994, p. 6.

5. For a wonderful description of the links between French businesspeople and African rulers, see Stephen Smith and Antoine Glaser, *Ces messieurs afrique: Le Paris-Village du continent noire* (Paris: Calman-Lévy, 1992).

6. See in particular Jean-François Bayart, "La politique africaine de la France: de Charybde en Scylla," *Politique Africaine*, 49, March 1993, pp. 133–136; also Bayart, *La politique africaine de François Mitterrand* (Paris: Karthala, 1984).

7. See the editorial "Dévaluation et politique," in *Marchés Tropicaux et Méditerranéens*, 2520, 25 February 1994, p. 339; Géraldine Faes and Rémi Godeau, "Dakar, 11 janvier 20 heures 50 . . . ," *Jeune afrique*, 1724, 20–26 January 1994, pp. 36–37; Kaye Whiteman, "The Party's Over," *Africa Report*, March-April 1994, pp. 13–28.

8. Jean-François Bayart, "Réflexions sur la politique africaine de la France," *Politique Africaine*, 58, 1995, p. 43.

9. Paul Collier, "Africa's External Economic Relations: 1960–1990," *African Affairs*, 90, 1991, p. 341.

10. Robert D. Putnam, "Diplomacy and Domestic Politics: The Logic of Two-Level Games," *International Organization*, 42(3), 1988, p. 432.

11. Ibid.

12. See the ministerial changes graphically displayed in Chris Allen, "Benin," in Bogdan Szajkowski (ed.), *Benin, the Congo, Burkina Faso* (London: Pinter, 1989), pp. 40–41.

13. On the role of ideas, see the essays collected in Peter A. Hall (ed.), *The Political Power of Economic Ideas: Keynesianism Across Nations* (Princeton: Princeton University Press, 1989); on how international ideas influence domestic coalitions, see Peter Gourevitch, "The Second Image Reversed: The International Sources of Domestic Politics," *International Organization*, 32(4), 1978, pp. 881–911.

14. Donald Horowitz, *Ethnic Groups in Conflict* (Berkeley and Los Angeles: University of California Press, 1987).

15. Dov Ronen, *Dahomey: Between Tradition and Modernity* (Ithaca: Cornell University Press, 1975), p. 104.

16. In a sad affirmation of Huntington's pessimistic analysis of praetorianism, Dahomey experienced coup after coup because no single faction could gain control and the only coherent institution in society was the army. See Samuel P. Huntington, *Political Order in Changing Societies* (New Haven: Yale University Press, 1968).

17. Dov Ronen, "People's Republic of Benin: The Military, Marxist Ideology, and the Politics of Ethnicity," in John Harbeson (ed.), *The Military in African Politics* (New York: Praeger, 1987), p. 112.

18. *Marchés Tropicaux et Méditerranéens*, 1517, 1 December 1974, p. 3529.

19. Daniel C. Bach, "Francophone Regional Organizations and ECOWAS," in Julius Emeka Okolo and Stephen Wright (eds.), *West African Regional Cooperation and Development* (Boulder: Westview Press, 1990), pp. 53–66.

20. A discussion of African Marxist-Leninist regimes can be found in Kenneth Jowitt, "Scientific Socialist Regimes in Africa: Political Differentiation, Avoidance, and Unawareness," in Carl G. Rosberg and Thomas M. Callaghy (eds.), *Socialism*

in Sub-Saharan Africa: A New Assessment, (Berkeley, Calif.: Institute of International Studies, 1979), pp. 133–173.

21. Michel Houndjahoué, "Notes sur les relations internationales du Bénin socialiste: 1972–1986," *Revue Études Internationales*, 8(2), June 1987, p. 371. See as well L. A. Obukhov, "The Ideological and Political Platform of the Revolutionary Democracy of Benin," in Jaroslav Cesar (ed.), *Dissertationes Orientales*, vol. 41, *The Most Recent Trends in the Socialist Orientation of Various African and Arab Countries* (Prague: Oriental Institute in Academia, Publishing House of the Czechoslovak Academy of Sciences, 1979).

22. Colin W. Lawson, "Soviet Economic Aid to Africa," *African Affairs*, 87(349), October 1988, p. 509.

23. Stephen D. Krasner, "Structural Causes and Regime Consequences: Regimes as Intervening Variables," in Stephen D. Krasner (ed.), *International Regimes* (Ithaca: Cornell University Press, 1983), pp. 1–22.

24. Dependency theory separates the world into countries that belong to the capitalist core and those that are part of an underdeveloped periphery. This theory rests upon a structural conceptualization of the core as homogenous and unitary in purpose and the periphery as divided, victimized, and without a capacity to use advanced technologies. The early proponents of this theory studied Latin America, but scholars such as Samir Amin, *Neo-Colonialism in West Africa* (New York: Monthly Review Press, 1973), Mahmood Mamdani, *Politics and Class Formation in Uganda* (New York: Monthly Review Press, 1976), Peter Anyang'Nyong'o (ed.), *Popular Struggles for Democracy in Africa* (Atlantic Highlands, N.J.: Zed, 1987), extended the theory to Africa. For an excellent critique of dependency theory as it pertains to Africa or elsewhere, see Paul Kennedy, *African Capitalism: The Struggle for Ascendancy* (New York: Cambridge University Press, 1988), pp. 119–123.

25. Jacques Latremolière, "L'indemnisation des entreprises nationalisés déterminera l'attitude de la coopération française à l'égard du Dahomey," *Marchés Tropicaux et Méditerranéens*, 1520, 27 December 1974, p. 3713.

26. People's Republic of Benin, Ministère des Affairs Etrangères et de la Coopération (16 March 1976), cited in Michel Houndjahoué, "Bénin: Révolution socialiste et politique étrangère à l'ère de la Diplomatie Nouvelle," *Le Mois en Afrique*, 225–226, October-November 1984, p. 34.

27. Roger Jouffrey, "Le Bénin depuis 1981," *Afrique contemporaine*, 127, July-August-September 1983, pp. 34–43.

28. Chris Allen, "'Good-bye to All That': The Short and Sad Story of Socialism in Benin," *Review of African Political Economy*, 54, 1992, p. 27.

29. Idem, "Reconstructing an Authoritarian State: The Limits of 'Democratic Renewal' in Benin," *Journal of Communist Studies*, 8(2), 1992, p. 63.

30. *African Contemporary Record 1976–1977*, 9, p. B556.

31. Quoted in Chaim Herzog, "UN at Work: The Benin Affair," *Foreign Policy*, 29, Winter 1977–1978, p. 144.

32. Ibid., p. 148.

33. Claude Wauthier, *Quatre présidents et l'Afrique: De Gaulle, Pompidou, Giscard d'Estaing, Mitterrand* (Paris: Éditions du Seuil, 1995), pp. 357–358.

34. See Robin Law, "Trade and Politics Behind the Slave Trade: The Lagoon Traffic and the Rise of Lagos, 1500–1800," *Journal of African History*, 24, 1983, pp. 321–348.

35. Laurent Zekpa and Antonin Dossou, "Impact du choc pétrolier au Nigéria sur l'économie Béninoise," *Revue Tiers Monde*, 30(120), 1989, pp. 895–905.

36. John Igue and Bio Soulé, *L'Etat entrepôt au Bénin: Commerce informel ou solution à la crise?* (Paris: Éditions Karthala, 1992).

37. On the concept of disengagement, see Victor Arzanya and Naomi Chazan, "Disengagement from the State in Africa: Reflections on the Experiences of Guinea and Ghana," *Comparative Studies in Society and History*, 29(1), 1987, pp. 106–131.

38. See Léon C. Codo, *Le Bénin dans les rapports Ouest-Africains: Stratégie d'insertion, bilatéralisme sous-régionale et engagements régionaux* (Bordeaux: Université de Bordeaux, Centre d'Etude d'Afrique Noire, 1987).

39. Zekpa and Dossou, "Impact du choc pétrolier au Nigéria sur l'économie Béninoise."

40. Daniel Bach has observed that international borders present opportunities for an extraction of rents that government officials exploit. His point is that an effective lobby has emerged among corrupt officials who resist regional integration in West Africa. Personal communication, 1995.

41. Elaine Sciolino, "U.S. Accuses Benin of Abetting Libyan Terrorism," *New York Times*, 20 May 1988.

42. For the full story, see *African Contemporary Record*, 19, 1986–1987, p. B7. See as well *Paris-Vogue*, December 1985–January 1986.

43. "Contract of Norwegian Oil Company Reported Revoked," *Aftenposten* (Oslo), 29 August 1985, translated in *Joint Publication Research Services*, JPRS-SSA-85-105, 20 October 1985, p. 36.

44. *African Economic Digest*, 6–12 December 1986, p. 7.

45. *Marchés Tropicaux et Méditerranéens*, 2221, 3 June 1988, p. 1445. See as well *African Contemporary Record*, 21, 1988–1989, p. B3.

46. *Marchés Tropicaux et Méditerranéens*, 2214, 15 April 1988, p. 914.

47. It is important to recognize that a country may default on bilateral loans with manageable disruptions to the national economy. Most such defaults precipitate negotiations to reschedule payments. Multilateral debt, however, must be assiduously repaid according to a prearranged schedule. In the event of a default on multilateral loans, the country will lose all access to international credit. Governments cannot endure such a situation, and thus few have ever gone into arrears on multilateral debt.

48. Richard Westebbe, "Structural Adjustment, Rent-Seeking, Liberalization in Benin," in Jennifer A. Widner (ed.), *Economic Change and Political Liberalization in Sub-Saharan Africa* (Baltimore: Johns Hopkins University Press, 1994), pp. 86–87.

49. John R. Heilbrunn, "Social Origins of National Conferences in Benin and Togo," *Journal of Modern African Studies*, 31(2), 1993, pp. 277–299.

50. The notion of democracy occurring in waves is from Samuel P. Huntington, *The Third Wave: Democratization in the Late Twentieth Century* (Norman: University of Oklahoma Press, 1991).

51. All quotes are from *Agence France Presse*, 14006, 27 July 1993.

52. *Jeune Afrique*, 1656, 1–7 October 1992, p. 10.

53. John R. Heilbrunn and Comi M. Toulabor, "Une si petite démocratisation pour le Togo . . . ," *Politique Africaine*, 58, 1995, pp. 85–100.

54. John R. Heilbrunn, "Togo: The National Conference and Stalled Reform," in John F. Clark and David E. Gardinier (eds.), *Political Reform in Francophone Africa* (Boulder: Westview Press, 1997), pp. 225–245.

55. *Economist Intelligence Unit–Benin*, 2, 1994, p. 36.

56. Ibid.

57. *Economist Intelligence Unit–Benin*, 3, 1996, p. 31.

58. Jennifer Ludden, "Benin: A Model of Openness in Turbulent Africa," *Christian Science Monitor*, 1 March 1996, p. 7.

59. The French company Elf-Aquitaine competed with the Americans for this contract. See "Bilan de la situation économique au Bénin," *Marchés Tropicaux et Méditerranéens*, 2658, 18 October 1996, p. 2219.

4

Exceptionality in External Affairs: Botswana in the African and Global Arenas

JAMES ZAFFIRO

Botswana has made a transition from the "Switzerland of Africa" to the "Sweden of Africa" in less than a decade. Its heightened diplomatic and military profile in regional, continental, and even global affairs today is truly puzzling for all but a few who have watched its leaders and diplomats skillfully maneuver in troubled waters since independence. How can we account for such a shift? Indeed, placing it within a wider foreign policy context over the same significant half decade of change and transformation in Botswana's external relations is the task of this chapter. How much of the change has been deliberate and homegrown in scope? How much is a result of external incentives and pressures?

In external relations as in domestic policy, we must tread carefully in interpreting Botswana's "exceptionality." After all, how many other African countries today are sending emergency aid to their neighbors,[1] volunteering troops for international peacekeeping,[2] and floating loans to the IMF?[3] In the 1990s, Botswana is positioning itself to build upon earlier foreign policy successes. In the course of this analysis, I will show how a regional and perhaps continental leadership role is possible for a state of limited means.

Key areas of current policy that most strongly capture the changing nature of external challenges and opportunities are considered, including: (1) deployment of Botswana Defence Force (BDF) units to UN peacekeeping missions, (2) initiation of formal relations with South Africa, (3) maturation of relations with the United States, (4) diplomatic leadership in regional conflict resolution, and (5) expansion of diplomatic and economic relations with Asia.

Domestic Environment

Little has changed since the mid-1980s when James Polhemus found evidence that Botswana's foreign policy makers responded mainly to "the realities of history, economics, and geography" and not domestic political demands.[4] Domestic political and economic priorities, particularly development needs and goals, are indistinguishable from regime foreign policy objectives. Founded in 1966, Botswana is small, poor, landlocked, arid, trade dependent, and surrounded by hostile neighbors and conflicts. Its foreign policy goals and strategies have always been motivated and shaped by its leaders' cautious, pragmatic, perceived need to acknowledge and come to terms with a set of relatively fixed environmental, geographic, colonially imposed, and regional constraints.

Commenting on the scant economic and geostrategic inheritance of his country at independence, Botswana's first president, Sir Seretse Khama, once said that his people could not just pick up their country and move it somewhere else. After the discovery of diamonds in the 1970s, there were surely some who were glad they could not. Diamond-driven, elite-serving development policies; an efficient, paternalistic bureaucracy; a frustrated, underemployed, foreign-educated professional cadre; and a tradition of civilian control of the military have been critical elements in the domestic environment for foreign policy. Southern African liberation pressures and threats, migrant labor, rapid urbanization, and population growth have also shaped the domestic context.

For Botswana, development policy *is* foreign policy, itself a means for pursuit of vital national and elite interests. Limited (until recently) official corruption; domestic political stability; presidential pragmatism and effective leadership; a climate of steadily improving regional security and stability; and the emergence of a fast-growing, diamond-based, export-oriented economy—and good luck—have all contributed to three decades of enviable foreign policy stability and success.

Botswana's foreign policy in the post–Cold War era must come to terms not only with a dramatically transformed international and regional environment but with a rapidly changing domestic context as well. It is at home that the greatest challenges—and dangers—to future foreign policy success lie. The economy is top-heavy, narrow, and capital-intensive. Diamonds are *not* forever, at least not in the mines of Orapa and Jwaneng. Unemployment is high. Foreign investment is not sufficient to fuel an Asian-style market takeoff.

Foreign reserves, in the face of severe income disparities and deteriorating living conditions for a majority of rural Batswana, compel more and more citizens to ask why these moneys are not being spent at home on basic needs. The share of votes garnered by opposition political parties in national, district, and local level elections is growing.[5] There were more opposition members of parliament (MPs) elected in the 1995 Botswana National Assembly—thirteen of forty-three—than ever before. For political reasons, future foreign policy must reflect changing domestic needs and interests.

The end of apartheid in Southern Africa may prove a mixed blessing for this front-line state, as colonially drawn "lines" fade and aid and investment spotlights shift southward. Botswana's initially shaky, "quasi-state" status may return as the diamonds run out; cities fill with educated, unemployed youth; and overgrazed, elite-owned rangeland deteriorates environmentally. As front lines dissipate, older, precolonial fault lines may begin to resurface: ethnic, linguistic, social, and economic. Foreign policy must realign. It may not have been possible to pick up Botswana and move it in 1966, but by the next round of national elections in 1999, the idea of the Botswana state may itself start to vibrate or "move" as the regional social, political, and economic tectonics continue their timeless shifting and scraping beneath the surface. Devising and pursuing innovative strategies aimed at decreasing external economic dependence must once again, as they briefly were in the beginning, become the central foreign policy objectives.

Presidential Politics and Foreign Affairs

Credit for the notable continuity, stability, and success of Botswana's foreign affairs must go, in large part, to the able leadership of the country's first two presidents. The current officeholder, Sir Ketumile Masire, squelching rumors of retirement, led his party to yet another national election triumph in 1994.[6] Attention now focuses on the question of electoral succession. Who will the ruling party candidate be? And how well will opposition parties do next time?

Presidential succession and civil-military relations remain key elements in any future foreign and defense policy equation. Since 1989, President Masire has had to contend with more than his share of factional strife within the ruling Botswana Democratic Party (BDP), aggravated by corruption scandals and forced resignations of top cabinet officials.[7]

The two main BDP factions have significantly different domestic economic policy agendas, each with important external policy implications. It will matter a great deal which eventually emerges victorious under a new presidential patron. The faction known as "Big-5" leads what one informed analyst labels "a trained mandarin class with a firm commitment to developing the economy"[8] in the context of a Western-oriented, paternalistic, bureaucratic state structure. The other faction, the "populist politicos," are led by Agriculture Minister Daniel Kwelogobe, who opposes heavy-handed, bureaucratic governance.

Big-5 controls the most powerful government positions currently. Presidential Affairs Minister Ponatshego Kedikilwe is also de facto minister of defense, internal affairs, and mass media. His portfolio includes the Botswana Defence Force. General Mompati Merafhe, who formerly commanded BDF and served as presidential affairs minister, is the current foreign affairs minister. Vice President Festus Mogae retains his position as head of finance and development planning. BDF Commander Seretse Khama Ian Khama, son of the late president, although not yet a political factor, has a strong, natural interest in siding with Big-5 technocrats if he is required to choose, both for his own political future as well as for stability in the country.

Foreign Policy Structures and Processes

Control over foreign affairs remains narrowly concentrated within the Office of the President (OP), which serves as a "superministry" encompassing foreign affairs, defense, mass media, police, public service, and even the National Assembly. In the early 1970s, a Department of External Affairs (EA) with a permanent secretary and a small headquarters staff (HQ) was created by President Seretse Khama.

It was generally understood, even after the appointment of a separate minister in 1974, that the president would remain Botswana's top foreign policy decisionmaker and diplomat. A decade later, EA remained small: It had fewer than sixty positions at HQ and was thinly spread across seven foreign embassies and high commissions abroad.[9]

Today, although foreign posts have proliferated, the basic structure of authority and decisionmaking has not changed fundamentally. Staff shortages, frequent reshuffling of key people, and lack of training and development continue to limit the potential of the department.[10] Efforts to address these chronic problems are outlined in National Development Plan 8 (1997–2003).[11] There are still periodic calls for a separate ministry of foreign affairs from ruling party backbenchers and opposition MPs, along with growing support for greater legislative influence on foreign affairs.[12]

Substantial policy influence rests with administrative elites in key ministries and departments, especially Finance and Development Planning. Opposition MPs and ruling party backbenchers as well are not trusted and have little influence with the public service cadre; they also do not have much access to information that might enable them to play a more active, informed role in debating external policy issues and priorities. Some permanent secretaries candidly view MPs as illegitimate players in policymaking, which in their view should remain the exclusive domain of cabinet officials and top public service managers.

The National Assembly serves as a forum for publicizing and ratifying "administratively generated" policies. Serious debate and actual decisionmaking occurs in the cabinet. Cabinet-level foreign policy deliberations and decisionmaking are more important today than under the tenure of President Khama, whose stature, experience, charismatic personality, and external affairs vision dominated, if not supplanted, the need for a foreign affairs debate. Few ministers have the time, interest, or access to information and advice necessary to participate actively in foreign policy making.

Key ministries have become increasingly sophisticated in involving themselves in relevant aspects of external affairs. Besides finance and development planning, commerce and industry, education, and mineral affairs are considered "top" portfolios and go to key presidential allies and experienced, trusted confidants.

The Military and External Affairs

At independence, Botswana's leaders decided that for financial and strategic reasons, they could ill afford to take the commonly accepted, sovereign step of creating an army.[13] A decade later, it was decided that territorial integrity and security of the citizenry necessitated creation of at least a symbolic armed defense force, and the Botswana Defence Force was born.[14] Another decade later, at the height of regional instability and South Africa's military actions against its neighbors, including Botswana, the BDF began to grow.

By 1990, most observers expected to see annual defense appropriations begin to recede, but instead, the early 1990s witnessed massive, unprecedented growth in military spending, arms purchases, force expansion, joint military maneuvers, creation of a more advanced air wing, and finally, by 1992, in international deployment of BDF troops in UN peacekeeping missions. This led to critical talk, both inside and outside Botswana, concerning continuing high levels of defense spending. Leaders stressed the connection between security and the uncertain regional situation in defending continued expansion.[15] The president contends that although recent levels of spending—roughly 10 percent of the recurrent budget for 1997–1998,[16] as compared with 12.7 percent for 1992–1993—may still seem too high, it must be acknowledged that the BDF did not inherit any physical infrastructure when it was created in 1976; only now is this being created. He has also made it plain that military spending and defense readiness remain essential to the country's stability and future.

Expanding the capabilities and experience of the BDF is good foreign policy. This extends to encouraging an international role for the BDF. African political factions embroiled in armed conflict are more likely to abide African mediators and peacekeepers on their territory than UN envoys or U. S. marines, French or Belgian paratroopers, or other foreign (non-African) troops. Botswana successfully demonstrated this preference in Somalia and Mozambique.

A cabinet member who inspected BDF troops in Somalia in 1993 briefed parliament on his return: "As I drove around Mogadishu, I was touched by the frequent shouts of Botswana, Botswana by young and old Somalis alike. The Somalis regard Botswana as blood brothers to whom they are willing to give information about arms caches, the discovery of which has been a major feature of the success of operations."[17]

Not surprisingly, Botswana, one of the few states that take membership in the OAU seriously enough to pay their dues on time, was also among a handful of African states pledging troops to serve in a humanitarian role in Rwanda.[18] As early as September 1992, long before the 1994 genocide, Botswana had provided BDF observers to a UN force stationed along the Rwanda-Uganda border.[19]

Botswana's diplomatic and military role in Mozambique was pivotal in helping to achieve and maintain the unsteady cease-fire between the Maputo government and Mozambique National Resistance Movement (RENAMO) forces. In September 1992, with President Masire as host, President Joaquim Chissano and Afonso Dhlakama of RENAMO met in Gaborone "because of the confidence they have in the leadership [of Botswana]"[20] to discuss prospects for peace in Mozambique. It was at that meeting that a common understanding for building peace was reached. In 1993, Botswana sent forces as part of the United Nations Operation in Mozambique (UNOMOZ) into the Tete region following withdrawal of Italian peacekeepers, and by mid-1994, it extended operations to Chimoio, Quelimane, and port and oil facilities at Beira.[21] There was even a request for the BDF to help train the new 30,000-troop integrated Mozambique National Defense Force, along with Britain, Portugal, and France.[22]

With five infantry battalions, armor, ground and air transport, and even a few secondhand jet fighters at its disposal, the BDF today is sufficiently large, trained, equipped, and led to be able to provide units in peacekeeping missions while still offering a limited domestic defense capability. Recent training and arming of the 4,500-member force emphasized rapid deployment and internal security.[23] By mid-1994, the BDF had efficiently rotated a total of 3,500 troops for peacekeeping in Somalia, Mozambique, and Rwanda.[24] Botswana's current leaders remain committed to building and maintaining a military force capable of future participation in UN and other multilateral missions. (For a discussion of African regional policies, see Chapter 12.)

Regional Policy

Given its landlocked position and extreme economic vulnerability, Botswana's primary external policy concern has always been bilateral relations with South Africa. Informal relations have been evolving continuously, but until the 1990s, Botswana studiously avoided South African pressures to establish normal diplomatic relations, not wishing to legitimize the apartheid state. Botswana officials interacted with their counterparts across the border only when an issue was perceived to be of direct benefit to national goals of survival, security, or economic well-being, such as renegotiation of the Southern African Customs Union (SACU) agreement, periodic high-level consultations over alleged ANC military infiltrations across Botswana, SADF raids on Botswana, and matters involving the treatment of Botswana citizens working in South Africa.

For both states today, opportunities for collaboration seem especially promising in the fields of mining, agriculture, education, the environment, AIDS policy, labor issues, and drought management. The mutual goal of expanding economic relations overshadows diplomatic, political, or security concerns, yet successful expansion will rest upon progress made across these "long-invisible" areas of relations. However, Botswana's tiny and new private industrial sector has begun to express concern about South African competition.[25]

Movement toward full normalization began in 1991 and intensified over the following two years. Both Botswana and South Africa opened representatives' offices in each other's capitals in June 1992.[26] At the same time, Botswana's leaders were working successfully to improve relations with the ANC. In July 1994, representative offices in Gaborone and Pretoria were upgraded to full diplomatic missions. Botswana's first high commissioner, veteran diplomat Oteng Tebape, presented his letters of credence to President Nelson Mandela in mid-September 1994. Offices in Johannesburg and Cape Town were upgraded to consulates. The former ANC representative to Botswana, Oupa Mokou, became South Africa's first ambassador to Gaborone in 1995.

Bilateral economic relations remain paramount, but they will become increasingly interwoven with changing regional, multilateral economic relations. For Botswana, rapid but narrow economic growth, uneven distribution of national income, recurrent drought, and a capital-intensive, mineral-based domestic economy have resulted in a heavy dependence on trade with Pretoria. The need for imports of all kinds, especially food, fuels, and manufactured goods, plays nicely into the hands of South African producers and exporters, who have been and remain Botswana's main source and suppliers, with or without apartheid. (For a South African perspective, see Chapter 9.)

Even with South Africa now formally a partner in SADC and the OAU, much of Botswana's future economic policy toward Pretoria will continue to depend mainly upon outside initiatives and actions, rather than those it takes on its own. The extent of Botswana's long-standing, asymmetrical economic integration with its southern neighbor will continue to make it extremely vulnerable to South African government or multinational corporations' activities in regional economic policy. A prime example is Botswana's near-total dependence on South Africa's road, rail, and shipping transport infrastructure for its exports.

Regional trade and integration arrangements have not lived up to initial expectations. Indeed, Botswana today is more economically dependent on South Africa than it was at the time of SADCC's founding. In August 1992, SADCC was transformed into the Southern African Development Community when its members signed the Windhoek Treaty, pledging to work along the same lines as the EU.[27] Member states must continue to face the sticky issue of balancing national and regional interests, especially in the areas of investment and trade.

The fact that the new SADC secretariat building sits in Gaborone is significant. Botswana has been a careful supporter of regional and continental institutions, from the standpoint of their relative utility in serving its national interests, and strong emphasis has been put on the SADC connection. South African membership brings new investment capital, technology, markets, and economic power to the grouping. Much will ultimately depend upon what sort of balance is struck between the traditional mission of the old SADCC—economic "liberation" and development via infrastructure rehabilitation and reduction of dependency on South Africa—and the new mission of SADC, a more truly regional trading bloc seeking to build a more globally competitive regional economy.[28]

Botswana's leaders need to strike a careful balance between bilateral and multilateral strategies for dealing with South African regional domination. For Botswana and its neighbors, any new world order will continue to be more directly mediated by South Africa than by any other player. Botswana can ultimately help itself by supporting decreased military spending and structures for regional military and security cooperation within the SADC framework.

Closer economic ties with a democratic South Africa offer Botswana the best way out of the coming economic slowdown as diamond-driven development declines, particularly if such ties can generate employment-producing, self-sustaining economic development. To empower itself, Botswana is better situated than any other SADC state to take advantage of South Africa's strong universities, sophisticated science and technology infrastructure, and economic base. Now that normal relations are politically acceptable, this process has begun in earnest.

Diamond-Driven Diplomacy: Reaping the Benefits

Botswana's leaders clearly want to play significantly larger roles in conflict resolution and avoidance, regional security, and continental peacekeeping today than ever before. Throughout the Cold War, a cornerstone of Botswana's foreign policy was the maintenance of friendly relations with a variety of states. One of the advantages of this strategy today, in the post–Cold War era, is that Botswana has a well-established global network of trusted diplomatic connections enabling it to aspire to a participatory role in virtually any African issue or conflict, at times extending even beyond Africa. Cultivation of networks and connections never stops. In late 1993, following peace talks and the accord between Israel and the Palestine Liberation Organization (PLO), Botswana resumed full diplomatic relations with Israel, making it one of only a handful of African states to do so.[29]

Because Botswana possesses Africa's only uninterrupted liberal democratic system and a strong economy, its leaders have advantages internationally that most of its neighbors do not have. Since 1970, Botswana's economy has grown at an annual rate of roughly 8.8 percent, one of the highest rates in the world.[30] Its reputation, resources, and experience in international diplomacy led to its selection as the host country for the 1993 ACP/EU Joint Assembly. At the same time, President Masire was serving as chairman of SADC. When the OAU established an observer mission to South Africa, it selected Botswana's long-serving (since 1980) UN ambassador, Joseph Legwaila, to head it. Legwaila had served in a similar capacity in 1989–1990 as UN assistant representative in Namibia during the transition to independence.

In 1993, Botswana's foreign minister, Gaositwe Chiepe, played an important role in gaining support for and approval of a formal OAU mechanism for conflict prevention, management, and resolution. Botswana also pushed for creation of a subcommittee of the Ad Hoc Committee of Heads of State to seek a solution to the Angolan conflict.[31] In South Africa, Botswana played a significant role, sending military and police officers to help train the new National Peace-Keeping Force (NPKF) in early 1994, along with twenty-three election observers, including five MPs.[32] Clearly, there is potential and some momentum for building a regional security apparatus for conflict resolution within SADC.

Beyond Mutual Admiration:
Botswana and the United States

U.S.–South African policy shaped bilateral relations until the arrival of Soviet-Cuban influence in Southern Africa in the mid-1970s. Local complexities of states in the region (to borrow the language of NSSM-39) were subordinated to globalist-containment logic. Declassified documents from Gerald Ford's administration strongly suggest that friendly relations with Botswana were explicitly viewed by then U.S. Secretary of State Henry Kissinger as a tool for broader strategic objectives in the region and nothing more.[33]

From independence, Botswana looked to the United States as an eventual substitute partner for a retiring Britain, specifically for development aid and diplomatic and strategic support. The relationship developed slowly until the mid-1980s. At that time, faced with South African military incursions, Botswana's leaders made a big push for unprecedented levels of U.S. high-technology arms transfers and diplomatic support. These efforts enjoyed only partial success, and Botswana was forced to turn to Britain and India to meet some of its most pressing military needs.

During the George Bush years, Botswana expected little substantive change in U.S.–Southern African policy, resigning itself to "dealing with Reaganism, at least a little while [longer]."[34] Particularly upsetting was the Bush pledge to continue "covert" military support to UNITA rebels in Angola, including the highly effective, ground-launched Stinger missile system, despite expressed opposition from FLS leaders. Botswana had asked the United States to sell them Stingers and was refused. (See Chapter 2 on Angola.)

During Bill Clinton's administration, bilateral relations changed little. In addition to multilateral security coordination in Africa, bilateral cooperation in natural resources management, wildlife conservation, basic education, family planning, AIDS prevention, private sector development, military training, and regional security continued.[35] The U.S. emphasis is now on regional, multilateral development assistance. The USAID mission in Botswana was phased out in 1994.[36]

Economic and commercial relations between the two countries grew following the 1989 visit of President Masire to Washington. Since then, the Ministry of Commerce and Industry, commercial banks, and Botswana embassies abroad, including those in the United States, have stepped up promotion and information activities. USAID and the Overseas Private Investment Corporation (OPIC) provided substantial support for private sector development during the early 1990s, emphasizing foreign and domestic investment, business linkages, management and training, and job creation.[37]

By 1994, direct U.S. private investment in the manufacturing sector totaled $150 million, three-quarters of which had flowed in since 1989. Some of the manufacturing enterprises to be affected were diamond polishing, the production of cooking oil (H. J. Heinz) and soap (Colgate-Palmolive), and a clay factory.[38] In addition, Botswana was chosen over South Africa as the site of a new Owens-Corning glass-reinforced pipe factory. A company spokesperson cited "Botswana's political stability" and "rapid economic growth," along with the continued uncertainty and violence in South Africa, as factors in its choice of Botswana.[39]

Controversy surrounded the construction of the BDF Mapharangwane air base facilities, dubbed "Operation Eagle" by the Botswana press. Criticism centered on its high cost (around $300 million),[40] alleged U.S. funding, and fears of a U.S. military presence in the country.[41] Joint military maneuvers in 1992 further fueled such speculation. Matters reached such a point by 1993 that Foreign Minister Merafhe presented documents to prove that the base was built "exclusively with Botswana public funds" and stated that "there are no foreign military bases or personnel in Botswana."[42]

Leaders view their ties with the United States as one important way of maintaining long-term security and territorial integrity in a still volatile region. Ties continue to be counterbalanced via ongoing defense cooperation with Commonwealth countries and ongoing efforts to construct an SADC defense and security regime.

The Lure of the Far East

Perhaps the most striking shift of emphasis in Botswana's foreign relations is in the growth of ties with East Asia, in particular China and Japan but also South Korea, Singapore, and Malaysia. (For similar trends in Kenya, see Chapter 6.) With the exception of relations with China, which date from the 1970s, and limited contacts with Asian Commonwealth states, this new emphasis has mainly been evident since 1989.

In the 1990s, diamond-driven economic growth gave Botswana's leaders the luxury of seeking representation that is more balanced worldwide outside of Europe, Africa, and North America by expanding diplomatic and commercial ties. By 1995, Botswana's foreign affairs budget had more than doubled from 1992.[43] While most other states cut back, Botswana opened a new embassy in the People's Republic of China (PRC), followed by a consulate-general office in Hong Kong, "to take care of trade and commercial interests in the Far East."[44]

What does Asia have to offer a landlocked, cattle- and diamond-based economy in Southern Africa? Diversification of economic partners and new sources of foreign aid, trade, and technology are more crucial than ever. In uncertain times, it is risky for a small, dependent state to put its foreign economic and security interests in one or even a few Western baskets.

The breakup of the former Soviet Union was one factor motivating Gaborone to move closer to the PRC. Another was the high cost of opening a mission in Tokyo, rather than China, to represent its regional interests. President Masire made an official state visit to the PRC—his second—to underscore the importance of these linkages. Agreements were signed in the areas of trade, railroad construction, and medical assistance.[45]

Beginning in the mid-1980s, Botswana stepped up efforts to woo Asian investment in manufacturing and to increase trade.[46] In 1989, a major agreement was signed for a Chinese shoe factory to be built in Botswana.[47] These efforts were redoubled in 1991, with successes in clothing and cosmetics manufacturing.[48] The PRC has been a small but dependable source of scholarships, medical aid, railroad construction, and other types of technical assistance.[49]

Since the late 1980s, official fascination with "Asian productivity" and admonitions to "learn the secrets of Asia's rapid economic success" have seemed sometimes to approach an almost mystical level. During his 1983 and 1991 China visits, Masire was deeply impressed with how hard Chinese workers applied themselves, and he has urged the Batswana to emulate them.[50]

The most crucial factors in expanding relations with Japan are development aid and investment potential. Since 1981, Tokyo has offered a growing variety of grants, soft loans, and technical assistance. At a time when Western sources are drying up, Japan is now providing skilled volunteers, drought relief, infrastructure construction (such as the Morupule power station and portions of the Trans-Kgalagadi highway), and equipment donations.[51] A major milestone in Japan's growing role in Africa came in 1993, when it sponsored the Tokyo International Conference on African Development. The Japanese Overseas Economic Cooperation promised to provide substantial financing, together with the IMF and the World Bank, for infrastructure projects, and Botswana is one of the early beneficiaries.

Japan has been increasingly willing to promote Botswana as a site for investment; by contrast, few actual projects have been forthcoming from European and North American governments. A Toyota assembly plant was opened in 1990, and expanded Japanese trade and investment topped discussions during President Masire's official visit to Japan in March 1992.[52] Emphasis was placed on inviting labor-intensive industrial investment, especially in leatherwork, textiles, and diamonds.[53]

The same is true for recent efforts to reach out to South Korea for additional technical assistance and investment, which led to construction of a Hyundai auto assembly plant.[54] Diplomatic relations were established with Malaysia in 1990, with promising trends in trade and investment rapidly following. A trade mission from Kuala Lumpur visited Gaborone in 1991, expressing interest in Botswana's beef, diamonds, and other minerals. Botswana noted that Malaysia was interested in helping to develop its fledgling textile industry.[55] A similar pattern describes relations with Singapore, which were first established in 1993. The two states are currently collaborating on civil service productivity, and President Masire made an official visit to Singapore in March 1994. Discussions centered on trade and investment promotion.

These actions demonstrate that Botswana foreign policy makers are not simply waiting for the world to come to them. As the center of power within the global economic order shifts to Asia, Gaborone has gone further than most of its neighbors to recalibrate regional and bilateral commitments and priorities. In an age when political analysis continues to lament the destructive economic legacy of European colonialism in Africa, Botswana is throwing open its doors to some of the promising new global economic powers of the twenty-first century.

This is not to suggest that long-standing ties with Western Europe, notably Britain and the EU, have been downgraded or are perceived by Gaborone as less important today. In particular, the growing EU-SADC connection is viewed as an absolutely crucial means of gaining greater economic support, through securing Lomé aid and loans, opening markets for Botswana's beef and diamond exports, and locating sources of badly needed investment capital in the years ahead. Bilateral economic ties with France, Germany, the Netherlands, Norway, and Sweden, in addition to those with Britain, remain significant for Botswana.

Conclusion

For Botswana, foreign policy is and must remain the pursuit of vital domestic interests beyond its own boundaries. Pragmatism demands that future external relations continue to be framed by Botswana's undiminished vulnerability to global economic and military forces that are largely beyond Gaborone's control. Diversified dependence is still dependence. A successful mineral-based export economy has yielded elite-serving economic growth in the short run, but it guarantees little in the way of equitable, sustainable development in the long run.

Ultimately, foreign policy success will rest on the country's long-term economic strategy. Less emphasis must be placed on cattle and diamonds. Even raw economic growth cannot continue indefinitely without an expansion of exports: A productive sector to export manufactured goods and services in the region and on the global market must be created. To build such a capacity requires foreign investment. That is why future relations with South

Africa, East Asia, the United States, and the EU, as well as within SADC, are so crucial. Failure in this regard means economic instability, greater unemployment and underemployment, a declining ability of government to fund social welfare programs, and ultimately, political instability.

Botswana has a regional, continental, and global role to play as it reshapes and fortifies its foreign and security policies. It is well placed to contribute to the management of Africa's most pressing problems: conflict, economic collapse, and lack of democracy. Part of its contribution will continue, one hopes, to be delivered by example.

Ali Mazrui recently asked several pertinent questions: Is Africa ready to deal with its own civil wars? Can Africa construct a peacekeeping force of its own? Should mechanisms and institutions be continental or regional?[56] Botswana has taken exemplary strides, both diplomatic and military, toward a "Pax Africana" in its efforts to promote conflict prevention (in Lesotho, 1994), containment (in Mozambique and Rwanda, 1993), and resolution (in Somalia, 1992–1994).

Botswana's contribution to African conflict resolution efforts will remain significant. The country's stature on the continent has never been higher. But simply having the diplomatic and economic wherewithal at a time when most African states cannot even afford to attend summit meetings and pay OAU dues is a necessary but not sufficient condition for explaining this pattern of external behavior.

What has been done diplomatically and militarily in recent years has been done sincerely, based on the belief that even a small state can make a difference. Such contributions should be seen as logical extensions of the country's long-standing commitment to principles of accommodation, tolerance, and respect for human life. Witness, for example, Botswana's refugee policy over the years.

Finally, one cannot completely avoid the "structure and process" aspects of foreign policy making and implementation in the wake of the changing foreign policy context in which Botswana finds itself today. Gone are the days when the small scale of Botswana's foreign affairs undertakings allowed presidential micromanagement. Pressures for the creation of a separate ministry of foreign affairs can be expected to increase. Botswana's leaders must pursue organizational specialization and professional diplomatic, managerial, and language training. If these leaders fail to do so, the next president and cabinet may find themselves poorly served by understaffed embassies and undertrained, overworked officials, especially on important foreign affairs and security matters. They also might be forced to cope with a confusingly complex and imprecise allocation of responsibilities between the Department of Foreign Affairs and the Office of the President.

Having the resources to expand diplomatic and commercial representation abroad is necessary but not sufficient for success. Botswana's thirteen

foreign embassies and missions are some of the most "skeletally staffed in
the world, with some staffed with only two diplomats."[57] Unless professional recruitment and training efforts are stepped up, the potential
economic benefits of new locations in Asia and elsewhere will never be
realized.

Botswana foreign policy can be expected to reflect domestic needs and
interests. Future leaders will be constrained by the same national, regional, and global factors that have set the parameters for external relations and security policy since independence. However, decisions and
commitments made today, in times of diplomatic and economic wealth
and leverage, may allow the next generation to continue to enjoy for a
while longer a measure of unparalleled political stability and economic
growth. They also may put Botswana in a better position than any of its
neighbors to pursue vital national goals—democracy, development, self-
reliance, and the unity or social harmony known as "Kagisano."

NOTES

1. "Botswana Pledges P2m Aid to Mozambique," *Daily News* (Gaborone) 6
April 1987, p. 1.

2. Nathaniel Motshabi, "Six African Countries Pledge Troops for Help in
Rwanda," *Daily News*, 16 June 1994, pp. 1, 5.

3. Sam Kamphodza, "Botswana to Loan IMF P12.5 Million!" *Mmegi wa Dikang*
(Gaborone), 17–23 June 1994, p. 9.

4. James H. Polhemus, "Botswana's Role in the Liberation of Southern Africa,"
in Louis A. Picard (ed.), *The Evolution of Modern Botswana* (London: Rex Collings,
1985), p. 241.

5. Jeff Ramsay, "The Opposition Could Have Won," *Botswana Gazette*
(Gaborone), 26 October 1994, p. 7.

6. Mesh Moeti, "I'm Not Going, Masire," *Mmegi wa Dikang*, 18–24 February
1994, p. 1.

7. See "New Party Within BDP?" *Mmegi*, 26 August–1 September 1995, p. 2;
"Botswana: Masire Squeezed in the Middle," *Africa Confidential*, 34(23), 19 November 1993, pp. 6–7.

8. John D. Holm, "Botswana: One African Success Story," *Current History*, May
1994, p. 202.

9. James Zaffiro, "Foreign Policy Decision-Making," in Stephen J. Steadman
(ed.), *Botswana: The Political Economy of Democratic Development* (Boulder: Lynne
Rienner, 1993), pp. 139–160.

10. See Republic of Botswana, *O and M Review: Report on Organization Review of
the Department of Foreign Affairs* (Gaborone: Management Services Division, Direc-
torate of Public Services Management, January 1994).

11. Author interview with Hon. Archibald Mogwe, ambassador of Botswana to
the United States, Washington, D.C., 24 March 1997. Mogwe was minister of state
for foreign affairs from 1974 to 1984.

12. James Zaffiro, "African Legislatures and Foreign Policy-Making," *Botswana Notes and Records* (Gaborone), 25, 1993, pp. 39–58.

13. See James J. Zaffiro, "State Formation and Pre-Independence Foreign Policy-Making in the Bechuanaland Protectorate," a paper presented at the 1991 Annual Meeting of the African Studies Association, St. Louis, Missouri.

14. See Richard Dale, "The Creation and Use of the Botswana Defence Force," *The Round Table* (London), 290, April 1984, pp. 216–235.

15. "Soldering Requires Dedication and Selfless Devotion—Magang," *Daily News*, 24 November 1992, p. 2.

16. "Mogae Presents Surplus Budget," *Daily News*, 11 February 1997, p. 1. The state president received 13 percent or P620 million, mainly for the Botswana Defence Force (BDF).

17. "BDF Soldiers Will Only Stay in Somalia for Minimum Period," *Daily News*, 12 February 1993, p. 2; "BDF Involvement in Somalia a Milestone," *Daily News*, 19 March 1993, p. 1.

18. Nathaniel Motshabi, "Six African Countries Pledge Troops for Help in Rwanda," *Daily News*, 16 June 1994, pp. 1, 5.

19. "Botswana Sends Mission to Rwanda," *Daily News*, 5 October 1993, p. 1.

20. "Chiepe Briefs Youth on Chissano-Dhlakama Talks," *Daily News*, 24 September 1992, p. 5.

21. "Key Assignments for BDF in Mozambique," *Daily News*, 18 February 1993, p. 1; "Merafhe Says Battalion Ready for Mozambique," *Daily News*, 23 February 1993, p. 3; "Battalion Leaves for Mozambique," *Daily News*, 6 April 1993, p. 1.

22. Albert Batungamile, "UN Representative Expresses Concern on Delay of New Defence Force Formation," *Daily News*, 2 June 1994, p. 3.

23. See Richard Dale, "The Politics of National Security in Botswana," *Journal of Contemporary African Studies*, 12(1), 1993, especially pp. 47–48, for details.

24. "BDF Troops Withdraw from Somalia to Pave Way for TNC," *Daily News*, 17 October 1994, p. 2; "BDF Can Be Fair, Gentle—Khama," *Daily News*, 13 April 1994, p. 1.

25. "SA Attempting to Squeeze Hyundai Botswana-Built Cars out of Market," *Daily News*, 5 May 1994, p. 2.

26. "SA Rep Presents Letters," *Daily News*, 22 June 1992, p. 1; "Mission in SA Has Staff of 7," *Daily News*, 23 February 1993, p. 3; "Tebape to Represent Botswana in SA," *Mmegi*, 7–13 May 1993, p. 2.

27. For the major points of the 1992 treaty, see "Towards a Southern African Economic Community," *New Ground* (South Africa), 14, 1993–1994, pp. 34–36; "New Economic Body Is Born," *Daily News*, 18 August 1992, p. 1.

28. Mpho Maine, "SADC: A Common Vision," *Mmegi*, 4–10 February 1994, p. 16; "SADC Conference Pinpoints Impediments to Integration," *Daily News*, 2 February 1994, p. 5.

29. "Botswana, Israel Resume Relations," *Daily News*, 9 December 1993, pp. 1, 5.

30. See Helene Norberg and Magnus Blomstrom, "Dutch Disease and Management of Windfall Gains in Botswana," in Magnus Blomstrom (ed.), *Economic Crisis in Africa* (London: Routledge, 1993), p. 162.

31. "Chiepe Defends OAU's Role in Resolving Conflicts," *Daily News*, 25 February 1993, p. 3.

32. "Botswana Takes Part in SA Peace-Keeping Force," *Daily News*, 28 February 1994, p. 1; "Five MP's to Observe South Africa's Elections," *Daily News*, 7 April 1994, p. 6; "Eight More Batswana Leave for SA," *Daily News*, 20 April 1994, p. 1.

33. For a detailed treatment of U.S.-Botswana relations from 1966 to 1989, see James J. Zaffiro, "U.S. Relations with Botswana," *TransAfrica Forum*, 9(3), Fall 1992, pp. 57–74.

34. "Living with Bush," *Mmegi*, 12–18 November 1988, p. 2.

35. "U.S. Principles a Beacon, Says Jeter," *Daily News*, 7 July 1994, p. 3; "Botswana, US Signs P12.6m Grant Agreements," *Daily News*, 15 July 1994, p. 1.

36. Mpho Maine, "USAID to Re-locate from Botswana," *Mmegi*, 4–10 June 1994, p. 12.

37. "U.S. for Botswana to Benefit Business," *Mmegi*, 17–23 May 1991, p. 6; Petrus Nzonzana, "Establish More Businesses," *Daily News*, 12 April 1991; and Ernest Gaelesiwe, "OPIC to Visit for Second Time," *Daily News*, 10 April 1991, p. 3.

38. Petrus Ngozana, "Political Stability Has Helped Secure Aid and Investment," *Daily News*, 15 June 1994, p. 3.

39. Gift Sipho Siso, "Botswana Beats SA for Pipe Project," *New African*, March 1994, p. 26.

40. "Botswana White Elephant," *Africa Confidential*, 17 May 1991; "Lavish Spending on BDF Not Justified, Temane," *Mmegi*, 2–8 August 1991, p. 1.

41. Keto Segwai, "Budget: 'Eagle' Grabs Lion's Share," *Mmegi*, 22–28 February 1991, pp. 1, 3; Mesh Moeti, "Huge Budget for Defence," *Mmegi*, 14–20 February 1992, p. 8; Goitsbeng Maphuting, "BDF Calls the Sho[r]ts," *Mmegi*, 21–27 February 1992, p. 8; "Defence Policy Dictated by Uncle Sam?" *Mmegi*, 28 February–5 March 1992, p. 8.

42. "Airbase Not Owned by Foreigners," *Daily News*, 1 March 1993, p. 5.

43. *Daily News*, 31 March 1995, p. 3.

44. "Parliament Approves over P26m for Department of External Affairs," *Daily News*, 25 March 1992, p. 4; "Botswana Opens Embassy," *Daily News*, 19 August 1991, p. 1.

45. "Sino-Botswana Relations Good," *Daily News*, 9 September 1991, p. 1; "Sino-Botswana Relations Should Be Nurtured," *Daily News*, 3 December 1991, p. 1.

46. "Scope of Trade with China Widens After Botswana Visit," *Daily News*, 9 May 1983, p. 1; "Chinese Trade Mission Here," *Daily News*, 17 December 1986, p. 1.

47. Keto Segwai, "Chinese Shoes for Botswana," *Mmegi*, 14–20 July 1989, p. 1.

48. Kwapeng Modikwe, "Chinese Invited to Invest in Botswana," *Daily News*, 16 September 1991, p. 1; "China Eager to Invest in Botswana," *Mmegi*, 4–10 June 1993, p. 5.

49. "Botswana, China Sign Protocol," *Daily News*, 8 February 1993, p. 1; "Botswana, China's Cooperation," *Daily News*, 28 January 1992, p. 5.

50. Charmaine Muir, "President Impressed by China," *Daily News*, 5 December 1983, p. 1; "Batswana Urged to Emulate the Chinese," *Daily News*, 26 September 1991, p. 1.

51. "Agreement for Funds to Buy Equipment Signed," *Daily News*, 17 November 1983, p. 1; "Japanese Volunteers Here," *Daily News*, 7 September 1992, p. 3; "Botswana, Japan Government Sign Grants," *Daily News*, 10 February 1993, p. 2;

"Botswana to Receive P61m from Japan," *Daily News*, 4 March 1992, p. 1; "Sebego in Japan for Signing of Loan Agreement," *Daily News*, 8 February 1993, p. 1; "Japan Provides Debt Relief," *Daily News*, 27 July 1994, p. 5.

52. "Masire Arrives in Japan," *Daily News*, 2 March 1992, p. 1; "Masire and Japan's Miyazawa Hold Talks," *Daily News*, 3 March 1992, p. 1.

53. "Sir Ketumile Invites Japanese Investors," *Daily News*, 8 October 1993, p. 1; "Botswana in Bid to Lure Japanese Investors," *Mmegi*, 21–27 February 1992, p. 7.

54. "Masire Appreciates Korea's Assistance," *Daily News*, 14 June 1991, p. 1; "Seoul Donates Drought Money," *Daily News*, 18 September 1992, p. 1.

55. "Malaysia Keen to Import Diamonds, Beef," *Mmegi*, 22–28 November 1991, p. 6; "Botswana Textiles Need Malaysian Technology," *Daily News*, 18 March 1992, p. 2.

56. Ali Mazrui, "Africa: In Search of Self-Pacification," *African Affairs*, 93, 1994, pp. 39–42.

57. "Botswana's Missions Understaffed," *Daily News*, 17 August 1993, p. 1.

Select Bibliography

Botswana Daily News (Gaborone) (government daily).

Carter, Gwendolen M., and E. Philip Morgan (eds.). *From the Frontline: Speeches of Sir Seretse Khama* (Bloomington: Indiana University Press, 1981).

Dale, Richard. "The Creation and Use of the Botswana Defence Force." *The Round Table* (London), 290, April 1984, pp. 216–235.

Hermans, Quill. "Impact of External Political and Economic Changes on Botswana." In *Botswana in the 21st Century*, conference proceedings (Gaborone: Botswana Society, 1994), pp. 117–131.

Mmegi wa Dikang (Gaborone) (a private weekly newspaper).

Polhemus, James H. "Botswana's Role in the Liberation of Southern Africa." In Louis A. Picard (ed.), *The Evolution of Modern Botswana* (London: Rex-Collings, 1985).

Zaffiro, James J. "Re-Designing Foreign Policy for the 21st Century: The New World Order from a Botswana Perspective." *Africa Insight* (Pretoria), 25(2), May 1995, pp. 98–107.

_____. "African Legislatures and Foreign Policy: The Botswana Case." *Botswana Notes and Records* (Gaborone), 25, 1993, pp. 39–58.

_____. "U.S. Relations with Botswana." *TransAfrica Forum* (Washington, D.C.), 9(3), Fall 1992, pp. 57–74.

_____. "Botswana's Foreign Policy and Exit of the Superpowers from Southern Africa." *Africa Insight* (Pretoria), 22(2), 1992, pp. 95–104.

5

The Foreign Policies of Ethiopia and Eritrea

CHRISTOPHER CLAPHAM

Few parts of the continent more strikingly illustrate the upheavals that have taken place in Africa's foreign policies than the area that, from 1952 until Eritrea's independence in May 1993, formally constituted Ethiopia. These upheavals have, moreover, occurred at several different levels. At one obvious level, that of the global system, the Horn was affected by a longer history of superpower engagement and competition than any other part of sub-Saharan Africa, and this in turn deeply affected the foreign policies of its constituent states; this engagement started with the close relationship established between Ethiopia and the United States in the aftermath of the World War II and was intensified by the Soviet-Somali agreement of 1963, continuing to the very end of the Cold War with the alliance between Mengistu Haile Mariam's Ethiopia and the USSR. At another level, that of the African state system, the secession of Eritrea after many years of bitter and extremely costly warfare marked the first and as yet only internationally recognized breach of the OAU-supported principle of state integrity.

At the level of domestic politics, Ethiopia has passed through two major traumas: first, one of Africa's few (perhaps its only) genuine revolutions and subsequently, the seizure of power by guerrilla insurgencies. Both had a marked influence on foreign policy. Beyond that, few if any other parts of the continent have been obliged to endure such a long experience of famine and warfare, most painfully evidenced by massive refugee movements and an appalling number of maimed human beings. These in turn have helped give rise to a new form of international relations, conducted to a large extent by private charitable agencies, that has been intricately (and at times bizarrely) incorporated into regional and domestic conflicts.

These shocks have challenged not just the people of the region but also the very idea of what "foreign policy" is. In particular, they have reduced to meaninglessness the idea that the study of foreign policy can be restricted to relations between states. As the nature of states changes, both territorially and through the transformation of domestic politics; as heavily armed and well-organized movements contest the power of formally constituted governments; and as much of the business of international relations comes to be conducted by private organizations, it becomes clear that every significant actor in the tangled politics of the region, whether drawn from inside or outside it, has its "foreign policy"; the foreign policies of, say, Oxfam or the Tigray People's Liberation Front (TPLF) are every bit as much a part of the picture as those of the people who, at any particular moment, hold formally recognized positions in the government in Addis Ababa. This chapter will accordingly attempt to sketch the foreign policies of Ethiopia and Eritrea, not just as states but also as parts of a multilayered conflictual region in which foreign policies, like every other aspect of politics, have been part of the currency of conflict.

The Foreign Policy of Ethiopian Centralism

The place to start, nonetheless, is with the foreign policy of the historical Ethiopian state, since this, more than anything else, defined the setting for the pursuit of other foreign policies by rival political actors. As an Orthodox Christian empire occupying the densely populated Ethiopian highlands north and west of the Great Rift, ancient Ethiopia developed a generally conflictual relationship with its neighbors, most of which—especially to the east, north, and northwest—were Muslim. The historical mission of Ethiopian statehood was, as far as possible, to subdue this unruly periphery, while seeking to control the trade routes that—leading south and west from the Red Sea coast between Massawa and the Gulf of Tadjoura—linked it to the international economy.[1] In the process, the representatives of the central Ethiopian state developed an ideology or manifest destiny that legitimated their right to govern the periphery in terms of empire and Christianity; in time, they associated this with a sense of Ethiopian nationalism.

The role of the world beyond Ethiopia's immediate borders in this mission of state formation was ambivalent. On the one hand, external powers represented a threat and were treated with deep suspicion, whether they came in the form of Roman Catholicism in the sixteenth and seventeenth centuries or European colonialism in the nineteenth and twentieth. On the other hand, external alliances provided essential resources with which to pursue the domestic and regional agenda, in the form of trade, technology, and, especially, armaments. The central goal of Ethiopian foreign policy, particularly as this developed from the middle of the nineteenth century onward, was to achieve the benefits (without succumbing to the perils) of association with the states of the industrialized world, an enterprise that characteristically relied on playing off the major outside states against one another. The most evident success of this strategy was in 1895–1896, when the Ethiopian empire was able to defeat the invading Italians with the help of firearms obtained from many sources, including the Italians themselves. Its most traumatic failure was in 1935–1936, when an isolated Ethiopia succumbed to the same enemy.

From the time of Emperor Haile Selassie's restoration in 1941, therefore, the search for a powerful protector was the first priority of Ethiopian foreign policy. The circumstances of that time—when Ethiopia (whose boundaries then matched those established again in 1993, without Eritrea or direct access to the sea) was virtually surrounded by territories controlled by Great Britain—made the United States ideally suited for the purpose. At that time, Washington was seeking allies in a region that had been made strategically sensitive by Arab nationalism and Middle East oil. The alliance was cemented on the U.S. side by a military training mission and support for the UN General Assembly decision in December 1950 that federated formerly Italian Eritrea with Ethiopia; on the Ethiopian side, it was cemented by the lease to the United States of a communications base in Eritrea and by participation in the UN force in the Korean War.

Before long, the dangers posed by Italian and then British imperialism had been replaced by those posed by African nationalism and potentially Soviet communism. Haile Selassie dealt very effectively with the threat that the demands for self-determination all around the continent might have presented to his anachronistic empire: He placed himself at the head of the newly emerging African diplomatic order and helped to draw up its constituent principles in ways that suited both the old Ethiopian state and the great majority of new African ones. The key to this process was the idea of juridical statehood, encompassing respect for existing boundaries (no matter how artificial) and noninterference in the internal affairs of other states (no matter how dictatorial), which was built into the charter of the OAU.

Externally, this formula served to isolate the threat to Ethiopia's integrity presented by the Somali Republic, which sought to incorporate Somalis living in Ethiopia into its own territory. Even though the Somali government wanted to bolster its position by reaching a military agreement with the USSR to counter the Ethiopian one with the United States, this posed no major danger as long as both the African consensus and the U.S. alliance supported Ethiopia. Internally, the same formula protected Ethiopian control over Eritrea, where armed opposition to full incorporation into the autocratic Ethiopian empire had started to arise by the time the OAU was formed in 1963. Some radical Arab states supported the Eritrean Liberation Front (ELF), which claimed that Eritrea belonged to the Arab world, but no African state did so.

The eventual failure of the formula of juridical statehood to protect Ethiopia's territorial integrity resulted overwhelmingly from the regime's domestic political inadequacies. The war in Eritrea had, by the early 1970s, escalated to a level at which it could be resolved only by a political settlement that lay beyond the capabilities of the regime. In other parts of the country, the seeds of what was to become the issue of "nationalities" were beginning to sprout. The reign of the emperor, who reached the age of eighty in 1972, was clearly coming to an end. The younger and more educated sections of the population were intensely alienated, and many of them sought to sweep away the "feudal" structures of the Solomonic monarchy with some form of Marxist revolution. Though the United States (then mired in Vietnam) was, in any case, reluctant to take on further commitments, it saw no future in associating itself with a regime that was evidently on its way out.

For a period, nonetheless, the revolution that broke out in 1974 was to give a new lease on life to the quest for centralized Ethiopian statehood that had formed the theme of Ethiopian imperial government and foreign policy since 1855. The group that eventually won the vicious, factional battles for control of the revolution during the later 1970s consisted of a core of radical young army officers with a following among the Marxist intelligentsia. Their project was essentially Jacobin: The revolution was to gain popular support by destroying the exploitative structures of the old regime and use this to create a purified Ethiopian nationalism. They were aided by the Somali invasion in 1977, which, coming two years after the land reform of 1975, enabled them to present the defense of the revolution as a sacred national duty. Those members of the urban intellectual class who favored some form of devolution or who sought to recognize the identities of the different ethnic and regional groups within the country were ruthlessly swept aside. Many were killed. Some went into exile and (along with refugees from the imperial regime) formed expatriate communities in the United States and elsewhere. A few took to the hills and established the insurgent movements that, in 1991, were eventually to come to power in both Addis Ababa and Asmara.

The new revolutionary project of centralized state formation aroused greater opposition and correspondingly needed greater external support than the old imperial one. In some areas, especially in the north, a "white" opposition of displaced imperial officials sought to mobilize local allegiances; radicals who had lost the fight for power in the cities challenged and soon displaced them. The upheavals of the revolution itself, starting with land reform, created the basis for a mobilization of the peas-

CHRISTOPHER CLAPHAM

antry. In some areas, this mobilization could (initially, at least) be used to recruit support for the regime, but in other areas, it was taken over by opposition movements. In every respect, the USSR made a better partner for this purpose than the United States. In a Stalinist form of Marxism, the new regime saw an ideology that could be used to combine social transformation with central power; for its part, the Soviet Union saw possibilities for communism in Ethiopia deriving from a social and economic base that in many respects mirrored that of Russia in 1917—Orthodox Christianity, a decaying monarchy, the agrarian question, the national question, and so forth. In addition, the Soviets had none of the qualms about the Ethiopian government's human rights record that were then starting to affect U.S. policy. The international setting in the five years that followed the collapse of South Vietnam in 1975 was uniquely favorable to Soviet expansion, and the USSR had unrivaled resources as a supplier of weapons. The shift in alliances that was already under way before the war with Somalia broke out in mid-1977 enabled the new Ethiopian government, with overwhelming Soviet and Cuban support, to gain a decisive victory. It also consolidated the Mengistu regime as a loyal supporter of Moscow. From 1977 onward, the supply of Soviet military hardware was unstinting, and Ethiopia—partly to demonstrate its credentials as a Soviet client but also to create a powerful domestic regime—was converted as far as possible into a model communist state.

Eventually, that project failed. Since its failure precisely coincided with the collapse of the superpower on which the Ethiopian government depended, it is tempting to regard the Mengistu regime as a victim of the transformation of the international system. This coincidence is, however, misleading. Long before the supply of Soviet arms dried up, the arms had ceased to serve their purpose because of the alienation of a population drained by unsustainable government demands—for taxation, military conscription, and endless other things—and because of the support for opposition movements, which counterproductive government brutality had only enhanced. Soviet weapons rapidly passed from the hands of the demoralized conscripts who were issued them into the hands of the insurgents who captured them. Mengistu's regime eventually fell, as Haile Selassie's had, because of its internal inadequacies. The quest to establish a centralized state, which had provided the motor for Ethiopian foreign policy over the previous century, fell with it. To find the basis for subsequent foreign policies, it is therefore necessary to look at the policies of the insurgent movements that opposed and eventually overthrew it.

The Foreign Policies of Peripheral Resistance

The insurgencies that, in May 1991, overthrew the Mengistu regime and established new governments in Addis Ababa and Asmara were successful because of the support they attracted and because of the decay in support for the central government. A number of recent writings, especially on Southern Africa, have persuasively challenged the Maoist orthodoxy that a "people's war" can only succeed with the support of the people.[2] Furthermore, the propaganda current during the "struggle," which ascribed the success of the Eritrean People's Liberation Front (EPLF) and Tigray People's Liberation Front entirely to the voluntary enthusiasm of a united population, certainly needs to be displaced by a more dispassionate postwar analysis. But the inevitable "revisionist" accounts of two of the most remarkable insurgencies of the second half of the twentieth century are unlikely to challenge the conclusion that the insurgents enjoyed substantially greater popular backing, at least in their own base areas, than the government they displaced. However, guerrilla warfare also requires resources from the international system, and the external relations of insurgency have easily been ignored or reduced to marginal status, precisely because any reference to external resources could readily be said to detract from the more ideologically appealing internal dynamics of the conflict. This imbalance needs to be redressed.[3]

A very brief genealogy of insurgent movements in northern Ethiopia may be helpful. Only in Eritrea did they predate the 1974 revolution. Owing to Eritrea's separate status as a former Italian colony and its consequent disposal by the UN as part of the post–World War II peace settlement, all Eritrean insurgent movements sought its establishment as an independent state within the Italian colonial boundaries. The first such movement, founded in 1961, was the ELF, which drew its core support from the Muslim peoples of western Eritrea. It sought international aid by identifying itself as a Muslim and even Arab resistance to the Christian Ethiopian empire. As the alienation of even Christian Eritreans from the Ethiopian central government intensified, many of these people joined the ELF; however, they were alienated from it in turn, partly by its personalist leadership and organizational ineffectiveness but also by an Islamic identity that, in the Eritrean context (since Eritrea is approximately equally divided between Christians and Muslims), could only be counterproductive. Defections from the ELF eventually led to the formation of a new movement, the EPLF, which adopted Marxism both for its effectiveness as an ideology of guerrilla warfare, and because it could be used to bridge over potentially disastrous religious divisions. By the late 1970s, this group had ousted the ELF, which split into a number of factions, and the EPLF went on to conduct the war that culminated in independence. Whether the EPLF represents all Eritreans regardless of religion or whether the ELF and its successors retain the allegiance of Muslims, especially in western Eritrea, remains a contentious issue.

In the adjoining Tigray region, armed resistance started with the attempt by local noblemen, led by former governor Ras Mengesha Seyoum, to contest the seizure of power by the revolutionary regime in Addis Ababa. Their position was in turn challenged by two movements led by Marxist intellectual refugees from the struggle in the towns; of these, the Ethiopian People's Revolutionary Party (EPRP) was more national in orientation, whereas the TPLF was explicitly regionalist.[4] The TPLF succeeded in displacing both of its rivals, and in the late 1980s, it helped to form a number of other movements, notably including the Ethiopian People's Democratic Movement (EPDM, which later became the Amhara National Democratic Movement [ANDM]) and the Oromo People's Democratic Organization (OPDO). Together, these organizations formed the Ethiopian People's Revolutionary Democratic Front (EPRDF), which seized power in Addis Ababa in May 1991. Unlike the Eritrean movements, these did not seek secession from Ethiopia but rather wanted to establish a federal or confederal system of government in which the rights of "nationalities" would be respected.

Denied formal access to the international system because they did not constitute "states" and defined as illegitimate due to the OAU's insistence on respect for the territorial integrity of its own members, these movements had to seek external support wherever they could find it. The USSR and its allies were excluded by their commitment to the central government. And Western states, despite their distaste for the regime in Addis Ababa, could scarcely be expected to aid Marxist revolutionary insurgencies; in any event, they too were broadly committed to the OAU consensus on respect for juridical statehood.

The insurgents were, however, able to profit from the long history of conflict in the Horn by attaching themselves to other states and movements opposed to Ethiopian centralism. One of these states, Siad Barre's Somalia, provided Somali diplomatic passports for EPLF and TPLF officials, but it was not otherwise in a position to do much to help. Sudan, however, directly bordered Eritrea and provided the most convenient access to Tigray.[5] Tacit Ethiopian central government support for the Sudanese People's Liberation Army (SPLA) in southern Sudan was countered by Sudanese support for the insurgencies in northern Ethiopia. Both EPLF and TPLF established their major external offices in Khartoum, which served, for all intents and purposes, as shadow foreign ministries conducting relations with the outside world. They also maintained missions in a number of other states, which correspondingly served as embassies. The TPLF, for example, maintained missions in the United States, Canada, the United Kingdom, Italy, Sweden, Somalia, and Saudi Arabia, staffed by representatives who were regularly replaced from the field.[6] In addition, the Sudanese authorities permitted (and were often scarcely in a position to prevent) EPLF and TPLF access through their own border regions; the EPLF especially maintained a major supply system into northern Eritrea from Port Sudan.

Though both movements met most of their need for arms through capture from government forces, they urgently required other resources, especially food, medicines, and cash. To some extent, they could raise cash through a highly organized support network, drawing on expatriate Eritrean and Tigrayan communities and other sympathizers, especially in North America and Western Europe. The EPLF in particular achieved a level of organization that was unmatched by any African government. For food and also to some degree for other resources, they predominantly depended on external aid supplied through northern NGOs. The relationship between humanitarian NGOs and opposition movements in African domestic conflicts goes back to the role played by Christian aid organizations in the Nigerian civil war of 1967–1970. The willingness of NGOs to supply aid to insurgent-controlled areas, in defiance of formal norms of state sovereignty, was also enhanced by non-African conflicts, such as that in Afghanistan. Contacts between NGOs and the Eritrean insurgents dated from the mid-1970s. In 1975, the EPLF established a nominally independent humanitarian organization, the Eritrean Relief Association (ERA), through which NGOs could channel relief aid without appearing to support an armed insurgency. The TPLF set up a similar body, the Relief Society of Tigray (REST), in 1978. For their part, in 1981, the NGOs (led by two Scandinavian Lutheran organizations) set up a Khartoum-based consortium, the Emergency Relief Desk (ERD), through which they could anonymously send aid to ERA and REST. This not only supplied food but also enabled the insurgents to raise cash by profiting from the difference between official and unofficial exchange rates on local purchases of food funded by external aid; in addition, it provided a means through which journalists could visit war zones under the protection of the insurgents.[7] During the great Ethiopian famine of 1984–1985, most NGOs supplied the bulk of their relief aid through channels controlled by the Ethiopian government (and in the process, of course, reinforced central government control, just as aid supplied through insurgent channels helped the EPLF and TPLF). Yet the famine greatly increased the level of interaction between insurgents and NGOs, and it enabled them to improve their contacts with Western governments.

As the global diplomatic climate changed from the late 1980s onward, the EPLF and TPLF were able to extend their diplomatic reach. Eventually, they were able to conduct relations with Western states on a basis comparable to that of formally constituted governments. The EPLF leader, Isaias Afewerki, visited the United States and other Western countries on a fairly regular basis from 1986 onward, and he was able to hold talks with senior officials in the Reagan and Bush administrations. When the TPLF leader, Meles Zenawi, first visited the West in 1989, he betrayed his diplomatic inexperience by revealing his admiration for the Hoxha regime in Albania.[8] The culminating point in this quest for external recognition came in May 1991, when U.S. Assistant Secretary of State Herman Cohen chaired talks in London between the central government and its opponents at precisely the moment when the TPLF and EPLF captured Addis Ababa and Asmara, respectively, and converted themselves into the new governments of Ethiopia and Eritrea.

A final and sensitive area of EPLF and TPLF diplomacy concerned their relations with one another. The two movements had an obvious interest in collaboration, and the TPLF launched its struggle with the aid of the already established EPLF. TPLF attacks on central government communications through Tigray greatly eased the pressure on the EPLF in Eritrea. The TPLF also readily accepted Eritrea's right to secession. The two movements nonetheless had significant ideological differences, derived in large part from their different local situations, and these led to an open breach between them in 1984–1988. This breach even extended to EPLF closure of relief aid access to Tigray through Eritrea during the 1984–1985 famine. These differences turned in particular on the issue of "nationality" or ethnicity. Tigray was fairly homogeneous in terms of ethnicity, and the TPLF sought a highly devolved system of government that placed heavy emphasis on ethnicity. By contrast, Eritrea was a multiethnic region, within which the EPLF sought a highly centralized government with a modest emphasis on ethnicity. They also differed over relations with the USSR, which the EPLF regarded with less hostility than the TPLF. The conflict was eventually patched up after the EPLF's victory at Afabet in 1988 made clear the advantages of alliance, and the EPLF provided aid for the TPLF in its victory over central government forces at Enda-Selassie in 1989. But the differences in attitude remained and were to affect post-1991 policy.[9]

Postinsurgent Foreign Policies

The question of what African guerrilla movements actually *do* when they come to power is fascinating and little explored.[10] At one level, the domestic and external trajectory mapped out for both the EPLF and the TPLF by equivalent victorious insurgencies in other parts of the world had been blocked by changes in the international system. Had these groups come to power twenty years earlier, they might have been expected—as happened in Cuba or Kampuchea—to establish explicitly Marxist-Leninist regimes, in close alliance with one of the world's two major socialist powers. Given their internal ideological orientation, the EPLF might well have looked to the USSR, and the TPLF/EPRDF might have turned to the People's Republic of China. In the circumstances of 1991, however, they had no option but to maintain close links with the United States, which indeed treated them in much more supportive fashion than might have been expected, given a Marxist past that the TPLF at least had only very recently abandoned; the EPLF, much more closely attuned to external developments, had downplayed its Marxist origins in favor of a more conventionally nationalist stance several years earlier. Part of the explanation for the U.S. readiness to support the new governments lay in its hostility to the previous Mengistu regime and to contacts with its opponents, which had started some years before the regime's fall. The coincidence that the insurgents gained power at the precise moment of the May 1991 London talks, when Herman Cohen was in personal contact with their leaders, may also have helped.[11] In any event, the United States maintained a protective attitude, which was aided by the fact that several of Cohen's closest associates continued to manage U.S. policy in the area even after the accession of the Clinton administration.

One result of this was that U.S. pressure to install multiparty democratic governments was relatively slight. In Eritrea, the EPLF announced, after seizing Asmara, that there would be a two-year transition period leading to independence, during which it would run the government. After that period ended, it inaugurated a four-year period leading to the promulgation of a permanent constitution, during which the EPLF instituted a purely cosmetic change by renaming itself the People's Front for Democracy and Justice (PFDJ) but otherwise continued to rule unchallenged. In Ethiopia (which in practice reverted to its pre-1952 boundaries from May 1991, though Eritrean independence was formalized only two years later), this easy option was scarcely available. Even after rapidly associating itself with the EPRDF, constituted of numerous newly created ethnic parties, it could not monopolize the political scene; rival movements—some demanding ethnic separation (such as the Oromo Liberation Front, or OLF) and others tacitly associated with Ethiopian centralism (such as the All Amhara People's Organization, or AAPO)—challenged the EPLF's claim to represent all Ethiopians through a set of ethnic alliances. But although the EPRDF's hegemonic ambitions very soon became evident, U.S. criticism of the harassment of opposition movements was at best extremely muted. In the field of economic policy, the main emphasis of external aid agencies was on postwar reconstruction rather than the imposition of economic conditionalities, and though both states announced their commitment to liberal economic policies, this commitment was in practice fairly lightly policed. In Ethiopia notably, the new government retained its commitment to state ownership of land, while in Eritrea, the intense commitment to autonomy that the EPLF had carried over from the experience of the independence struggle continued to affect all relations with outside organizations, whether governmental, intergovernmental, or private.

The regional scene provided further backing for a supportive relationship with the United States. To the south, the U.S. involvement in Somalia gave both the Ethiopian and Eritrea governments ample opportunities to demonstrate their goodwill by aiding U.S. initiatives and helping as far as they could to rescue the United States from the imbroglio into which it had pitched itself. To the east, the seizure of power by an Islamist regime in Sudan in 1989 added to U.S. concerns and aided relations with Eritrea and Ethiopia. The poor state of U.S. relations with Daniel arap Moi's Kenya may also have helped the connection.

Continentally, both Ethiopia and Eritrea emerged as members of the small group of African states, along with Yoweri Museveni's Uganda and the Rwanda Patriotic Front (RPF) regime in Rwanda, that were critical of the consensus represented by the OAU. In fact, Isaias Afewerki roundly dismissed the OAU as "an utter failure" in his first address to the organization as Eritrea's president. The protection given to successive Ethiopian central governments during the Eritrean war of independence, which stemmed from the OAU's insistence on the territorial integrity of African states, continued to rankle. The EPRDF regime in Ethiopia, inheriting a skillful foreign policy bureaucracy, was more circumspect in its challenge to cherished continental norms than its Eritrean ally. But the commitment to the OAU principles of nonintervention and respect for existing frontiers, which had been so critical to Ethiopian foreign policy in the years up to 1991, no longer meant so much under the new dispensation.

At the same time, some of the alliances that the new regimes had maintained during their years as insurgent movements were reversed after they came to power. Most important of these was the understanding with successive Sudanese governments that had enabled both EPLF and TPLF to operate out of Sudanese territory and maintain their shadow foreign ministries in Khartoum. In the immediate aftermath of May 1991, the EPRDF government repaid its debts to Khartoum by expelling the SPLA from its bases (and refugee camps) in southwestern Ethiopia, greatly aiding the Sudanese regime in its civil war in the south; the Eritreans, too, sought to emphasize their separateness from Ethiopia by looking instead to Sudan. Before long, however, the relationship began to fade. For one thing, the al-Bashir regime in Khartoum was uncomfortably reminiscent of the Mengistu one in Addis Ababa in its determination to enforce central rule regardless of the cost in human suffering. Looking at their own histories, the EPLF and EPRDF realized they had far more in common with the SPLA. For another, the Islamist bent of the Khartoum government posed implicit and perhaps explicit threats to states with substantial Muslim populations.

The suspicion of Sudanese intentions was greatest in Eritrea. The even distribution of Muslims and Christians in Eritrea, the preponderance of Christians in the EPLF (which nonetheless had a substantial Muslim element), and the presence of large numbers of Muslim Eritreans in refugee camps in Sudan all helped to make the Islamist threat a very real one. The EPLF, too, after a long war fought at enormous cost, was intensely resentful of any slight on its territorial integrity or national independence. Before long, fighters of the Eritrean Islamic Jihad, an Islamist group tacitly backed by Hassan el-Tourabi's National Islamic Front, started to infiltrate western Eritrea from Sudan. Though EPLF forces dealt with these incursions without much trouble, Isaias issued a public warning to Sudan in January 1994 and in December broke relations between the two states. In 1995, the Eritreans hosted the conference of Sudanese opposition groups in Asmara, which led to the formation of the Sudanese Democratic Alliance, an organization that linked the southern Sudanese SLPA to northern opposition movements. Sadiq al-Mahdi, former Sudanese prime minister and leader of the Ansar Muslim brotherhood, took refuge in Eritrea in 1996. Meanwhile, Isaias Afewerki—in a startling reversal of African diplomatic norms—announced his willingness to provide military support to any movement committed to overthrowing the government in Khartoum. Eritrea's relations with its other Muslim neighbors were also strained. Eritrea contested ownership of a strip of land along its frontier with Djibouti, and in December 1995, it attacked Yemeni forces on the Hanish islands, a small group of uninhabited islands in the southern Red Sea the ownership of which was uncertain.

Paradoxically, given that the EPLF and its predecessors had spent some thirty years fighting for Eritrean independence from Ethiopia, Eritrea's closest regional ally thus became the government in Addis Ababa. This was, of course, dominated by the TPLF, with which the EPLF had, despite their differences in the later 1980s, generally enjoyed good relations. But the situation emphasized the potential dangers for Eritrea of independent existence in a region of very intense international and domestic conflict. The other major regional state, Saudi Arabia, had historically supported the ELF and was regarded with deep suspicion in Asmara. Eritrea moved quickly to establish good relations with Israel, but if the Ethiopian government ever fell into the hands of a hostile regime, Eritrea would be dangerously exposed. This in turn was reflected in Eritrean support for the EPRDF, which probably extended as far as the use of Eritrean forces for internal security duties within Ethiopia.

Whereas the Eritrean government had a clear set of foreign policy objectives in maintaining independence and internal political order against both foreign and domestic threats, the position in Ethiopia was far more confused. The rationale that had underpinned Ethiopian foreign policy for more than a century—that is, the need for external backing to help maintain the powerful central government required to protect the state against external conquest or internal fragmentation—had been whisked away. This occurred when the Mengistu regime was overthrown and replaced by an EPRDF government that favored ethnic confederation and a guarantee of self-determination for "nationalities" within Ethiopia that explicitly included the right of secession. Moreover, there was no prospect of an Ethiopian government gaining the type of military aid it had received from the USSR and, before that, from the United States.

Ethiopia's regional relationships paralleled Eritrea's. Although Meles Zenawi had been far more reluctant than Isaias Afewerki to risk an open breach with Khartoum, Sudanese involvement with Islamist groups within Ethiopia aroused suspicions. An open break followed when the attempted assassination of President Husni Mubarak of Egypt (who was in Addis Ababa for an OAU meeting in June 1995) was traced to agents of the Sudanese government. The outraged Ethiopian government broke diplomatic relations, and the SDA attack on towns close to the Sudanese border with Ethiopia early in 1997 can scarcely have been launched without Ethiopian connivance. In 1996, Ethiopian helicopters attacked the western Somalia bases of another Islamist group, al-Ittihad, which was responsible for bomb explosions in Addis Ababa hotels: Even though Somalia had effectively ceased to exist as a state, Ethiopia's relations with its Muslim periphery continued to pose problems.

Conclusion

Two less "typical" states than Ethiopia and Eritrea—Sub-Saharan Africa's oldest state and its newest—could scarcely be imagined. Their foreign policy trajectories were correspondingly distinctive. To a large extent, these related not so much to the problems of postcolonial statehood familiar in most of the rest of the continent but to much older relationship patterns between highland and lowland, Christianity and Islam, and central autocracy and peripheral resistance. Foreign policy was ultimately no more than a part, albeit a very significant part, of ongoing conflicts whose nature was essentially domestic and regional. At times, these conflicts had pushed regional actors—both states and nongovernmental organizations and especially insurgent movements—into an intense search for the external alliances needed to support local political agendas. This search had in turn brought the region to the attention of the superpowers and prompted a disastrous level of militarization. And while famine and food dependence, with their associated external relations of relief aid, were not entirely due to internal political conflict, they were certainly massively exacerbated by it.

By the mid-1990s, at least a partial resolution of Ethiopia's internal conflicts had been achieved with the independence of Eritrea and the installation in Addis Ababa of a government with at least some commitment—no matter how disputed by its opponents—to regional autonomy. As a result, the two states of Ethiopia and Eritrea enjoyed a greater level of internal peace than at any time, probably, since the early 1960s, and their demands on the international system were correspondingly muted. Even their perennially fragile economies showed some signs of improvement. At the same time, the problems of the Horn of Africa as a whole are not definitively resoluble, and any apparent settlement can only be partial and temporary. The complete collapse of the Somali state and the problems raised—both for its domestic viability and for its external relations—by the Islamist regime in Sudan create intense difficulties for neighboring countries. Despite the unifying impact of a long liberation war, Eritrea is permanently divided, by religion and geography, between very different communities. And it remains to be seen whether the EPLF regime can maintain a powerful state within this territory. It is also not clear that the EPRDF regime in Ethiopia, drawing its core support from a relatively small and peripheral section of the country's population, can maintain a balance between the forces of Ethiopian centralism and peripheral fragmentation. Not only foreign policy but also the nature and even the existence of the states themselves must therefore remain uncertain.

NOTES

1. I explored this theme in my "Ethiopia," in Timothy M. Shaw and Olajide Aluko (eds.), *The Political Economy of African Foreign Policy* (Aldershot, England: Gower, 1984), pp. 79–93.

2. See, for example, Norma Kriger, *Zimbabwe's Guerrilla War: Peasant Voices* (Cambridge: Cambridge University Press, 1992), and William Minter, *Apartheid's Contras: An Enquiry into the Roots of War in Angola and Mozambique* (London: Zed, 1994).

3. I have attempted a general survey of the external relations of African insurgencies in *Africa and the International System: The Politics of State Survival* (Cambridge: Cambridge University Press, 1996), chap. 9.

4. The conflict in Tigray has been examined in a thesis by John Young, "Peasants and Revolution in Ethiopia: Tigray 1975–1989" (Ph.D. thesis, Simon Fraser University, Canada, September 1994); a revised version of this is John Young, *Peasant Revolution in Ethiopia: The Tigray People's Liberation Front, 1975–1991* (Cambridge: Cambridge University Press, 1997).

5. Tigray region had no external borders, but the TPLF claimed, quite fictitiously, that the Wolkait district of Gondar region, lying between Tigray and the Sudanese border, had "historically" been part of Tigray.

6. Interview with TPLF officials, Addis Ababa, January 1995.

7. See William DeMars, "Tactics of Protection: International Human Rights Organisations in the Ethiopian Conflict, 1980–1986," in Eileen McCarthy-Arnolds, David R. Penna, and Debra Joy Cruz Sobrepena (eds.), *Africa, Human Rights and the Global System* (Westport, Conn.: Greenwood Press, 1994), chap. 5, and Barbara Hendrie, "Relief Behind the Lines: The Cross-Border Operation in Tigray," in

Joanna Macrae and Anthony Zwi (eds.), *War and Hunger: Rethinking International Responses to Complex Emergencies* (London: Zed, 1994), chap. 7.

8. *The Independent* (London), 28 November 1989.

9. These differences are examined in John Young, "The Tigray and Eritrean Peoples Liberation Fronts: A History of Tensions and Pragmatism," *Journal of Modern African Studies*, 34(1), 1996, pp. 105–120.

10. I have attempted a sketch of postinsurgent government in the Horn in my "The Horn of Africa: Consequences of Insurgency," *Africa Insight*, 23(4), 1993, pp. 184–189.

11. This coincidence has given rise to the bizarre myth among sections of the Ethiopian exile community that the EPLF and EPRDF took power only because Cohen invited them to do so; both movements were in fact poised for a victory that nothing could have averted, and Cohen's intervention at most only helped to smooth the transition.

BIBLIOGRAPHICAL NOTE

There has been no book-length study of Ethiopian foreign policy. Two general overviews, both now outdated, are Negussay Ayele, "The Foreign Policy of Ethiopia," in Olajide Aluko (ed.), *The Foreign Policies of African States* (London: Hodder and Stoughton, 1977), and Christopher Clapham, "Ethiopia," in Timothy M. Shaw and Olajide Aluko (eds.), *The Political Economy of African Foreign Policy* (Aldershot, England: Gower, 1984).

Much of the literature takes the form of studies of the Horn of Africa as a whole and of the relationships between local actors in the region and the superpowers. For an overview, see John W. Harbeson, "Post–Cold War Politics in the Horn of Africa: The Quest for Political Identity Intensified," in John W. Harbeson and Donald Rothchild (eds.), *Africa in World Politics: Post–Cold War Challenges* (Boulder: Westview Press, 1995). See also Terence Lyons, "The International Context of Internal War: Ethiopia/Eritrea," in Edmond J. Keller and Donald Rothchild (eds.), *Africa in the New International Order* (Boulder: Lynne Rienner, 1996). Studies of superpower relations with the region include Paul B. Henze, *The Horn of Africa: From War to Peace* (London: Macmillan, 1991); David A. Korn, *Ethiopia, the United States and the Soviet Union* (London: Croom Helm, 1986); and Robert G. Patman, *The Soviet Union in the Horn of Africa* (Cambridge: Cambridge University Press, 1990). Steven R. David, *Choosing Sides: Alignment and Realignment in the Third World* (Baltimore: Johns Hopkins University Press, 1991), chap. 4, provides an interesting analysis of the calculations facing local rulers in their relations with the major powers.

For an overview of guerrilla insurgencies in the region, there is still no satisfactory successor to the now outdated John Markakis, *National and Class Conflict in the Horn of Africa* (Cambridge: Cambridge University Press, 1987). On the Eritrean conflict, see Ruth Iyob, *The Eritrean Struggle for Independence* (Cambridge: Cambridge University Press, 1995). As already noted, the best studies of cross-border relations and humanitarian relief are found in William DeMars, "Tactics of Protection: International Human Rights Organisations in the Ethiopian Conflict, 1980–1986," in Eileen McCarthy-Arnolds, David R. Penna, and Debra Joy Cruz

Sobrepena (eds.), *Africa, Human Rights and the Global System* (Westport, Conn.: Greenwood Press, 1994), and Barbara Hendrie, "Relief Behind the Lines: The Cross-Border Operation in Tigray," in Joanna Macrae and Anthony Zwi (eds.), *War and Hunger: Rethinking International Responses to Complex Emergencies* (London: Zed, 1994). I have as yet seen no study of the foreign policies of the new governments that took over in 1991.

6

Kenyan Foreign Policy

JONA RONO

Kenya continues to be a relatively stable and important country in Africa despite the challenges facing it as a result of the collapse of the state system in many neighboring countries and the difficulties of the democratization process. It has continuously maintained civilian government since gaining independence in 1963; it accomplished one presidential transition from Jomo Kenyatta to Daniel arap Moi in 1978; and it transformed itself, albeit with difficulties, from a one-party to a multiparty state in the 1990s. In terms of economic development, Kenya, despite many setbacks, has made important strides and has continued to be a model for other states.

This chapter analyzes Kenya's foreign relations to explain achievements and failures in the following contexts: the domestic scenario; general policy orientation premised upon security; decisionmaking structures; relations with neighboring countries; regional organizations; continental organizations, especially the Organization of African Unity; and relations with major powers and organizations such as the United Nations, the International Monetary Fund, the World Bank, and the Commonwealth. Overall, the chapter attempts to refute the negative image of Kenya widely held in Western capitals by exploring the perceptions of the Kenya government.

The Domestic Scenario

Kenya became independent on 12 December 1963 after a bitter struggle against British rule. The issue central to the independence struggle, and in particular Mau Mau, was land tenure. Over the years, white settlers had annexed the best land for themselves and systematically excluded Africans.

At independence, two political parties existed: the Kenya African National Union (KANU) and the Kenya African Democratic Union (KADU).

In 1964, KADU recognized the gains to be made in joining KANU and dissolved itself, and prominent KADU leaders, such as Daniel arap Moi and Ronald Ngala, joined the KANU government.

Following the Zanzibar revolution of 1964, military mutinies occurred in Tanganyika, Uganda, and Kenya. Though these uprisings were quickly put down, interestingly with the help of the British, they signaled the beginning of an ideological divide propelled by the Cold War. Within KANU, a socialist opposition group developed around Vice President Jaramogi Oginga Odinga. He resigned from the government in 1966 to form the Kenya People's Union (KPU). KPU was banned, and Odinga was detained in 1969 following KPU's challenge to the Kenyatta government and tensions stirred by the assassination of Tom Mboya.[1] The KPU found it difficult to extend its power base beyond the Luo, Odinga's ethnic group, partly because of intense government resistance.

Kenyatta pursued a foreign policy that emphasized cooperation with neighboring countries, support of continental liberation movements, and a mixed economy that strongly encouraged foreign investment and hence close ties with Western countries. After his death in 1978, there was a smooth transition despite a precarious political environment, allowing Vice President Moi to become president. There were attempts to topple Moi in a coup d'état in August 1982, and later the wind of change of multiparty democracy blew through Kenya, but Moi was able to hold off a fierce challenge and win another term of office in 1992 and again in December 1997.

Kenyatta and Kenya's Foreign Policy

Robert Jackson and Carl Rosberg decried the lack of institutions in Africa and hence the emergence of personal rule. In the context of foreign policy, the most important policy formulation institution is the presidency, often supported by the respective ministries of foreign affairs.[2]

Kenyatta's style of leadership was reflected in his foreign policy. Kenyatta assumed the presidency at a time when he had achieved heroic status among Kenyans and condemnation as a leader "unto darkness and death" by the colonial government.[3] At independence, Kenyatta apparently had already made up his mind about Kenya's path in foreign affairs. Subsequent policy documents, such as the KANU Manifesto and the Sessional Paper No. 10 of 1965, clearly spelled out Kenyatta's wishes: that Kenya would be built along the lines of free enterprise, tied to the West, and that the accumulation of foreign capital would be necessary for economic growth, which led to the Foreign Investment Protection Act of 1964.

The comments put forward by John Okumu and Samuel Makinda outlining various factors influencing foreign policy are partially accurate.[4] It is the contention here that the input by the head of state is paramount. Kenyatta at independence was the hero who brought "Uhuru" (freedom, independence) but settlers and the British government had earlier been hostile. The *Kenya Weekly News,* the mouthpiece of the British settler community, described Kenyatta as being "stained with the mark of the beast," and in 1958, the chief secretary of the Kenya Colonial Administration, Walter Coutts, made perhaps the most representative of British commentaries: "All sensible people will know that these leaders of Mau Mau are not fit to return to civilized society much less assume the mantle of political leadership. Anyone who supports the contrary view stamps himself as a supporter of bestiality, degradation and criminal activity."[5]

The British were quick to change their opinion of Kenyatta on realizing the extent of his domestic and international support and, perhaps above all, his willingness to cooperate with Britain, the settlers, and foreign investors. Sir Patrick Renison was recalled and replaced by a conciliatory governor, Malcolm McDonald, who became high commissioner at independence. Kenyatta came out strongly to allay the fears of the settler community:

> The government of an independent Kenya will not be a gangster government. Those who have been panicky about their property, whether land or buildings or houses, can now rest assured that the future African government, the Kenya government, will not deprive them of their property or rights of ownership. We will encourage investors in various projects to come to Kenya and carry on their business peacefully in order to bring prosperity to this country. We are going to be an orderly and responsible government . . . we want to run our country in the most peaceful and friendly way.[6]

Kenyatta was determined to be a good neighbor within the East African region and protect Kenya's territorial integrity. Being an "elder statesman," he was consulted on continental matters. He became the chairman of the OAU Congo Conciliation Committee during the Congo crisis in 1964. He was also consulted by the warring Angolan factions, and he held conciliatory meetings in Nakuru and Mombasa in 1975.[7]

On territorial integrity, Kenyatta made it very clear that Kenya would not concede any of its territory. In September 1963, he cautioned the British government against negotiating away the Northern Frontier District (NFD), which the Somali government was claiming. This problem was never solved before Kenyan independence, and Kenyatta had to engage forces against the "shifta" (often translated as "bandits") guerrillas in 1967.[8]

In brief, Kenyatta's personality had a strong influence on foreign policy, and he maintained Kenya in a close relationship with Western states. Others perceived his stance as a "wait and see" policy because Kenyatta was cautious and conservative. This perhaps stemmed from Kenyatta's maturity, his experience abroad, and his detention for about a decade in remote areas of Kenya. Okumu best summed up foreign policy under Kenyatta:

> [Kenya] has effectively maintained a "low profile" on many of the burning issues in Africa and elsewhere, a style of diplomacy that is best described as quiet diplomacy. It is a style which avoids radical aggressiveness which she cannot defend or promote. It is a diplomatic posture which recognises that the uses and functions of foreign policy of a poor nation are to promote economic and social modernisation, tasks which require the services of development diplomats.[9]

Foreign Policy Under Moi

Foreign policy under the Moi administration has become more of a presidential prerogative, more aggressive, and consequently, more controversial. Foreign policy under Kenyatta, as discussed above, was characterized by a noncommittal, wait-and-see attitude. Kenyatta disliked air travel, and he often sent Vice President Moi or the foreign minister to represent him. In contrast, Moi has proven to be as active as any foreign minister. He has visited many countries, including the United States, China, Japan, and Australia, trying to establish links useful to Kenya. Positive nonalignment was to be the official maxim of the country's foreign policy.

Moi emphasized what came to be known as Nyayo philosophy, following the "footsteps" of Kenyatta with the objective of achieving three espoused principles—love, peace, and unity—as well as the more concrete objective of maintaining close links with the West. In regional foreign policy, Moi put the Nyayo philosophy into practice in the following areas: good neighborliness, peacemaking, and peacekeeping.

Good Neighborliness

Kenya's foreign policy of "good neighborliness" came to be President Moi's cornerstone policy in regard to nearby countries. However, some scholars believe this policy has been ambiguous at best. Samuel Makinda wrote: "It is a little difficult to see what Professor Okumu calls a 'good neighbour policy' on the part of Kenya. It is indeed difficult to see which of the East Africa community partners was interested in pursuing a 'good neighbour policy,' unless one takes that policy to mean an absence of real war."[10]

It was Kenya that had a greater interest in this policy. Makinda and Okumu agree that Kenya stood to gain more because it was more economically advanced than its neighbors. Makinda's statement is proven correct when relations between Kenya and the neighboring countries are closely examined.

After 1967, when Tanzania launched its socialist program, the Arusha Declaration, Kenya was suspicious of Tanzania's policies and motivations. Radio broadcasts emanating from Tanzania described Kenya as a "man-eat-man" society. Though Kenyatta and Julius Nyerere participated in cordial summits, the fundamentals of regional cooperation, such as federation and common currency, had already been abandoned. Relations reached their lowest ebb when Tanzania closed its border with Kenya and signaled the collapse of the East African Community (EAC) in 1977. President Moi attempted to mend the relationship, with a measure of success, when relations were normalized in the early 1980s, but it was not until the 1990s that full cooperation could be resumed.

Kenya and Uganda have had stormy relations; indeed, the countries are not unlike two quarreling brothers. In 1969, Uganda under Milton Obote also launched a socialist program, similar to that of Tanzania, known as the Common Man's Charter. Under this policy, unskilled workers from Kenya working in Uganda were expelled despite Kenyatta's intervention. Relations with Uganda under President Idi Amin were even more unpredictable. Initially, they were good, and Amin even visited Kenyatta in Mombasa, but Amin soon claimed part of Kenyan territory. By the time of the Entebbe raid in 1976, Kenya had already had enough of Amin and was only too willing to aid in the operation to rescue the Israeli hostages.

Presidents Godfrey Binaisa and Yusufu Lule were not in office long enough to permit any assessments of their policies toward Kenya. However, during the Obote II period, 1980–1985, relations were relatively tranquil. Kenya even willingly assisted Obote on his way to exile.

Relations with President Museveni's Uganda have been most difficult. Though Moi brokered a peace accord between the National Resistance Army (NRA) and Tito Okello's government in 1986, a process that took four months, Museveni appears to have little regard for Kenya and its president. In fact, on a number of occasions, the two countries have been on the verge of war, with troops amassed at the borders. The bone of contention for Kenya seems to be the government's perception that Museveni wishes to dominate the politics of the region. When socialism was in vogue, Museveni was the militant who rescued Uganda from dictators like Obote and Amin, but now that democracy and the free market are the norm, he is able to explain the importance of a no-party state convincingly, even though it is one and the same thing as a one-party state.

Moi handled challenges posed by Uganda by attempting to maintain good relations, bearing in mind that Uganda is Kenya's leading trading partner. The claim of the presence of a guerrilla group known as FEM (February Eighteen Movement) and its military wing FERA (February Eighteen

Resistance Army) appeared from the Kenya government's perspective to be a creation of the NRA/NRM (National Resistance Army/National Resistance Movement). Articles in *Time* and *Newsweek* about the nonexistence of FEM and FERA are indicative of tensions between the government and the international media.[11] Kenya points to the apparent role played by Museveni in supporting the Rwanda Patriotic Front (RPF) in 1994 to support claims that he is sponsoring forces of instability in the region. Paul Kagame, RPF's commander, once served as a senior officer in the NRA.

The election of Benjamin Mkapa as president of Tanzania in late 1995 proved to be the turning point needed to normalize relations between the three East African states. After a number of diplomatic shuttles between Kampala and Nairobi, Mkapa brought together the "three Ms"—Moi, Museveni, and Mkapa—at a summit in Arusha that launched the Secretariat for East African Cooperation, which is now based there. Kenya's ambassador to the UN, Francis Muthaura, was named secretary-general, with deputies from Uganda and Tanzania.

The Sudanese situation has also been difficult. Kenya has been torn between providing relief to southern Sudan and maintaining good relations with the Sudanese government. The Sudanese government has accused Kenya of aiding the rebel movement known as SPLM/SPLA (Sudanese People's Liberation Movement/Sudanese People's Liberation Army), and several peace summits chaired by Moi have borne no fruit as yet.[12]

The friendship between Ethiopia and Kenya has stood the test of time. Ethiopia is the only country in the region that has never had a major quarrel with Kenya, despite the fact that Mengistu had established a Marxist dictatorship. This peaceful coexistence was necessary because a Kenya-Ethiopia security pact was needed to counter Somali aggression. (For a discussion of the changing fortunes of Ethiopia and Eritrea, see Chapter 5.)

Relations with Somalia have been difficult. Ever since Kenya's independence in 1963, Somalia's five-pointed star has meant the existence of Somali irredentism for nationalists who claim an expanded Somalia; the star represents the five territories of Somalia—one of which is northern Kenya. This led to numerous skirmishes between the shifta and Kenyan security forces. President Moi's efforts were successful because Somali President Siad Barre declared that he had no claim to Kenyan territory, but he had other pressing domestic problems that eventually forced him into exile and precipitated the disintegration of Somali society.[13]

Peacemaking, Peacekeeping, and Southern African Liberation

The New York–based International Peace Academy's Conference on Internal Conflicts in Africa, held in March 1992 at Arusha, acknowledged Kenya's regional role in peacemaking and peacekeeping. Kenya's reputation in this regard came as a result of efforts to reconcile warring factions. As chairman of the OAU (1981–1983), Moi expended a lot of energy in trying to resolve the Chadian conflict, and after that term, he worked to reconcile conflicts in Uganda, Sudan, Mozambique, Ethiopia, and Somalia. This peacemaking role was further amplified during the crisis in the Great Lakes region. Moi hosted the Nairobi 1 and 2 summits to try to prevent a humanitarian calamity as the rebel forces in Zaire fought their way to the capital. Appreciating Moi's efforts and the severity of the situation, Presidents Mandela, Mugabe, Mkapa, and Museveni and other heads of state attended the Nairobi summits.

Peacekeeping has become a major foreign policy tool for Kenya. Its armed forces remain among the most disciplined on the continent, and they have been involved in peacekeeping in Iran, Iraq, Namibia, Chad, and the former Yugoslavia. This has earned Kenya a good reputation, especially in Namibia where its role was appreciated by the Namibian government. (This is similar to the role of Botswana, discussed in Chapter 4.) It was perhaps partly as a result of these peacekeeping efforts that Kenya obtained 182 votes to win a two-year tenure to the nonpermanent seat of the UN Security Council.

Although detractors have accused Kenya of paying lip service to the liberation struggle in Southern Africa, it in fact made a tangible contribution to this effort. The government made substantial contributions to the OAU Liberation Committee, and Moi held a "Harambee" (fund-raising effort) to assist SWAPO. Kenya also became one of the few countries that accorded diplomatic status to the African National Congress and provided all the facilities necessary for the ANC office to run efficiently. Certain politicians may have undermined Kenya's official antiapartheid stance by having informal contact with the Pretoria regime. For example, during the 1983–1984 inquiry into the activities of Charles Njonjo, a former attorney general and minister for constitutional affairs, it was revealed that Njonjo had fairly extensive contacts with Pretoria. When Nelson Mandela was released from prison, Kenya had exploratory contacts with South Africa, to the chagrin of the ANC. This is now a thing of the past because Kenya has established full diplomatic relations with the new South Africa.

Relations with the West

Relations between Kenya under Moi and Western countries could be classified in two phases, before and after 1988. Prior to 1988, relations with most Western countries were cordial, cemented by the stable political situation, a healthy economy, and favorable conditions for Western multinational corporations. Kenya accordingly received massive economic assistance from the West, both at the multilateral level, through the European Union and the World Bank, and on a bilateral level, from individual countries.

Financial assistance has provided about 40 percent of Kenya's development spending in health, water, food, education, transport, and energy sectors. Through the aid programs, Western countries have played a key role in Kenya's development policies, such as the Sessional Paper No. 1 of 1982 on District Focus for Rural Development and Sessional Paper No. 1 of 1986. At the same time, close political relations have been maintained, most notably with Britain, the former colonial power. In fact, there have been few disagreements between the two countries, apart from a couple of incidents. The first was over Britain's obstinacy in regard to the Rhodesian crisis after Rhodesia's unilateral declaration of independence in 1965. Kenya opted to vote against Britain and threatened to sever diplomatic relations.

The second incident, developing from the early 1980s, concerned the harboring of Kenyan dissidents who clamored for multiparty democracy and was centered on writer Ngugi wa Thiong'o and others. Moi and British Prime Minister Margaret Thatcher had a close personal friendship, signaled by such things as the building of the Margaret Thatcher Library at Moi University, and even at the height of calls for multiparty democracy, Britain did not join other Western countries led by the United States in applying economic sanctions. However, it did voice concern over certain issues, although in a subdued manner.

In 1988, Kenya's relations with the West began undergoing change, with the government being hostile to changed Western perceptions. With the end of the Cold War and the rapprochement between the superpowers that culminated in the emergence of the United States as the sole superpower in 1990, Western countries started looking more critically at governments in developing countries that they had previously supported, without question, as long as they were anticommunist. They increasingly pushed the following formula for good governance: multipartyism and democracy, free and fair elections, privatization, and transparency and accountability in the management of public funds.

This resulted in the West's increased criticism of Kenya. The main accusations and criticisms regarded the deterioration of human rights, including such issues as detention without trial, and internal political developments, such as expulsions from KANU. By 1990, economic aid became tied to political and economic reform programs in recipient nations.[14]

The Kenya government believed that the Western powers, especially the United States, had become uncompromising and had adopted aggressive and interventionist policies toward it. These changing attitudes were reflected, for example, in relations with Norway and the United States. Kenya severed diplomatic relations with Norway in 1990, following the latter's granting of political asylum to Kenyan dissidents and extended adverse media coverage on Kenya that appeared to have the consent of the Norwegian government. Kenya had benefited from Norwegian development assistance in the form of loans and grants, and the severing of relations with Norway adversely affected Kenya's relations with other Scandinavian countries that had been active in promoting rural development. The tensions that ensued, however, were short lived, as normal diplomatic relations resumed following the improved human rights situation in Kenya after 1992.[15]

Relations between Kenya and the international financial institutions, the International Monetary Fund, and the World Bank had traditionally been smooth, but following the end of the Cold War, Kenya was called upon to be more accountable. This followed a series of revelations that senior government officials and certain Asian businessmen had colluded to steal billions of Kenya shillings from Kenya's treasury. The classic example of this theft was the Goldenberg scandal, in which an Asian businessman together with officials of the Kenyan Central Bank and the Ministry of Finance, managed to illegally take 14.8 billion shillings out of the treasury. Following this revelation, the IMF and World Bank called for reforms in the financial sector.

After the 1992 elections, the government appointed new leadership to the Central Bank and Ministry of Finance, and within a short time, the two helped to redeem the image of Kenya's financial sector in the eyes of the IFIs. However, problems in regard to governance issues threatened relations after the mid-1990s, especially in the 1997 elections and the run-up to them.

Kenyan-U.S. Relations

Kenyan-U.S. relations were traditionally cordial, until the dramatic changes in the early 1990s. After Kenyan independence, the United States was willing to provide development aid and investment, but it also had other interests centered upon the strategic importance of the Indian Ocean in the Cold War conflict with the Soviet Union and Kenya's willingness to cooperate with the U.S. military. Kenya was important to the United States for two primary reasons: because of its favorable ideological position in regard to private investment and capitalism and because it was in need of aid, especially food (of which the United States had significant amounts to give). The United States worked through a program known as the Surplus Food Disposal Program, later renamed Food for Peace, perhaps by the State Department's public relations experts.

U.S. envoys to Nairobi were primarily concerned about the spread of communism. The contacts Kenya had with the USSR and China were viewed suspiciously by the United States, and thus envoys such as Ambassador William Attwood occupied themselves with strategizing how communism could be stopped from spreading into Kenya and other African states. Attwood wrote a book entitled *The Reds and the Blacks,* which was later banned by the Kenya government. Perhaps through U.S. influence, such books as *Quotations from Chairman Mao* were also banned in Kenya, and communist-inclined university lecturers were closely monitored.

The United States, conscious of the Soviet military buildup in Ethiopia and Somalia, provided Kenya with military hardware, including the F-5 fighter aircraft. Kenya reciprocated by supporting the United States publicly in the fight against communism. Several examples demonstrate this. First, Moi set a day of prayer for U.S. hostages held in Teheran in 1979, repeatedly called for their release, and said that he was willing to help the United States "in any way" to secure that release. Second, Kenya joined the Western boycott of the 1980 Olympic Games in Moscow. Third, Kenya permitted air and naval facilities in Mombasa to be used by the U.S. Rapid Deployment Force. These facilities were later used by the United States in its failed mission in Somalia in 1994.

This cozy relationship came to an end in 1990. Washington no longer needed small allies such as Kenya in its strategic global master plan. In what amounted to betrayal as Kenya's leaders saw it, the United States demanded immediate changes in the way the Kenyan government was being run. Washington demanded that the one-party political system be replaced by a multiparty system. Pleas by Moi that Kenya was not cohesive enough to undergo multiparty transformation were not convincing.

In the Kenyan government's perception, the United States orchestrated an anti-Kenya campaign in 1992 to freeze aid from all Western countries and multilateral agencies, such as the IMF and World Bank. Encouragement was given to anti-Moi elements to demand changes in the name of human rights and pluralism, though the Kenyan government claimed these were ethnically based demands. Some prominent Kenyans, such as lawyer Gibson Kamau Kuria, traveled to the United States and were provided funding by the Kennedy family to facilitate these changes.

Kenyan leaders believed that the outspoken U.S. ambassador Smith Hempstone was posted to Nairobi by the Bush administration to openly campaign against the Moi administration. Hempstone supported the formation of the opposition Forum for Restoration of Democracy (FORD) and helped to fund publications critical of the government. Despite the overt U.S. support for multipartyism, FORD split along ethnic lines and was defeated by Moi's KANU in the 1992 elections. The country was rocked by ethnic violence, and a bloodbath was predicted, but Kenya's resiliency has prevailed, and it has had to meet all the demands imposed by the United States, the IMF, and the World Bank—but with mixed results.

In 1996, Kenya seemed to be headed for a gradual economic revival and improved political stability, but the tensions prior to the 1997 elections brought about greater instability. Incidents such as the inadvertent detention of the female U.S. ambassador, A. E. Brazeal, in a roadblock and threats by KANU secretary-general Joseph Kamotho to expel *Newsweek* and *Time* reporters for filing "negative and false stories" about Kenya— leading to a commentary by Jimmy Carter that such expulsions would adversely affect Kenya's human rights image—eventually passed over. The Kenya government maintains—admittedly, controversially—that the United States should by now have learned that ethnic cohesion in Africa is more important than liberal democracy, having watched the horrors in Rwanda, Burundi, and Somalia. However, the ethnic violence within Kenya in 1997 and 1998 has only served to increase pressure on the Moi administration, especially as Western powers perceive the government to be a partial instigator of that violence.

Relations with Communist Countries

Though Kenya established diplomatic relations with the two major communist powers, the PRC and the USSR, little of substance took place between these nations. On a visit to the USSR in May 1964 during Kenyatta's presidency, Vice President Odinga managed to obtain aid to build a 200-bed hospital in Kisumu, a radio station, a sugar factory, a paper mill, an irrigation project, a fish cannery, and a food-processing facility. Kenya was also offered 300 scholarships.[16]

Relations with the Soviets soured when the Kenyan government discovered armaments hidden in the basement of Odinga's ministry building, ostensibly meant for the overthrow of Kenyatta's regime. After that, no high-ranking Kenyan official visited the USSR before its collapse, though Kenya maintained diplomatic relations with Moscow.

Relations with China did not take off until recently. The earlier coolness in Nairobi's relationship with Beijing was perhaps caused by Chou En Lai's 1964 remark that Africa was ripe for revolution. This was not taken kindly by Kenya in light of the Zanzibar revolution and the army mutinies that followed. The cool relations resulted in mutual withdrawal of diplomatic personnel. However, during the Moi administration, relations have warmed up, resulting in two presidential visits to China and Chinese assistance in the building of both the Moi International Sports Centre in Nairobi and Moi University Teaching Hospital in Eldoret.

Relations with Other Countries

Indian-Kenyan relations date back to antiquity, as monsoon winds bounced Indian traders in sailing ships to East African shores, a journey of two to three weeks. Years later, the British took many Indian indentured laborers to build the Kenya-Uganda Railway in 1895, and a sizable

Indian community settled in Kenya. This has turned out to be a prosperous community partly because of the privileges they enjoyed under British rule and also because they are a hardworking community.

Relations between Kenya and India have always been intimate, helped by the admiration Kenyan freedom fighters have had for Indian nationalists such as Mahatma Gandhi and Jawaharlal Nehru. Kenyan Indians, among them Makhan Singh and Pio Gama Pinto, also contributed to Kenya's independence struggle. The bone of contention has been the conspicuous prosperity of the Indian community and its failure to integrate with Africans. Such exclusivity had led Idi Amin to expel the Indians from Uganda in 1972. In Kenya, no such drastic action has occurred, and it is unlikely to happen in the future, though some populist politicians have harped on the so-called Indian question.

On the economic front, Indian companies such as Panafrican Paper Mills of Orient Paper and Industries Ltd., Raymond Woollen Mills, and Ken-India Insurance Company, among others, have invested in Kenya. There is renewed interest in investments from India, particularly in appropriate small-scale industries. In the field of education, about 25,000 Kenyans have received their education in India.[17]

Japan is another important country for Kenya. Nairobi has a diplomatic mission in Tokyo, and bilateral aid from Japan has steadily increased. Japan has financed some costly projects, such as the Jomo Kenyatta University of Agriculture and Technology, a forestry institute, Moi Airport, and Kilifi Bridge. The imbalance of trade is, however, 1:14 in favor of Japan. This has to be evaluated if any meaningful relationship is to be maintained.[18]

Kenya has established diplomatic missions in several Middle East countries, namely, Egypt, Iran, Saudi Arabia, the United Arab Emirates, and Israel. The relations have mainly centered on Kenya's dependence on the oil produced by some of these countries. Relations with Israel, however, have been strained. When Kenya allowed Israeli troops to fuel in Nairobi during the Entebbe raid, it was accused of supporting imperialism. Kenya did sever relations with Israel during the Arab-Israeli War of 1973, in line with OAU recommendations, but it continued to maintain informal contacts until 1993, when relations were again normalized. Kenya had hoped that the Arab world would provide cheaper fuel as a show of solidarity. But this never occurred, and relations seem to be purely premised on the supply of oil and on a new security issue regarding Islamic fundamentalism.

Kenya Foreign Policy Decisionmaking Structures

The Department of Foreign Affairs was established in the Office of the Prime Minister (now President) in 1964. Joseph Murumbi became the first minister of state in charge of foreign affairs, and Robert Ouko was the first permanent secretary. Murumbi was succeeded briefly by Argwings Kodhek in 1966, then by Njoroge Mungai. Munyua Waiyaki was the minister for foreign affairs between 1968 and 1983. Other notable and long-serving ministers include Elijah Mwangale, Robert Ouko, Ndolo Ayah, and now Stephen Kalonzo Musyoka. The Department of Foreign Affairs later attained its own identity and became the Ministry of Foreign Affairs and International Cooperation.

Josephat Karanja, later Kenya's vice president, went to London as Kenya's first high commissioner, Adala Otuku was posted to Moscow as ambassador, and Burudi Nabwera represented Kenya in Washington, D.C. These pioneer diplomats made their presence felt in international diplomatic circles. Waiyaki was the chief architect of Kenya's antiapartheid policy. Ouko made Kenya's presence felt at the EAC and in the late 1980s when he vigorously defended the Moi administration internationally.[19]

At the level of permanent secretary, several illustrious Kenyans have made their mark. Bethwell Kiplagat, permanent secretary between 1983 and 1991, was an articulate diplomat whose oratory was admired by the Nairobi diplomatic corps. He was also the architect of Moi's peace diplomacy and an authority on Mozambique, Sudan, and Somalia. His successor, Sally Kosgei, became the first female Kenyan high commissioner in London and also the first female permanent secretary. She was articulate in defending Kenya, authoring such publications as *Nailing Lies*,[20] which attempted to counteract publications by Africa Watch and Amnesty International that were critical of Kenya's human rights record. She was also behind attempts to change the attitude in Western capitals regarding Kenya's political and economic reforms.

Most of Kenya's diplomats are trained either abroad, in Oxford, Washington, or Islamabad, among other places, or at the University of Nairobi's Institute of Diplomacy. As yet, however, there is no diplomatic cadre separate from the ordinary civil service. Officers from other ministries often find their way into foreign affairs and vice versa. There has been a quiet debate on whether this is healthy; the debate exploded publicly in 1996 when potential investors complained that Kenyan diplomats abroad were not particularly concerned about informing their hosts on investment opportunities. The mini–press war that ensued was enlivened by open disagreement between Kenya's ambassador to the United States and the permanent secretary in the ministry.

Some writers have lamented the low-profile role played by African diplomats in Western capitals. A.H.M. Kirk-Greene called for the study of the role of the African diplomat in a rather humorous paper entitled "The Sad Case of the Missing African Diplomat." He said that closer attention must be paid to the structure and staffing of ministries of external affairs in texts on international relations and diplomacy in their African context: "At present, the basic literature on foreign policy and international relations all too often conveys the impression that the African diplomat if he exists at all, is irrelevant to international diplomacy."[21] In my assessment, African diplomats have made their presence felt. It now falls to the academic or academically inclined diplomats to write about their experiences.

Although a detailed study of the Ministry of Foreign Affairs and International Cooperation is beyond the scope of this chapter, it will suffice to state that the ministry is involved almost on a daily basis in shaping and formulating foreign policy. The thirty-six missions abroad file reports that assist the permanent secretary and the ministry in advising the president on policy matters. The Monday morning "prayer" meeting in the ministry's boardroom often serves as a brainstorming session. Seminars on various aspects of foreign policy have been held, and recommendations have been presented to the government.

The biannual conference of Kenyan ambassadors and high commissioners also serves as a useful forum for exchanging views on various foreign policy issues. Recommendations are then presented to the government for further action. The seventy-five foreign missions and twenty-three international organizations based in Nairobi also have some influence on the formulation of policy.

The establishment of the UN Environment Programme (UNEP) made Kenya in 1972 the first developing country to be chosen as the headquarters of a UN organization. In 1976, the UN Human Settlement Secretariat (UNSS-Habitat) was also established in Kenya. This has positively influenced various aspects of foreign policy. For example, Kenya is party to several conventions on biodiversity, such as the Convention on International Trade in Endangered Species (CITES), and is the only country that regularly disposes of illegally acquired but widely traded wildlife products such as ivory, rhino horn, and leopard skin by public burning.

Toward Economic Diplomacy

The end of the Cold War has had a profound impact not only on Kenya but on all the neighboring countries. Tanzania has long abandoned the socialist path, Ethiopia's Marxist revolution fell apart (see Chapter 5), and Uganda under Museveni has toned down its revolutionary rhetoric in favor of a market economy that is now booming. Somalia and Sudan, however, are still mired in their internal wars.

Kenya had long followed the path of the capitalist market economy, but global changes had their impact in the 1973 and 1983 fuel crises and the coffee booms of 1977 and 1986. Economic and political systems survived the test induced by the major powers and the World Bank when aid was frozen between 1991 and 1993. Kenya depends on the West for machinery, chemicals, and industrial inputs, and it relies on Middle East petroleum to drive the economy. Agricultural exports such as tea, coffee, soda ash, horticultural products, sisal, wattle bark, and pyrethrum depend on world market prices decided in the West. Thus, foreign policy has to cater to these aspects in a world increasingly focused on economic power.

In recent years, President Moi's major foreign policy preoccupation, like that of many African leaders, has been the wooing of foreign investors. In May 1994, while on transit to China, the president took time to meet members of the Indian business community and urge them to invest in Kenya. In November of the same year, he traveled to Britain to address a Confederation of British Industry (CBI) conference on investment in Kenya. Government incentives include investment allowances of up to 85 percent on plant and machinery in manufacturing and hotel sectors, liberal depreciation rates, and remission of the customs duty. Export processing zones (EPZs) have also been set up and enjoy special incentives.

Within the East African region, Kenya has put a great deal of effort into reviving three important economic institutions: the EAC; the Preferential Trade Area (PTA), now COMESA; and the Inter-Governmental Authority on Development (IGAD). The EAC established a secretariat, which became operational in 1996. Kenya also participated actively in the formation of the recently launched Indian Ocean Rim Association for Regional Cooperation (IORARC).

Since independence, Kenya has done well in the development of tourism, which has grown eightfold in terms of arrivals and seventeen-fold in earnings and today ranks as the highest foreign exchange earner for Kenya. Sport has also been used as a tool for economic diplomacy. Kenya has enjoyed unsolicited publicity as a tourist destination through its long-distance athletes, especially during the Olympic and Commonwealth Games.

Security is a major concern for Kenya. In the early 1990s, an influx of about 500,000 refugees, caused by civil wars in Somalia, Sudan, and Ethiopia, strained the country's security and resources. The government's patience with refugees finally ended in 1995, when Moi ordered the UN High Commissioner for Refugees (UNHCR) to repatriate refugees responsible for the worsening security situation.

Conclusion

Kenya's foreign policy has arguably stood the test of time. This was initially because of Kenyatta's pragmatic approach to issues, which meant that Kenya could cooperate with any country in the world—as long as it was in the best interest of Kenya. Kenya's priority at independence was economic development and security. The government elite recognized that the West was economically better placed to deal with these needs, hence the evolution of closer relations. These relations, though unbalanced in favor of the West, were built on the foundation of seventy years or so of British colonial rule and the strong presence of Western multinational corporations.

The pragmatic approach toward domestic and foreign affairs has served Kenya well. The challenges ahead are many and difficult. The domestic scenario is threatened by ethnic intolerance and violence, unemployment in the midst of a rapidly growing population, and insecurity as a result of armaments infiltrating in from countries such as Somalia. On the international front, there is a growing disinterest in and marginalization of Africa. The withdrawal of U.S. troops from Somalia and the absence of Western intervention in Liberia and Sierra Leone are clear signals that Africa must look for homegrown, regional solutions—and peacekeepers—to cope with its problems. (The growing significance of regionalism is taken up in many chapters, notably in Chapters 3, 7, 9, and 12.)

The government has some good ideas, such as striving for an export-oriented economy, rewriting the constitution to promote better ethnic cohesion, and strengthening the security apparatus to create an environment conducive to foreign investment. The Moi government calls for help and understanding from friendly countries rather than what it considers to be stereotyped condemnation by the Western media. The tragedies of Somalia, Rwanda, and Burundi should serve as lessons for the international community, although there admittedly remains more to be done to solidify Kenyan democracy.

NOTES

1. The banning of the KPU and detention of Odinga should also be understood in the context of ethnic rivalry between Odinga and Kenyatta. Rivalry also characterized the relationship between Mboya and Odinga, though both were Luo. Mboya had support from the United States.

2. Robert Jackson and Carl G. Rosberg, *Personal Rule in Africa: Prince, Autocrat, Prophet, Tyrant* (Berkeley and Los Angeles: University of California Press, 1982), p. 1.

3. For a complete biography of Kenyatta, see Jeremy Murray-Brown, *Kenyatta* (New York: E. P. Dutton, 1973).

4. John Okumu, "Kenya's Foreign Policy," in Olajide Aluko (ed.), *The Foreign Policies of African States* (London: Hodder and Stoughton, 1977), p. 136; Samuel M. Makinda, "From Quiet Diplomacy to Cold War Politics: Kenya's Foreign Policy," *Third World Quarterly*, 5(2), April 1983, pp. 300–319.

5. Harry Ododa, "Continuity and Change in Kenya's Foreign Policy: From Kenyatta to Moi Government," *Journal of African Studies*, 13(2), Summer 1986, p. 50.

6. Jomo Kenyatta, *Suffering Without Bitterness* (Nairobi: East African Publishing House, 1968).

7. Despite Kenyatta's best efforts, these meetings were fruitless, partly because of superpower rivalry and South Africa's interest in stopping African liberation.

8. Katete Orwa, "Foreign Relations and International Cooperation," in Ministry of Information and Broadcasting (ed.), *Kenya: An Official Handbook* (Nairobi: Colourprint, 1988), p. 308.

9. Okumu, "Kenya's Foreign Policy," p. 136.

10. Makinda, "From Quiet Diplomacy," p. 305.

11. Joshua Hammer, "Never Count a Big Man Out," *Newsweek*, 27 March 1995, p. 13. Museveni's National Resistance Army set a dangerous precedent when Rwanda's president was assassinated in a plane crash in 1994. This resulted in interethnic violence that claimed more than 500,000 lives. There are dangers for Kenya should the NRA arm Kenyan opposition parties, such as Ford-Kenya, whose supporters have close ethnic links with Uganda.

12. Kipyego Cheluget, "Kenya and the Search for Peace in the Nile Valley," in Kipyego Cheluget (ed.), *Kenya's Quarter Century of Diplomatic Relations: Issues, Achievements and Prospects* (Nairobi: Government Press, 1990), pp. 3–16. SPLA/M stands for Sudan People's Liberation Army/Movement.

13. V. B. Thompson, "Conflict in the Horn of Africa: Kenya-Somalia Relations Since the Ogaden War, 1978–1986," paper presented at the African Studies Association conference, Chicago, 28–31 October 1988.

14. Many in the Kenya government consider it ironic for the United States and European countries to have taken this stand, given the fact that Europe recently colonized Africa and violated human rights. The U.S. human rights record at home is not that good, and its role in aiding and abetting apartheid in South Africa is well documented.

15. A major issue concerned the arrest of a former MP, Koigi wa Wamere, who was caught smuggling arms into Kenya, and the open support offered to him by the Norwegian embassy in Nairobi.

16. Ododa, "Continuity and Change in Kenya's Foreign Policy," p. 53.

17. "Indian Exports to Kenya Boom," *Kenya Trade and Travel* (New Delhi: Kenya High Commission), 1(1), 1994, p. 2.

18. Kul Bhushan, *Kenya Factbook, 1995–1996* (Nairobi: Newspread International, 1995). I am grateful to Bhushan for his help with this information.

19. Ouko was murdered in February 1990; his remains were discovered a few days later. To date, the case has not been solved.

20. Ministry of Foreign Affairs and International Cooperation, *Nailing Lies* (Nairobi, 1991).

21. Paper presented by A.H.M. Kirk-Greene at a seminar organized by the Institute of Diplomacy and International Studies, University of Nairobi, held in Mombasa, December 1991.

SELECT BIBLIOGRAPHY

Government Documents

Ministry of Foreign Affairs and International Cooperation, *Nailing Lies* (Nairobi, 1991).

Ministry of Information and Broadcasting (ed.), *Kenya: An Official Handbook* (Nairobi: Colourprint, 1988).

Articles and Books

Bhushan, Kul. *Kenya Factbook, 1995–1996* (Nairobi: Newspread International, 1995).

Cheluget, Kipyego (ed.). "Kenya's Quarter Century of Diplomatic Relations: Issues, Achievements and Prospects" (Nairobi: Government Press, 1990).

Makinda, Samuel M. "From Quiet Diplomacy to Cold War Politics: Kenya's Foreign Policy." *Third World Quarterly*, 5(2), April 1983, pp. 300–319.

Murray-Brown, Jeremy. *Kenyatta* (New York: E. P. Dutton, 1973).

Ododa, Harry. "Continuity and Change in Kenya's Foreign Policy: From Kenyatta to Moi Government," *Journal of African Studies*, 13(2), Summer 1986, pp. 47–57.

Okumu, John. "Kenya's Foreign Policy," in Olajide Aluko (ed.), *Foreign Policies of African States* (London: Hodder and Stoughton, 1977).

7

Nigeria: Aspirations of Regional Power

Stephen Wright and Julius Emeka Okolo

Nigeria is Africa's most populous country and potentially one of its strongest in terms of exerting influence on neighboring African states and, at times, on events outside the continent. Within the West African subregion, Nigeria is unequaled in terms of the size of its economy, military, and population, leading to its claims to be a subregional "hegemonic power."

Following Nigerian foreign policy since the country's formal independence in October 1960 is something akin to riding a roller coaster: There are high and low points and plenty of anticipation. During the First Republic of 1960–1966, foreign policy orientations were modest and conservative, formally espousing nonalignment or "positive neutralism" but remaining closely tied economically to the former colonial power, Britain, and reflecting the caution of the predominantly Muslim leadership under Prime Minister Alhaji Abubakar Tafawa Balewa. A fierce civil war fought between Biafra and the federal forces during 1967–1970 was internationalized by both parties. France became openly sympathetic to the Biafran cause, though stopping short of formal recognition, and this significantly hampered Nigerian-French relations after the end of the war. The Soviet Union became a major arms supplier to the federal government, taking advantage of Britain's momentary twinge of conscience, but by the end of the war, Britain was again the main military supplier to Nigeria.[1]

The 1970s witnessed a burgeoning economy, based on petroleum exports, that allowed Nigeria to push itself into international prominence. Successive leaders were able to pursue forceful West African and continental policies, often couched in moralistic and "manifest destiny" terms.

Such policies required European nations and the United States to pay greater attention to the country that was increasingly touted—not only by Nigerians—as the "champion" of Africa, able to protect and preserve the interests of Africa's less fortunate, both on the continent and in the diaspora. As two prominent scholars put it: "There can be no nobler task for Nigeria to accomplish than to employ prudently Nigeria's leverage to obtain accelerated justice and freedom for all blacks."[2]

From the early 1980s to the present, Nigerian political economy has lessened such policy influence, undermined some of the country's aspirations, and led to a grudging acceptance of more realistic assessments of its capability. Julius Ihonvbere summed up these factors in a critical manner: "Its aspirations have been checkmated by several internal contradictions—dependence, foreign domination, corruption, political instability, poor leadership, inconsistency in policy formulation and implementation, technological backwardness, and a marginal location and role in the international division of labor."[3]

Economic crises, an unevenly implemented structural adjustment program, failures to democratize, and a changing global order are other critical factors contributing to Nigeria's troubled fortunes and status in the late 1990s.

Political Economy and the Decisionmaking Environment

Since the early 1970s, petroleum has accounted for more than 90 percent of Nigeria's annual export revenues and has been considered by many observers as the basis for building a credible foreign policy.[4] As the fortunes of the Organization of Petroleum Exporting Countries (OPEC), of which Nigeria is a member, rose during the 1970s, the national economy boomed, with oil revenues peaking in 1980 at around $25 billion. A miniboom during the Gulf War of the early 1990s provided a brief respite after the steady collapse in prices over the 1980s—petroleum earned only $4.2 billion in 1989—but not from other associated economic problems faced by the country. These included external debt of $37 billion by 1997, chronic social dislocation accentuated by the SAP, and the repeated failure to implement a democratic transition.

Agriculture had been the backbone of the economy during the 1960s, contributing some 70 percent of the GDP at independence. The large physical size of the country, combined with its distinctive types of terrain and climate, provided useful diversity of production. Unfortunately, a combination of oil's sorcery and government neglect led to the rapid decline of the agricultural sector, which contributed only 36 percent of the GDP by 1985. Over the same period, agriculture's share of export revenues fell from 81 percent to just 5 percent. Efforts through structural adjustment to diversify export revenues, for example into cocoa, failed miserably in the 1990s.

Other factors in Nigeria's political economy were equally significant. Federalism has been a constant feature of political life since 1954, though its specific structure of implementation has altered over time. During the First Republic (1960–1966), there was a weakened central government and strong regional governments, each with their own foreign policies. Lessons from the civil war, combined with the strengthening of the federal center through control of oil revenues and a strong centralized military rule, brought greater coherence to foreign and domestic policy. The military's control of the government since 1966 for all but the four years of the civilian Second Republic (1979–1983) has influenced both the character of policy and, more substantially, the style of decisionmaking.

Internal cleavages have provided significant inputs into the foreign policy mechanism. Nigeria is composed of more than 250 ethnic groups, but several are dominant, notably the Hausa-Fulani in the north, the Yoruba in the west, and the Igbo in the east. Clashes between them and minority groups contributed to the civil war, but rivalries have also significantly impaired the ability of civilian governments to govern effectively. More recently, ethnicity appears to have intensified with the impact of structural adjustment, the creation of new states within the federal structure, and the increasingly bitter competition for survival.[5]

Smaller ethnic groups have tried to assert their voice in policymaking, most effectively seen after the civil war with the rise in influence of groups from the "Middle Belt," and in the 1990s with the Ogoni from the oil-producing southeast delta area. The Ogoni challenge to the federal government for greater revenue sharing, more effective development spending, a measure of environmental protection, and greater devolution of political power from the federal level to state and local government levels threatened the military's control of the country's political economy and its spoils of office.[6] These tensions echoed well beyond the borders of Nigeria, becoming a significant foreign policy issue—for state and non-state actors—and impacting relations with many non-African states as well as large oil multinationals, particularly Shell, and international organizations, including the European Union and the Commonwealth.

The federal government's repression of the Movement for the Survival of Ogoni People (MOSOP), culminating in the execution of nine of its leaders in November 1995 along with the continued detention of other leaders, brought international ostracism and outrage, though it had a minimal impact within Nigeria or on the country's vital oil industry. Both the federal government and the dissident minorities carried out major international campaigns to press their respective cases. The overt failure of due judicial process led to international action against the government, including sanctions on arms trade and travel by members of the military government into the EU and the United States, Nigeria's undignified (temporary) dismissal from the Commonwealth (which was led by a Nigerian secretary-general, Emeka Anyaoku), and the principled action of South Africa's president, Nelson Mandela, calling for harsher international sanctions against Nigeria. (See Chapter 9 for a South African perspective.) The Nigerian boycott of the African Soccer Cup in South Africa in January 1996 appeared to be a nationalistic response to Mandela's criticism. The ire of the EU and the United States was not sufficient to include the oil trade in the sanctions they imposed.

Religious diversity also impacts policy orientation, with Christians and Muslims fairly equally divided within the country. Membership of the Organization of the Islamic Conference (OIC), the issue of diplomatic relations with Israel, and support for parties in the Gulf War have been among the foreign policy issues affected by religious pressures. In addition, university faculty and students have been outspoken in airing views on foreign policy matters, although they have had few successes in influencing policy. The abrogation of the Anglo-Nigerian defense pact in the early 1960s is one of only a few exceptions. Human rights groups, vociferous and numerous, have combined with external forces to increase political conditionality pressures on Nigerian military regimes, especially in the late 1990s, but they have also recorded little success in shaping either domestic or external policy. Many of the leaders of these human rights groups have found themselves in jail or exile or, worse still, as victims of a growing wave of political assassinations.

Another substantial issue in policy formulation is that of social class. Whose interests are served by the Nigerian state and its foreign policy? More traditional surveys of Nigeria assume a rational purpose to foreign policy designed to benefit the majority. This view is increasingly being challenged. Whether in the brief years of civilian government since independence or in the decades of military government, it is evident that policy has not significantly benefited the "average" Nigerian, male or female. Labor unions have consistently been dominated by governments, civilian or military, and have exerted little influence over policy formation.

Massive corruption has skimmed billions of dollars in oil revenue into private hands. This, combined with kickbacks and fraud across the whole economic spectrum, has severely undermined Nigeria's development potential and discouraged foreign investment (beyond the oil sector). For example, a government-appointed panel admitted that $12.4 billion in oil revenues could not be accounted for between 1988 and 1994.[7] Structural adjustment has done little to undermine this graft; if anything, it has increased it. Glaring inequalities now exist between rich and poor, with a rapidly shrinking middle class forced to eke out an existence in any way possible. Privatization has allowed the wealthy to capitalize on economic opportunities, without much of the trickle-down effect anticipated by the external reformers. Military governments, installed as self-proclaimed reformers, appear unable or unwilling to facilitate meaningful reform within Nigeria's political economy and equally unable to forge a greater sense of national unity.[8] Widespread suspicion that the military will conspire to extend its rule beyond the transition date of October 1999—or hand over power to carefully vetted civilians—gives little cause for optimism in terms of real societal change.

It is within the context of these societal and political economy characteristics that foreign policy decisionmaking must be placed. Formal civilian structures, such as the National Assembly and political parties, have been present only for short spells and have had a very limited impact on policy. The Ministry of External Affairs has had a more productive role to play, though it is often limited by the command structure of military governments.[9] An informative study of the foreign policy process undertaken by Ibrahim Gambari, both a scholar and a former external affairs minister, considered the interplay of the sizable bureaucracy with the military command. Gambari found (with some bitterness) that though there was considerable policy discussion and formulation within the ministry, critical decisions were formulated by the military leadership, often with little recourse to the ministry. Furthermore, the country's intelligence services played significant roles in policymaking, but these services were not under the control of the External Affairs Ministry. Useful debate on foreign policy was carried out by the Nigerian Institute for International Affairs (NIIA), the Nigerian Institute for Policy and Strategic Studies (NIPSS), and the Nigerian Institute for Social and Economic Research (NISER), but there was little in the way of a formal mechanism to channel those ideas into government. Greater training and specialization were called for within the ministry itself.[10]

Although these formal relationships provide some insights into policy formulation, much more informative and accurate is the focus on informal mechanisms—the role of business interest groups, the Manufacturers Association of Nigeria, the "Kaduna mafia,"[11] religious lobbies, and personal connections, as well as the outlook of a handful of elite advisers around the head of state.[12] Other agencies, such as nongovernmental organizations, women's groups, the media, and academic associations, have sporadic rather than consistent impact on the decisionmaking machinery. External pressures are also important, shifting from those of European governments in the early days of independence to those of key international financial institutions, the IMF, and the World Bank, in the 1980s and 1990s. The end of the Cold War has possibly increased the leverage of these latter groups over Nigeria and many other African states, as there is now little alternative to them in debt rescheduling or foreign investment negotiations.

Developing Regional Stature: 1960–1983

At independence, the power of regional governments within Nigeria— northern, western, and eastern—weakened the federal center and undermined the concept of a Nigerian "national interest," however that would have been defined. Political elites, maintained in power by manipulating ethnic, religious, and regional interests, and sustaining political parties at the local rather than national level had little to gain by strengthening the appeal of the federal government or of its foreign policy. The constitution gave concurrent powers to federal and regional governments to pursue "industrial development," enabling elites to take foreign policy positions favorable to their own narrow interests. Each regional government maintained a separate delegation in London, leading to confusion over foreign policy articulation. Despite paying lip service to nonalignment, Nigeria remained closely linked to Britain, influenced by the conservative perspective of Tafawa Balewa, and distanced from the radicalism of Ghana's Kwame Nkrumah, who succinctly criticized Nigeria as "big for nothing."[13]

Two military coups in 1966 altered the political balance, and in 1967 General Yakubu Gowon irreversibly altered the federal structure by splitting the country into twelve states, setting in motion a set of political forces that resulted in the country being divided into thirty-six states by October 1996. Ethnic and religious sentiments, combined with economic muscle from proximity to the oil production, contributed to the eastern region's decision to secede, sparking the civil war between 1967 and 1970. The war led to innovative foreign policies, with each side aiming at the diplomatic isolation of the other. Eastern Europe and the Soviet Union became drawn in on the federal side, particularly to provide weapons, whereas strong French support and humanitarian NGOs provided assistance to the Biafran secessionists. The Nigerian military quickly expanded from 10,000 to 250,000 troops, gaining advanced hardware on the way; as a result, Nigeria in the 1970s possessed the strongest military force in independent sub-Saharan Africa.

The experience of the civil war, the bloated military, the international connections forged during the war, and the new revenues accruing from the boom in oil exports all contributed to a new dynamism and stature in foreign policy in the 1970s, especially but certainly not exclusively inside international organizations.[14] A succession of military and civilian leaders—Yakubu Gowon (until 1975), Murtala Muhammed (1975–1976), Olusegun Obasanjo (1976–1979), and Shehu Shagari (1979–1983)—maintained similar foreign policy profiles. Their formal foreign policy supported liberation movements, opposed apartheid, and promoted non-alignment; the focus was also turned upon developing the country's influence over West African and, wherever possible, continental affairs. Oil revenues allowed Nigerian foreign aid to be spread liberally around Africa, though not necessarily with much corresponding influence, particularly because of the absence of trade relations with other countries in the continent. Since independence, more than 80 percent of Nigeria's trade has been with Europe, the United States, and Japan, and official trade with African neighbors has remained static.

Debates about Nigeria's true foreign policy capability during this period still rumble, with revisionist scholars arguing that policy was more posture and rhetoric than power and capability and that Nigeria was not quite the African giant and leader that many claimed it to be. Trade with neighboring states remained negligible, limiting any contact Nigeria may have had around the continent, and the "oil weapon" was, of course, double-edged. Nigeria could hardly afford to cut exports to key European countries or the United States, and it could not realistically hope to cut oil being traded to South Africa. As Kayode Soremekun concluded, "Shagari was being unduly euphoric about the use of the oil weapon against South Africa and her Western friends."[15]

William Graf placed a study of Nigeria within a political economy context, and he was critical of the overambitious reach of Nigerian policymakers in the 1970s. In his view, "The 'golden era' of Nigerian foreign policy, roughly from 1975 to 1980, coincides with the peaking of the state class's relative economic power on the strength of its control over a strategic resource and its share of oil revenues."[16]

Nigeria's position within the global political economy was marginally improved in the 1970s by the loosening of the Cold War and the post–Bretton Woods growth of new economic centers in Europe and Japan, as well as by the reluctance of the United States to intervene internationally in the post-Vietnam, post-Watergate era of Presidents Ford and Carter.[17]

In this fluid international context, Nigeria was pandered to and courted by Northern states and was able to carry out high-profile roles: backing the Popular Movement for the Liberation of Angola in 1975; helping with the creation of the Economic Community of West African States in 1975; taking the lead in negotiations for the Lomé Convention between 1973 and 1975;[18] boldly, perhaps extravagantly, hosting the Festival of Black Arts and Culture (FESTAC) in 1977; working on the nationalization of British Petroleum operations as a feature of the broader intervention in the Zimbabwe independence negotiations in 1979;[19] participating in the peacekeeping efforts in Chad from 1980 to 1982; leading the various boycotts of Olympic (1976 and 1984) and Commonwealth (1978) Games; and hosting an Organization of African Unity summit in 1980 that led to the continental economic program contained in the Lagos Plan of Action

(LPA). All these activities raised the country's international exposure and stature but, significantly, did not threaten, in any major way, established interests held in Western capitals or by multinational corporations. Shagari's ruling National Party of Nigeria (NPN) and, more important, its ruling elite did not stand to benefit from a radical nationalist policy that would destabilize important connections with the West.

One could make a case that this stature peaked during the early part of Shehu Shagari's first term as president, as the legitimacy of civilian rule combined with maximum oil revenues. As Tom Forrest pointed out, building an economic base purely on oil made the country extremely vulnerable because "economic expansion became dependent on an increase in real oil earnings," and "after a short period of financial surplus, expenditure tended to outstrip revenue, leading to large internal budget deficits."[20] By the overthrow of the Second Republic in December 1983, the poor performance of the political class, the arrogant and flamboyant display of its corrupt wealth, the failure to listen to military demands for tough action in disputes against neighboring Chad and Cameroon, and declining economic fortunes all combined to diminish the country's stature and point to the limitations in Nigerian capability—and encourage the military to again try its hand at government.[21]

Constraints on Status and Stability: 1984–1998

One should again stress the important distinction between pronouncements on policy and actual implementation—related to the issue of apparent influence versus real capability—in assessing the true nature of Nigeria's effectiveness in foreign policy. As has been stated elsewhere, it may be "more accurate . . . to see the achievements in the sphere of foreign policy in the 1970s and early 1980s as separate or sporadic successes rather than as linked events in a constant chain of political power. These successes were also partly assisted by favourable external events,"[22] notably the support of the U.S. government for a strong Nigerian role to help promote Namibia/Zimbabwe settlements, as well as to serve as an entry point for U.S. trade into Africa.

There is a clear distinction between this period and the later 1980s and 1990s, when Nigerian economic capability relatively diminished, further reducing the effectiveness of its foreign policy. However, some scholars argue that there has been underlying weakness since independence but that this became especially noticeable in the 1990s. Julius Ihonvbere summarized their arguments:

> [They contend] that a neocolonial, underdeveloped, dependent, foreign-dominated, distorted, disarticulated, politically unstable, debt-ridden and crisis-ridden, social formation cannot provide credible leadership or operate

a viable, credible, respectable, and consistent foreign policy. It is contended that Nigeria, in spite of its vast human and material resources, cannot make claim to leadership in Africa as long as it is characterized by mindless corruption, mass poverty, gross inequality, mismanagement, waste, and social, political, and economic tension, contradictions, and conflicts. Thus, to this group ... Nigeria's assumed "power," "influence," and "credibility" are merely rhetoric, propaganda, and "issue-based" diplomacy rather than evidence of any credible, viable, and consistent basis of foreign policy.[23]

At least eight specific factors help to explain the contemporary influences and constraints on Nigeria's foreign policy and suggest why the country has arguably less capability in the late 1990s to succeed in its goal of being a regional hegemon and African champion.[24] Many of these factors are common to other states discussed in this volume and are shaped by the changing characteristics of the post–Cold War environment.

First, the economy in general has continued to stagnate and has not responded to SAP measures to the extent predicted by the World Bank. In the early 1980s, Shehu Shagari resisted dealing with the IMF for as long as possible, but his immediate military successors, Muhammadu Buhari and Ibrahim Babangida, were forced to the table to negotiate terms for major structural adjustment agreements. Much was made of Babangida's reluctance to accept financial assistance from the IMF, but SAP was introduced after September 1986, and loans from the World Bank were accepted to ease the growing economic problems.[25]

By the late 1990s, privatization and devaluation occurred, but they have provided only mediocre improvements to the economic performance of the country. Throughout the 1990s, a succession of public protests, strikes, and riots have been targeted against government policies, but such popular movements have been repeatedly suppressed by an increasingly aggressive military government.

The military government of General Sani Abacha was under the watchful eye of the IMF and World Bank, as well as the debt regimes, and was therefore somewhat constrained in what it could do, although there had been deviations from SAP since 1993 when Abacha seized power. The oil earnings on which the country still heavily relies remain stagnant.[26] Prospects for the much vaunted $3.6 billion liquified natural gas (LNG) project are good, as are the prospects for the possible privatization of the oil fields, but gains will not be seen until the twenty-first century. There is little optimism that gains will, in any case, trickle down to the people through better development policies. And as Joe Garba remarked in 1987: "The problems of economic development and the provision of a better standard of living for our people will become the preoccupation of foreign policy."[27]

The second factor is related to the first: Increased economic conditionalities have been matched by increased political conditionalities, not only by the IMF but also by the EU and the United States independently. The failure to meet deadlines to transfer political power to civilians in 1990, 1992, 1993, 1994, and 1998, as well as the annulment of the 1993 elections that saw Chief Moshood Abiola, a Yoruba Muslim entrepreneur, elected as president, have brought minor sanctions on the military leadership by the EU, the Commonwealth, and the United States and made it difficult for Sani Abacha to seek external support and economic relief. Increasing pressures to improve human rights across Africa came at a time when Nigeria suffered under its most repressive government since independence, a situation highlighted by the execution of the Ogoni Nine and the harassment of prodemocracy movements.[28] Within the United States, the major African-American lobby, TransAfrica, turned its energies toward Nigeria and pressured the Clinton administration, albeit unsuccessfully, to take a hard line against Abacha.

The transition program of the late 1990s aims to return government to civilian rule in October 1999, following elections in the same year. Conditionalities will not be significantly relaxed before the transfer, especially given the record of the military in pulling justifications out of thin air to halt the transition program. The prospect of Abacha being elected to the presidency as the sole candidate in August 1998 was fortuitously prevented by his sudden death in June 1998. The new government under General Abdulsalam Abubakar offered fresh hope for political change.

The third factor to consider is related to the end of the Cold War. One element of nonalignment was the ability to play off the superpowers against each other to gain preferential treatment. With the Cold War ended, the possibilities for doing this are very limited. Russian influence has all but disappeared from Africa, and Nigeria's tortuous relationship with that country in building the Ajaokuta steelworks (construction is a decade late, and there is little prospect of the project being economically viable) does not augur well for future ties. Africa, specifically West Africa, appears to be less strategically important to outside powers than before, which leaves less on which Nigeria can play. The Liberia crisis continues with little involvement by the United States, as does the internal war in Sierra Leone.

This is not all negative for Nigeria, however, because the situation provides opportunities, particularly within West Africa, for Nigeria to play a stronger (hegemonic?) role in peacekeeping, such as within ECOMOG in Liberia throughout the 1990s and in Sierra Leone in 1997–1998, and in general brokering of relations within the continental community of states. Nigeria may be poorer than it used to be and therefore unable to play the "subimperial" role anticipated in the late 1970s. But it remains much stronger economically and militarily than most states in Africa, especially in the West African subregion. It also appears more willing to use its military muscle in the post–Cold War era than before. Talk of a nuclear element to defense policy persists, though it is not as vociferous as in the late 1970s.[29]

Nigeria's efforts to maintain high-profile diplomacy have been seen throughout the 1990s. In 1991, for example, the Babangida government hosted summits of both ECOWAS and the OAU, and it continues to shoulder the financial burden of ECOWAS and ECOMOG. However, critics point out that there has been little solid gain for Nigeria from these activities, and the cost has been tremendous, estimated by some to be more than $1 billion during the 1990s.

A fourth, related factor involves liberalization and globalization. The economic reforms in Central and Eastern Europe during the 1990s have opened up new economic opportunities in stabler environments that Nigeria finds difficult to match. The integration of the EU markets and the EU's proximity to the burgeoning markets of the Czech Republic, Hungary, and Poland, to name a few, push Nigeria and other African, Caribbean, and Pacific states (ACP) to one side and threaten the vitality of the Lomé agreements that Nigeria has worked so hard to produce since the 1970s.[30] Nigeria today possesses little or no power to arrest these developments, even though its economic potential is still fairly significant. Few consider Nigeria to be critical in the upcoming EU-ACP-Lomé 2000 round of renegotiations, contrary to the country's status in previous negotiations.

Wider trends within the global economy, including globalization and the emerging New International Division of Labor, again hasten the marginality of Nigeria. In a nutshell, the question is where Nigeria fits into the global economy. How can Nigeria strengthen its competitiveness, its technology base, and its labor skills to withstand the pressures of and be competitive within the global economy? The LNG project, while lucrative, maintains the country essentially as a commodity producer.

The fifth factor ties to the fact that since the 1970s, successive leaders have focused foreign policy on the West African subregion, based upon ECOWAS. Hopes were high in the 1970s, buoyed by side payments and aid from Nigeria's oil fortunes and Nigeria's ability to circumvent the strong French role in the subregion.[31] Since the early 1980s, however, ECOWAS has failed to deliver on its expectations. Nigeria was itself largely to blame in 1983 and 1985 with its expulsion of millions of ECOWAS workers, contrary to the spirit if not the law of ECOWAS. Moreover, Nigeria's ailing economy has not allowed it to make the same sort of payments to keep ECOWAS on track,[32] and it has been unable to capitalize on France's waning interest in the region (not to be exaggerated, though), most noticeable in the CFAF devaluation of 1994. All the obstacles to closer integration that were seen in the late 1980s remain in place. Unofficial trade is buoyant, largely due to the efforts of Nigerian entrepreneurs, but there appears to be little prospect that Nigeria will see the diplomatic and economic gains within ECOWAS that had been anticipated.

The sixth factor stems from the fact that a large measure of Nigeria's credibility, status, and moral leadership in Africa derived from its support for the liberation struggle and Front-Line States. Though Nigeria's actual successes here were arguably limited, this should not devalue the genuine commitment and financial allocations made to end colonialism and apartheid in Southern Africa. The successful establishment of a majority government in South Africa in April 1994 marked the end of that chapter of the liberation struggle, and one area of African unity and Nigerian "high-profile leadership" was thereby closed. There is not another equally visible issue around which Nigeria can so easily rally other African states. The New International Economic Order (NIEO) has an old and hollow ring to it; promoting continental unity for economic or strategic purposes seems unobtainable. This absence of a clearly articulated regional foreign policy or regional agenda is difficult to overcome.

The seventh factor, related to the previous point, is the emergence of postapartheid South Africa, which has eclipsed Nigeria as the regional power and the "champion of Africa." With a larger and more diversified economic base than Nigeria, South Africa has attracted significant interest from international investors, and it has negotiated special assistance from the EU along with qualified membership in the Lomé Convention. It also is the most likely nation to reach the status of a newly industrializing country (NIC); furthermore, the Southern African Development Community appears to be a better regional economic vehicle for South Africa than ECOWAS is for Nigeria. The charisma and legitimacy of Nelson Mandela contrasted markedly with the international ostracism of Abacha, and South Africa's triumphal assertiveness within the Commonwealth coincides with Nigeria's ignominious exclusion. The voice championing African issues is now South African rather than Nigerian. And the ultimate insult is that the pariah status that South Africa once held has now been placed—by South Africa among others—on Nigeria.

The eighth and final factor to mention concerning Nigeria's foreign policy position is the increased emphasis since 1995 on extensive public relations programs designed to reassert the stature of Nigeria and the stability and human rights record of the regime. The country's external image has already been battered by the bad publicity surrounding some of its citizens' involvement in the "419" or advanced fee fraud scandals and the international drug trade, making the country one of the largest narcotics transshipment points in the world. Furthermore, some of Nigeria's outstanding academics and playwrights are now in exile abroad, attacking the military regime from outside and pursuing a private foreign policy beyond the control of the government in Abuja.

Most African states do not wish to alienate Nigeria, and some, such as Kenya, are assertively supporting the embattled regime, thereby maintaining a semblance of African unity. However, a number of states show a growing reticence to side openly with Nigeria for fear that by doing so, they will be the next to undergo political scrutiny from outside the continent.

Conclusion

Nigerian governments have been leading actors in Africa and have pursued foreign policies commensurate to the country's perceived standing. During the 1970s, a clear policy focus, matched by some economic muscle, gave the country an important stake in the African continent, and its policy overtures beyond the continent were consequently listened to with some respect. In this sense, the country gained status within the global community, which at times translated into real influence.

Since the early 1980s and increasingly during the 1990s, a combination of forces has brought a deterioration in both domestic and external factors that influence foreign policy options and orientations. It would be wrong to claim that Nigeria has lost all its capability in policy; rather, it has failed to exert influence to the extent that it did previously. As in other African states, a troubled position in the contemporary global economy limits its options, and the country's failure to develop a diversified competitive economy and to democratize indicates a continuing weakness in pursuing foreign policy issues beyond the continent. The ongoing inertia of ECOWAS, combined with the real potential of South Africa, appear also to limit the continental role.

But Nigeria still retains some options and potential. Transfer of power to a capable civilian government in 1999 or soon thereafter could provide fresh impetus to the economy, to human rights, to relations with the major powers, and to better policies overall. Unfortunately, this appears unlikely. Nigeria's potential is considerable, especially within the West African subregion. Without corrective actions, however, it will simply remain potential, and the country's aspirations of continental and regional leadership will remain unfulfilled, as will its hopes of becoming the continent's largest democracy.

NOTES

1. E. Wayne Nafziger, *The Economics of Political Instability: The Nigerian-Biafran War* (Boulder: Westview Press, 1983).

2. A. Bolaji Akinyemi and Joy Ogwu, "Policy Towards Overseas Africans and the Black World," in National Institute for Policy and Strategic Studies (NIPSS) (ed.), *Nigeria's African Policy in the Eighties* (Kuru: NIPSS, 1981), p. 142. See also Ade Adefuye, *Culture and Foreign Policy: The Nigerian Example* (Lagos: NIIA, 1992).

3. Julius O. Ihonvbere, *Nigeria: The Politics of Adjustment and Democracy* (New Brunswick, N.J.: Transaction, 1994), p. 35.

4. For general surveys of Nigerian political economy, see William Graf, *The Nigerian State: Political Economy, State Class and Political System in the Post-Colonial Era* (London: James Currey and Portsmouth: Heinemann, 1988); Julius O. Ihonvbere and Timothy M. Shaw, *Towards a Political Economy of Nigeria: Petroleum and Politics at the (Semi-)Periphery* (Aldershot, England: Avebury, 1988); Claude Ake (ed.), *Political Economy of Nigeria* (Harlow, England: Longman, 1985); I. William Zartman (ed.), *The Political Economy of Nigeria* (New York: Praeger, 1983).

5. Eghosa E. Osaghae, "Structural Adjustment and Ethnicity in Nigeria," Research Report No. 98 (Uppsala, Sweden: Scandinavian Institute of African Studies, 1995). Also, E. Ike Udogu, "The Allurement of Ethnonationalism in Nigerian Politics," *Journal of Asian and African Studies*, 29(3–4), 1994, pp. 159–171.

6. Eghosa E. Osaghae, "The Ogoni Uprising: Oil Politics, Minority Agitation and the Future of the Nigerian State," *African Affairs*, 94, 1995, pp. 325–344. Also, Ken Saro-Wiwa, *Genocide in Nigeria: The Ogoni Tragedy* (Port Harcourt, Nigeria: Saros, 1992).

7. Kayode Soremekun, "Oil and the Democratic Imperative in Nigeria," in Dele Olowu, Kayode Soremekun, and Abebayo Williams (eds.), *Governance and Democratisation in Nigeria* (Ibadan, Nigeria: Spectrum, 1995), pp. 97–109.

8. Stephen Wright, "State-Consolidation and Social Integration in Nigeria: The Military's Search for the Elusive," in Henry Dietz and Jerold Elkin (eds.), *Ethnicity, Integration and the Military* (Boulder: Westview Press, 1991), pp. 179–207.

9. General reviews of Nigerian foreign policy and decisionmaking include Gabriel O. Olusanya and R. A. Akindele (eds.), *The Structure and Processes of Foreign Policy Making and Implementation in Nigeria 1960–1990* (Lagos: NIIA and Ibadan: Vantage, 1990); Kenoye Kelvin Eke, *Nigeria's Foreign Policy Under Two Military Governments, 1966–1979: An Analysis of the Gowon and Muhammed/Obasanjo Regimes* (Lewiston: Edwin Mellen, 1990); and NIPSS, *Nigeria's African Policy in the Eighties.*

10. Ibrahim A. Gambari, *Theory and Reality in Foreign Policy Making: Nigeria After the Second Republic* (Atlantic Highlands, N.J.: Humanities Press, 1989).

11. Shehu Othman, "Nigeria: Power for Profit—Class, Corporatism, and Factionalism in the Military," in Donal B. Cruise O'Brien, John Dunn, and Richard Rathbone (eds.), *Contemporary West African States* (Cambridge: Cambridge University Press, 1989), pp. 113–144. See also Okechukwu Okeke, *Hausa-Fulani Hegemony: The Dominance of the Muslim North in Contemporary Nigerian Politics* (Enugu, Nigeria: Acena, 1992).

12. Interesting insights came from Joe Garba, *Diplomatic Soldiering: The Conduct of Nigerian Foreign Policy 1975–1979* (Ibadan, Nigeria: Spectrum, 1987).

13. For a general overview of this period, see I. A. Gambari, *Party Politics and Foreign Policy: Nigeria Under the First Republic* (Zaria, Nigeria: Ahmadu Bello University Press, 1980). Also, Larry Diamond, *Class, Ethnicity and Democracy in Nigeria: The Failure of the First Republic* (Syracuse, N.Y.: Syracuse University Press, 1988), and Claude S. Phillips Jr., *The Development of Nigerian Foreign Policy* (Evanston, Ill.: Northwestern University Press, 1964).

14. Timothy Shaw and Olajide Aluko (eds.), *Nigerian Foreign Policy: Alternative Perceptions and Projections* (London: Macmillan, 1982); Olajide Aluko, *Essays in Nigerian Foreign Policy* (London: George Allen and Unwin, 1981).

15. Kayode Soremekun, "Presidential System and Petroleum Policy (1979–1983)," in Kayode Soremekun (ed.), *Perspectives on the Nigerian Oil Industry* (Lagos: Amkra, 1995), p. 94.

16. Graf, *The Nigerian State*, p. 236.

17. George Obiozor, *Uneasy Friendship: Nigeria/U.S. Relations* (Enugu, Nigeria: Fourth Dimension, 1992); Bassey E. Ate, *Decolonization and Dependence: The Development of Nigerian-U.S. Relations* (Boulder: Westview Press, 1987).

18. Abiodun Alao and Aderemi Ajibewa, "Nigeria and the European Economic Community," in A. B. Akinyemi, S. O. Agbi, and A. O. Otubanjo (eds.), *Nigeria Since Independence: The First Twenty-Five Years, Volume X: International Relations* (Ibadan, Nigeria: Heinemann, 1989), pp. 105–116.

19. Olayiwola Abegunrin, *Nigeria and the Struggle for the Liberation of Zimbabwe: A Study of Foreign Policy Decision Making of an Emerging Nation* (Stockholm: Bethany, 1992).

20. Tom Forrest, *Politics and Economic Development in Nigeria* (Boulder: Westview Press, 1995), p. 135.

21. Toyin Falola and Julius Ihonvbere, *The Rise and Fall of Nigeria's Second Republic, 1979–84* (London: Zed, 1985). Also, Shehu Othman, "Classes, Crises and Coup: The Demise of Shagari's Regime," *African Affairs*, 83(333), October 1984, pp. 441–463.

22. Stephen Wright, "Limits of Nigeria's Power Overseas," *West Africa*, 27 July 1981, p. 1685.

23. Ihonvbere, *Nigeria: The Politics of Adjustment and Democracy*, p. 36.

24. Some of these issues are also discussed in Julius Emeka Okolo and Stephen Wright, "Nigeria," in Timothy M. Shaw and Julius Emeka Okolo (eds.), *The Political Economy of Foreign Policy in ECOWAS* (New York: St. Martin's, 1994), pp. 125–146.

25. Thomas J. Biersteker (ed.), *Dealing with Debt: International Financial Negotiations and Adjustment Bargaining* (Boulder: Westview Press, 1993). Also, U. Joy Ogwu and R. Omotayo Olaniyan, *Nigeria's International Economic Relations: Dimensions of Dependence and Change* (Lagos: NIIA, 1989).

26. E. Wayne Nafziger, *The Debt Crisis in Africa* (Baltimore: Johns Hopkins University Press, 1993), pp. 57–63.

27. Garba, *Diplomatic Soldiering*, p. 218.

28. Human Rights Watch/Africa, "Nigeria: Permanent Transition—Current Violations of Human Rights in Nigeria," 8(3A), September 1996.

29. G. Aforka Nweke, "Nuclear Power and Nigeria's Defence Policy," in A. E. Ekoko and M. A. Vogt (eds.), *Nigerian Defence Policy: Issues and Problems* (Lagos: Malthouse, 1990), pp. 144–161.

30. Stefan Brüne, Joachim Betz, and Winrich Kühne (eds.), *Africa and Europe: Relations of Two Continents in Transition* (Münster: Lit Verlag, 1994).

31. Jibrim Ibrahim, "Towards a Nigerian Perspective on the French Problematic in Africa," in Haruna J. Jacob and Massoud Omar (eds.), *France and Nigeria: Issues in Comparative Studies* (Ibadan, Nigeria: Credu Nigeria, 1992); also, Femi Otubanjo and Seye Davies, "Nigeria and France: The Struggle for Regional Hegemony," in Akinyemi, Agbi, and Otubanjo (eds.), *Nigeria Since Independence*, pp. 73–86.

32. Julius Emeka Okolo and Stephen Wright (eds.), *West African Regional Cooperation and Development* (Boulder: Westview Press, 1990).

8

Senegal's Foreign Policy: Responding to Internal and International Pressures for Change

PETER J. SCHRAEDER
(WITH NEFERTITI GAYE)

Scholars historically sought to explain the formulation and implementation of African foreign policies by focusing on one of three sets of narrowly defined arguments: the continuation of "dependency" relationships between the newly independent African states and their former colonial powers; the positions of African states within the larger geopolitical setting of the Cold War struggle; and the overriding importance of the personal whims of authoritarian African leaders—the so-called "big-man" theory of foreign policy. The following analysis of Senegalese foreign policy demonstrates that these classic dependency, Cold War, and personal rule–oriented explanations were at best exaggerations and at worst mere caricatures of more complex and dynamic foreign policy processes.[1] Even during the Cold War era, Senegal's foreign policy could not be explained by mere reference to the superpowers or by the personal beliefs of the first two Senegalese presidents, Léopold Sédar Senghor (1960–1980) and Abdou Diouf (1981–present). Other, often neglected or downplayed factors, such as religion, regional interests, and traditional culture, must be examined if one wishes to achieve a more complex, nuanced, and valid understanding of Senegalese foreign policy. One can moreover argue that these and other factors are even more salient in a post–Cold War era in which Senegalese policymakers are confronted with twin challenges responding to rising popular demands for the further democratization of the political system and reacting to the dilemma of growing marginalization within an increasingly competitive international system.

Foreign Policy Context:
Domestic and International Environments

Several factors are important in understanding the context of the formulation and implementation of Senegalese foreign policy. First, Senegal is a former French colony that has maintained strong links with the former metropole. The resilience of this cultural factor is demonstrated by the Senegalese constitution's recognition of French as the "official language" of all government activity[2] and the self-classification of the elite as belonging to a greater French-speaking community (la francophonie) whose cultural center is France. Although the privileged status of French is gradually being eroded by a "national languages" movement intent upon making indigenous languages more integral to government business, as well as by the increasing numbers of elite children who are learning English as a second language in Senegal and at universities abroad, the commitment of the French elite to la francophonie remains very strong.

The French connection is also important in regard to the ideological context of foreign policy. As explained by Sheldon Gellar, it is difficult to understand Senegalese politics "without some appreciation of the influence of the French left on Senegalese intellectuals particularly during the postwar era (1945–1960)" when most of the elite attended school in France and adopted various forms of socialism as their guiding philosophies.[3] During the Senghor years, an African socialism derivative of the French experience and often presented as the "middle way" between Soviet Marxism and U.S. liberalism, served as one of the cornerstones of foreign policy.[4] Although adopting classic elements of liberalism, such as reducing the role of the state and enhancing the private sector, in their quest to restructure the economy during the 1980s and 1990s, President Diouf and his principal advisers nonetheless remain the standard-bearers of the ruling Parti Socialist (PS, Socialist Party) and continue to maintain Senegal's privileged ties within the Socialist International.[5]

A third factor—a profoundly nationalist spirit that seeks to make Senegal an influential regional foreign policy actor—is fueled by at least two traditions: the once privileged place of Senegal within French colonial Africa and a vibrant traditional culture. What in essence constitutes a sense of regional superiority (e.g., the elite argues that Senegalese French is the "purest" of francophone Africa) is first explained by the fact that the northern town of St. Louis and subsequently the current capital of Dakar served as the cultural and politico-military center of Afrique Occidentale Française (AOF, French West Africa), the colonial unit that grouped together the currently independent states of Benin, Burkina Faso, Côte d'Ivoire, Guinea, Mali, Mauritania, Niger, and Senegal.[6]

Of even greater importance to understanding Senegalese aspirations to regional leadership is the fact that the physical location of the AOF capital and the current Republic of Senegal were built upon an extremely vibrant series of Wolof kingdoms that were expanding and incorporating less powerful local ethnic groups in a quest for regional hegemony.[7] The ongoing "Wolofization" of Senegalese society is underscored by 1988 census results: Whereas the Wolof ethnic group comprises roughly 44 percent of the population, 71 percent of the people speak Wolof as either their first or second language.[8] It is precisely for this reason that ethnicity has not become a divisive factor in national politics, with the vast majority firmly embracing a "Senegalese" national identity.[9] Two significant exceptions to this trend, discussed below, are a guerrilla insurgency largely led by the Diola ethnic group that since 1982 has sought independence for Senegal's southern Casamance region and the bloody urban attacks against peoples of Mauritanian descent during the 1989 border conflict with Mauritania.

Regional aspirations have been dampened, however, by a poor resource base and an economy marked by "stagnation and decline."[10] Despite well-intentioned efforts to diversify and modernize an economy heavily dependent on primary exports, most notably groundnuts, the net result has been a decline in real per capita income since independence. Even "after fifteen years of structural adjustment programs," explains Gellar, "Senegal in the mid-1990s is still facing an uphill economic battle saddled by foreign debt, chronic government deficits, a poorly functioning banking system, and high unemployment rates, particularly among high school and college graduates."[11]

High unemployment rates among a rising urban population constitute one of the driving forces behind sometimes violent confrontations between government forces and heavily politicized student groups and workers' unions.[12] As captured by the film *La Génération Sacrifiée?* (The Sacrificed Generation?), coproduced in 1995 by a Senegalese and a U.S. filmmaker, rising numbers of increasingly educated yet discouraged Senegalese youth are entering a job market that, in their eyes, offers them nothing but positions as street vendors, maids, and cooks. The concept of a "sacrificed generation" has become especially poignant in the aftermath of France's decision in 1994 to unilaterally impose a 50 percent devaluation on the common currency (CFA franc) shared by Senegal and other members of the CFA franc zone; the net result of this move was a 50 percent decline in the purchasing power of an already economically marginalized population. "It is a testament to the resilience of Senegalese culture, extended family relationships, and perhaps of greatest importance, the strength of religious values, especially those of Islam," explained a diplomat associated with the Senegalese Ministry of Foreign Affairs in 1996, "that Senegalese society has been able to cope with severe economic marginalization that has led other African countries such as Rwanda and Somalia to descend into political chaos and armed violence."[13]

This allusion to religious values is characteristic of the important and growing role of Islam.[14] Policymakers are especially attentive to the concerns of the Islamic brotherhoods, the religious leaders of which—known as marabouts—are capable of mobilizing the Muslim faithful (approximately 94 percent of the population) through an intricate series of patron-client ties in which thousands of lesser marabouts declare their allegiance to more senior leaders.[15] Two Muslim brotherhoods—the Mourides and the Tijaniyya, based in the holy cities of Touba and Tivaouane, respectively—are especially powerful and claim the allegiance of approximately two-thirds of the Senegalese faithful.

The power of the marabouts derives from the population's belief in the spiritual and often magical powers of their personal religious guides (e.g., one can go to a marabout to seek potions providing protection from potential enemies). Most important, the marabouts enjoy almost complete financial autonomy from state control due to a highly complex system of alms collection by *taalibe* (disciples) who are capable of channeling enormous amounts of money into a designated cause. The marabouts therefore can mobilize a potent reaction to undesired state policies with little or no fear of state retribution. A dramatic case in point occurred in the mid-1980s when the Diouf administration was forced to withdraw an invitation to Pope John Paul II to visit the country because leading marabouts threatened to have their taalibe occupy the runways at the international airport. Although the pope was subsequently reinvited and actually visited Senegal in 1991 to the wide acclaim of both Muslims and Christians, the marabouts had clearly served notice that sensitive issues had to be raised with them in advance.

A final important domestic factor that influences foreign policy stems from the fact that Senegal has enjoyed over thirty-five years of uninterrupted democratic rule. Whereas specialists rightfully underscore the imperfect nature of this democracy—for example, a highly centralized presidential system has ensured the victory of the ruling PS party throughout the independence era—they equally underscore its enduring character on a continent in which almost every country has experienced at least one military coup d'état.[16] As succinctly noted by Leonardo A. Villalón, a specialist of Islam and democracy in Senegal, the sincere commitment of policymakers to democratic principles "has at the very least ensured that Senegalese society has never been subjected to the repression, exploitation, arbitrariness, or indeed terror at the hands of the state known by all too many of its neighbors."[17]

Foreign Policy Continuity and Change

Although policy changes have definitely occurred in the decades since independence, they have largely constituted gradual shifts in emphasis rather than radical breaks with the past. This tendency toward continuity or at best gradual change is primarily due to the relatively stable nature of Senegal's political system, under which Senghor's *dauphin* (chosen successor) peacefully assumed power in 1981 when Senghor voluntarily retired from the political scene.

Four sets of principles or policy orientations are essential to a comprehensive understanding of Senegalese foreign policy. The first principle is promotion of la francophonie. Originally conceived by Senghor as part of a wider, "culturally" informed policy that embraced the promotion of *négritude* (the celebration of the uniqueness of black African culture), this principle led in 1966 to Senegal's hosting of the first meeting on African soil of the World Festival of Negro Arts, as well as Senghor's personal involvement in the launching of what eventually would become regular Franco-African summits. Although the wider cultural aspects of Senghor's vision did not outlast his presidency, the Diouf administration has firmly embraced the promotion of la francophonie, and it took a lead role in launching a regular, worldwide summit of francophone leaders, the third of which was held in Dakar in May 1989 (the most recent conference was held in Ouagadougou, Burkina Faso, in December 1996). It is notable that, in the aftermath of the death in 1993 of President Félix Houphouët-Boigny of Côte d'Ivoire, President Diouf has emerged as one of the inheritors of the mantle of leadership within francophone Africa.[18]

A firm commitment to African unity and integration constitutes a second consistent theme of foreign policy. Diplomats from the Ministry of Foreign Affairs offer three rationales for their country's staunch support for regional cooperation.[19] The simplest reason is the firm belief that there is strength in numbers. In order to effectively compete within an increasingly competitive international economic system, West African states must band together and pool their valuable resources. A second rationale revolves around the desire to promote the economic development (usually perceived as industrialization) of West Africa. Underscoring that most West African countries are economically impoverished, Senegalese policymakers argue that West Africa must forge an integrated and self-sustaining regional economy capable of reducing dependence on foreign actors. Third and most important, regional economic schemes are perceived by Senegalese policymakers as the best means for creating the self-reliant development needed to reduce this dependence on foreign actors. It is expected that by strengthening ties with like-minded neighbors, the stronger, regional economic entity that will emerge will be capable of reducing foreign influence and strengthening West Africa's collective ability to bargain with foreign entities on a more equal basis.

There has been an extremely active quest to pursue regional cooperation schemes. These have ranged from the creation of formal federations with neighboring countries, such as the extremely short-lived Mali Federation in 1960 and the longer but also unsuccessful federation with Gambia from 1982 to 1989, to several looser forms of cooperation and integration, most notably the Comité Inter-États de Lutte Contre la Sécheresse dans le Sahel (CILSS, the Inter-State Authority in the Fight Against Drought in the Sahel); the Economic Community of West African States; the Organisation Commune Africaine et Malgache (Joint African and Malagasy Organization); the Organisation de Mise en Valeur du Fleuve Gambie (OMVG, Organization for the Development of the Gambia River Valley); and the Organisation de Mise en Valeur du Fleuve Sénégal (OMVS, Organization for the Development of the Senegal River Valley). Although the reasons for the limited success of these cooperation schemes is beyond the scope of this chapter, suffice it to note that difficulties have not resulted from a lack of interest or effort on the part of the Senegalese foreign policy establishment.[20]

A third guiding principle of foreign policy that evolved out of Senegal's preferential relationship with France is adherence to the concept of nonalignment, albeit with a de facto pro-Western tilt that was gradually strengthened during the 1980s and 1990s. During the Senghor administration, nonalignment was conceived of in the Gaullist sense of the term. "Like the French," explains Gellar, "Senghor thus opposed the domination of world politics by the two major superpowers, regarded France as the natural leader of an independent Europe and a champion of Third World interests, and saw an alliance between Europe and Africa as the best hope for providing a 'Third Force' to counteract superpower domination."[21] Despite the fact that such a policy "extended the Gaullist vision of the U.S. as an imperialist power in Europe into Africa," it nonetheless promoted the shared interests of Washington and Paris in preventing the spread of communism to the African continent.[22] As discussed below, the Diouf administration reinforced this Western tilt by gradually seeking closer ties with the United States and other Western countries during the 1980s in a process that was accelerated in the aftermath of the Cold War's end.

The promotion of a moderate brand of Islam through increased interaction with the Islamic world constitutes a fourth guiding principle of foreign policy. Due to the rising influence of Islam within the Senegalese political system, especially as concerns the increased stature of the marabouts, it is only natural that this element would also express itself within the foreign policy realm.[23] Senghor initiated a series of diplomatic overtures to the Arab world, such as inviting the PLO to open its first diplomatic mission in sub-Saharan Africa in Dakar and taking the lead in seeking financial redress from the oil-rich Gulf states in the aftermath of the dramatic oil-price "shocks" of the mid-1970s. However, it was only under the Diouf administration that Senegal achieved prominent international status as a Muslim country at the crossroads of sub-Saharan Africa and the Middle East.

The most notable indicator of this shift in Senegalese foreign policy was Diouf's extremely popular decision, just weeks after taking office on 1 January 1981, to attend the Third Islamic Conference held in Saudi Arabia.[24] "Words do not begin to describe the pride I felt in seeing the president make the pilgrimage to Mecca as both a Muslim and as the President of Senegal," explained one diplomat associated with the Ministry of Foreign Affairs. "This is something that Senghor as a Catholic could never do nor truly understand."[25] To further strengthen Senegal's image in this regard, Diouf presided over the Sixth Islamic Conference held in Dakar in December 1991. This conference was notable for two reasons: It marked the first time that the conference had been held in sub-Saharan Africa since the organization's founding in 1973, and it took place in the immediate aftermath of the Gulf War, to which Senegal sent a contingent of troops and achieved the sad distinction of losing the greatest number of troops on the Allied side (ninety-three soldiers died in a tragic plane crash after the cessation of hostilities).

The intertwining of numerous foreign policy interests or principles makes it difficult to clearly distinguish the origins of a particular policy. In the case of Senegalese involvement in the Gulf War, for example, one could conceivably cite several factors.[26] Western-based scholars could offer explanations that focus on Diouf's desire to curry favor with the United States as the sole remaining superpower in the post–Cold War era or the desire to take part in an operation in which France was also playing a leading role. One could also focus on the religious factor: A Muslim state had been invaded, and the guardian of the holy sites of Mecca (Saudi Arabia) was also threatened. Although each of these reasons surely played a role in Senegal's final decision, the most important factor, as is usually the case in Senegalese foreign policy, was derived from Senegal's regional relationships and domestic politics. Specifically, involvement in the war constituted an extension of Senegal's 1989 border conflict with Mauritania. Iraq was one of the principal military suppliers of Mauritania, and it had been viewed as a destabilizing threat to the region. By taking part in operations against the Iraqi regime, Senegalese leaders were in essence resolving one of their regional problems at its source. Indeed, Senegal's military involvement in the war was extremely popular at all levels of society precisely for this reason.

As the end of the twentieth century approaches, diplomats associated with the Ministry of Foreign Affairs have underscored four important security challenges that either are the direct result of or have been intensified by the ending of the Cold War.[27] First, officials have raised concerns over the rise of Islamist movements that are perceived as largely funded by outside sources (Libya during the 1980s and Iran during the 1990s) and potentially capable of taking advantage of Senegal's unemployed and disaffected youth. Diplomats have also raised concerns over the recent rise in military coup d'états—the so-called *contagion kaki* (khaki contagion)[28]—that are threatening the democratization process in francophone Africa. During spring 1996, for example, Senegalese diplomats cautiously observed a successful coup in Niger and an unsuccessful mutiny in Guinea (not to mention a successful coup d'état in neighboring Gambia during the previous year). Both the Islamist and military security challenges are perceived as closely related to a third dilemma of the 1990s: the devastating economic aftermath of the 1994 devaluation of the CFA franc and the rising short-term costs associated with implementing SAPs imposed by the IFIs. Finally, officials correctly note that the end of the Cold War has ushered in a new set of international priorities in which foreign patrons are no longer willing to aid countries, such as Senegal, that are attempting to reorganize their economic and political systems.

The common solution pursued by policymakers to resolve each of these perceived dilemmas has been the intensification of regional diplomacy. In regard to the perceived Islamist threat, Senegal has increasingly coordinated policy with Mauritania and Mali, most notably by sharing information and mounting joint activities against recognized threats to regional security. In response to the successful coup in Niger, President Diouf, together with Presidents Omar Bongo of Gabon and Alpha Oumar Konare of Mali, publicly denounced illegal seizures of power. Diouf also sent Prime Minister Habib Thiam to Guinea to offer a message of support to President Lansana Conte.[29] As for combatting the negative effects of devaluation and the perceived marginalization of Africa, Diouf in March 1996 presided over the first preparatory meeting signaling the creation of L'Afrique Aide l'Afrique (AAA, Africa Aids Africa), a humanitarian mutual-aid society composed of African states and designed to offer African responses to African crises. In short, although Senegal is certainly not willing to forgo the pursuit of policy relationships outside of Africa, an important outgrowth of perceptions of marginalization within the international system is the rising tendency among Senegalese leaders to seek African solutions for what in essence are African problems.

Decisionmaking Structures and Processes

As underscored by Minister of Presidential Services and Affairs Ousmane Tanor Dieng in a 1989 speech, an important hallmark of the foreign policy establishment is the firm belief that foreign policy constitutes the *domaine réservé* (privileged realm) of the president. The legitimizing power of this belief, according to Dieng, is derivative of an "unwritten law" shared by policymakers and laypersons alike that the president embodies certain unique characteristics that demand his "personal handling" of the "major foreign policy issues of the day."[30]

The president is indeed granted a wide array of foreign policy prerogatives under the constitution. He is recognized as the commander in chief of the armed forces (Article 39), is empowered to name Senegalese diplomats abroad and accredit those from foreign countries (Article 40), and is granted the authority to negotiate, ratify, and approve international agreements (Article 75) except in certain specified realms (e.g., peace treaties and agreements with international organizations) that require ratification by the National Assembly (Article 76). One must be careful, however, not to equate a system based on presidential dominance with the principal theme of early studies that foreign policy begins and ends with the desires of African presidents. Other formal and informal actors must be taken into account.

First, personal advisers appointed by the president can have an important impact on the policymaking process. In the Office of the President, Babacar Carlos Mbaye and Amadou Diop are charged with overseeing bilateral and multilateral foreign affairs, respectively. The often overlooked role of these two actors is potentially significant in that they not only serve as a sort of filter in terms of what information should reach the president's desk but also aid the president in providing directives to various ministries concerned with international affairs. Their impact is also dependent on the nature of presidential management style. Under the current administration, for example, it has been noted that Diouf is much less "restrictive" than was Senghor and therefore allows much more "dialogue" among his key advisers during working sessions at the Office of the President.[31]

Appointed by the president primarily to manage the day-to-day functioning of the government (and therefore not beholden to the National Assembly), the prime minister also maintains a diplomatic cabinet under the guidance of an adviser; therefore, he plays a potentially influential role in policymaking. The current system constitutes a significant change from that of the early 1960s when the Office of the President and the Office of the Prime Minister were constitutionally independent of each other. During this period, an intensifying power struggle between Senghor and Prime Minister Mahmadou Dia led to the revision of the constitution in 1963 to create a system based on presidential dominance. The current prime minister, Habib Thiam, has long-standing professional and personal links with President Diouf, and he relies upon Paul Badji to coordinate the Office of the Prime Minister's involvement in foreign affairs in conjunction with the Office of the President and the foreign affairs bureaucracies.[32]

The Ministry of Foreign Affairs is the largest and most active of the foreign affairs bureaucracies within the policymaking establishment, taking responsibility for much of the daily administration of foreign relations. Depending on his "personality" and "special skills," the minister of foreign affairs (currently Moustapha Niasse) therefore is potentially a key player within the policymaking network. The combination of his access to the president and a far-reaching foreign affairs bureaucracy provide important tools to set the policy agenda.[33] Indeed, according to Elhadj Mbodj, director of the Institut des Droits de l'Homme et de la Paix (Institute of Human Rights and Peace) at Cheikh Anta Diop University, former Minister of Foreign Affairs Ibrahima Fall was the driving force behind the Diouf administration's more "progressive" stance toward African issues.[34]

A second, often neglected actor within the foreign affairs bureaucracy is the Senegalese military, currently headed by Minister of Armed Forces Cheikh Amadou Kane. Despite strong adherence to the ideal of civilian control, the military nonetheless has played important behind-the-scenes roles in shaping Senegal's political history.[35] During the 1963 constitutional crisis between Senghor and Dia, pro-Senghor military forces prevailed over those wishing to depose the president. More recently, Army Chief of Staff General Taverez Da Souza was removed from office in 1988 amid charges that he had convened meetings with other high-ranking officers to discuss the potential necessity of military intervention to end the political disturbances following the 1988 presidential elections.

These examples are not unique but instead are indicative of an important institution that, according to Momor Coumba Diop and Moussa Paye, increased its influence during the 1980s and 1990s due to Senegal's internal and external security problems.[36] For example, military officers have called for the strengthening of the armed forces (most notably the purchase of helicopters) to seek a military solution to the intermittent guerrilla war in the Casamance region, and they have also strongly argued in favor of "hot pursuit" operations against neighboring countries (e.g., Gambia and Guinea-Bissau) that at worst have been accused of providing sanctuary to the rebels and at best of being unable to adequately control their national territories.[37] Overall, the military has played an influential role as a tool of foreign policy throughout the Diouf administration, ranging from Senegal's involvement in a number of peacekeeping operations, such as the ECOWAS-sponsored Ceasefire Monitoring Group in Liberia, to Diouf's decision to use military force in 1981 to restore President Daouda Diawara to power in Gambia.[38]

As is the case in many African countries that either democratized or increasingly liberalized their political systems during the 1990s, Senegal's

National Assembly became a more vocal arena of national debate under the Diouf administration. Largely reduced to the role of a "rubber stamp" institution during the Senghor years (there was no opposition voice between 1964 and 1978), the National Assembly increasingly has questioned government policies since the lifting of multiparty restrictions in 1981, most notably in the aftermath of the 1993 legislative elections in which candidates from five opposition parties won a total of 36 seats in the 120-seat National Assembly. The two most important foreign affairs components of the National Assembly include the Committee on Foreign Affairs, headed by Daouda Sow, and over twenty "friendship groups" that promote formal and informal contacts between Senegalese representatives and the country in question.

The willingness of representatives to challenge the executive branch in the realm of foreign policy remains relatively tepid, however, and when a challenge is made, it is largely restricted to issues related to the economy, typically the costs and impacts related to foreign-sponsored SAPs. In addition to embodying a weak constitutional role relative to that of the executive, as well as an ongoing negative public image as constituting nothing more than *applaudisseurs* (literally, "applauders" of government policies), the National Assembly is seriously hampered in regard to foreign affairs by the lack of economic resources that would allow committees and representatives to hire staffs and independently conduct research and fact-finding missions. "If we want the National Assembly to truly play its constitutionally mandated role," explains Representative Sémou Pathé Guèye, a member of the opposition Parti de l'Indépendance et du Travail (PIT, Independence and Workers Party), "we must put an end to the disastrous conditions under which Representatives work."[39] As further lamented by Iba Der Thiam, the head of the *Jappoo* (Wolof for "union") party alliance, representatives do not even enjoy something as simple as individual offices within which they can work and privately receive members of their constituency.[40]

A variety of nongovernmental actors also influences the policymaking process. Due to the liberalization of the print and broadcast media during the 1980s, for example, the daily government newspaper, *Le Soleil*, which serves as a good source for documenting official foreign policy stances, is now challenged by the daily publication of two rival newspapers, *Le Sud* and *Wal Fadjri*, as well as by a host of sporadically published newspapers such as *Le Témoin* and *Démocraties*.[41] These private newspapers play an important agenda-setting role and, at the very least, offer a more critical perspective of foreign policy. For example, the German government's March 1996 decision to include Senegal in the list of nondemocratic countries for which requests for political asylum would be routinely considered was picked up by the press and turned into a public debate, prompting Minister of Communication Serigne Diop to hold a widely reported special meeting with the German ambassador to Senegal.[42]

The growing numbers of Senegalese living and working abroad due to economic stagnation and decline at home have also affected the policy-making process. Although exact numbers are unavailable, the seriousness with which the government treats these groups is demonstrated by the simple yet telling June 1993 decision to rename the Ministry of Foreign Affairs the Ministry of Foreign Affairs and of Senegalese Abroad. When one examines the growing tilt toward warmer relations with the United States, for example, one is left wondering to what degree this has been in-fluenced by the large numbers of Senegalese who sought their fortune in the United States and are now capable of mobilizing financial resources for a variety of business undertakings in their country of birth. Indeed, the Senegalese government as of 1996 was attempting to facilitate the cre-ation of an investment consortium of Senegalese living in the United States as a unique means for attracting greater investment into Senegal and promoting expanding trade links between the two countries.

Public opinion has also exerted an influential, albeit intermittent, influ-ence on the policymaking process. The strengthening of the democratiza-tion process portends greater popular input on policymaking as policies are increasingly held accountable to public opinion. It has been argued that public opinion, fueled primarily by radio broadcasts by Radio France Internationale, was the primary factor that led to bloody clashes between Senegal and Mauritania in 1989.[43] Despite the fact that this conflict was neither desired nor promoted by Diouf or President Ould Taya of Mauri-tania, both of these leaders, despite efforts to contain public passions, were confronted by violent clashes that spiraled out of control.

Finally, one must also take into account the formal and informal roles played by marabouts within the policymaking process. The formal role of marabouts is marked by the fact that they occupy important positions within the foreign policy establishment. For example, prominent marabouts, such as Cheikh Tidiane Sy of the Tijaniyya brotherhood, are often named as ambassadors to influential Muslim countries (in Sy's case, Egypt). More important, the marabouts play a significant informal role within the policymaking process, most notably demonstrated by their ability to reduce tensions in the aftermath of the 1989 border conflict be-tween Senegal and Mauritania via an unofficial form of shuttle diplomacy across the river that separates these two countries.

Foreign Policy Relationships

Building upon Senghor's conceptualization of international relations as a series of *cercles concentriques* (concentric circles) extending outward with

Senegal at the middle, four sets of countries are usually cited as constituting the cornerstone of Senegalese foreign policy: (1) immediate neighbors, (2) the remainder of Africa, (3) the Arab world and other Muslim countries, and (4) the Western democracies. Although such an order suggests prioritization, it is doubtful that Senghor would have placed France and other Western democracies last, and policymakers are usually quick to note that priority often depends upon the issue to which one is speaking.[44]

The first circle of foreign policy revolves around the promotion of stable and prosperous relationships with immediate neighbors—Mauritania, Mali, Guinea, Guinea-Bissau, and Gambia. Until the 1980s, however, regimes perceived either as threatening la francophonie or as promoting the spread of "radical" expansionism tied to the Eastern bloc were viewed with suspicion and led to conflictual regional relationships. In three cases—Sekou Toure's Guinea, Luiz Cabral's Guinea-Bissau, and Modibo Keita's Mali—Senegalese policymakers viewed "radical" regimes as posing varying threats to Senegalese security; often, conflictual relations only improved after the regime in question was overthrown.

Concerns over the potential threat posed by radical neighbors reached its height in July 1981 when a self-proclaimed group of African Marxists led by Samba Kukoi Sanyang took power through a coup d'état in Gambia. The coup was perceived as one of the first serious foreign policy "tests" of the recently inaugurated Diouf administration, and it raised concerns within the policymaking establishment that a "radical cancer" situated in the center of Senegal could prove destabilizing to the entire subregion.[45] At the very least, policymakers were fearful that the continued existence of a radical regime would embarrass the Diouf administration, which would be put to the electoral test for the first time in 1983.[46] As a result, Diouf ordered the Senegalese military to intervene and to restore former President Dawda Jawara back to power. This military episode was followed by the creation of the Senegambia federation, which collapsed in 1989.

During the 1980s and 1990s, the winding down of the Cold War was accompanied by a new period of regional instability in which Senegalese policymakers were confronted by two overarching security issues.[47] The most pressing security concern—maintenance of the territorial integrity of the Senegalese state—was pushed to the forefront by the emergence in 1982 of an ongoing guerrilla insurgency in the Casamance region, led by the Mouvement des Forces Démocratiques de Casamance (MFDC, Movement of Casamance Democratic Forces); in the extreme, the insurgency has called for secession and the creation of a separate Casamance nation. The response to this armed movement has fluctuated between aggressive military campaigns (1990–1992 and 1994), as favored by the Ministry of Defense, and a series of diplomatic initiatives seeking to politically isolate the most radical elements of the MFDC, as was the case with short-lived truces and peace accords that were signed in May 1990, April 1992, and July 1993. During 1996, the Senegalese government and the MFDC agreed to another cease-fire, which quickly unraveled.

A second source of conflict with regional neighbors has stemmed from the management and development of shared border resources. In addition to the 1989 border conflict between Senegal and Mauritania, which has its origins in the ownership and control of the rich wetlands on Senegal's northern border,[48] a border dispute that emerged with Guinea-Bissau during the 1980s took on added urgency due to the discovery of oil within the disputed area. After Guinea-Bissau agreed to (but subsequently rejected) international arbitration that twice ruled in Senegal's favor, Senegalese authorities took the unexpected step of offering Guinea-Bissau a percentage of the oil profits if they recognized Senegalese sovereignty over the territory. Guinea-Bissau accepted, and a formal protocol between the two nations was signed on 12 June 1995. The primary reason for Senegalese generosity was an unstated linkage that called for the Guinea-Bissau government to take, in return for a portion of the oil profits, a much more active role in denying the Casamance insurgents both access to illegally transhipped weapons and safe havens on the Guinea-Bissau side of the border.[49] This accord is indicative of a rising consensus within the policymaking establishment that resolution of the Casamance issue is "central" to the fashioning of stable, long-term regional relationships.[50]

A second concentric circle of foreign policy revolves around Senegal's involvement with other African states beyond its immediate frontiers. Throughout the Senghor and Diouf administrations, one of the cornerstones of this continental approach has been the desire to take a lead role in a variety of organizations committed to promoting regional integration and African unity, as perhaps best noted by Diouf's tenure as chairman of the OAU in 1985–1986. Especially during the Senghor administration, however, these relationships had a tendency to reflect larger Cold War and francophone-anglophone rivalries. In the case of the Angolan civil war, for example, ideological concerns clearly predominated: Senghor not only supported the Western-backed UNITA forces under the leadership of Jonas Savimbi (a highly unpopular decision due to Savimbi's alliance with the South Africans) but also became the only African head of state who refused to recognize the Cuban and Soviet-backed MPLA government that assumed power in 1975. In addition to backing different sides in the Angolan civil war, Senegal and Nigeria suffered strained relations due to larger francophone-anglophone rivalries. Adopting the stance of both France and Côte d'Ivoire, the Senghor administration had a tendency to treat Nigeria as an expansionist anglophone threat to francophone interests in West Africa.[51] (For the Nigerian perspective, see Chapter 7.)

The inauguration of the Diouf administration in January 1981 heralded a more balanced approach to bilateral relationships with those African nations beyond its immediate frontiers. Although clearly supportive of la francophonie and eager to maintain close ties with the West, Diouf's approach toward Angola and Nigeria suggested that larger issues of African unity would also be taken into consideration. In the case of Angola, the Diouf administration ordered the closure of UNITA's office in Dakar and diplomatically recognized the MPLA government. In the case of Nigeria, the administration sought a closer partnership as the means for furthering regional integration in West Africa. In addition to serving as the president of ECOWAS in 1991–1992, Diouf took the important step of committing a contingent of Senegalese troops to the Nigerian-dominated ECOMOG peacekeeping effort in Liberia.

The promotion of links with the Arab world and other Muslim countries constitutes a third concentric circle of foreign policy. Building upon Senegal's heritage as a Muslim nation at the crossroads of North and sub-Saharan Africa, both the Senghor and Diouf administrations have sought to make Senegal a pivotal link between these two worlds; Diouf has taken a particularly active role, as witnessed by his attendance at and subsequent chairmanship of the Islamic Conference. Diouf has sought a more balanced set of relationships even with those powers that were the target of often strident critiques during the Senghor years. The ongoing civil conflict over the future disposition of the former Western Sahara (claimed and annexed by Morocco, with a small portion also falling under Mauritanian sovereignty) offers a telling insight: Whereas Senghor firmly embraced Morocco's claims because of his ideological and regional rivalries with former Algerian President Houari Boumedienne (the primary financial backer of guerrillas seeking independence), Diouf successfully sought to engage Boumedienne's successor, President Chadli Benjedid, in a dialogue that positioned Senegal as a moderate voice of caution within the Muslim world and a voice that needed to be taken seriously.

The Diouf administration's pursuit of closer Arab ties has not been completely balanced, and it has not been free of conflict. Privileged links have been sought especially with Morocco, due to that country's unique position as the birthplace of Senegal's politically powerful Tijaniyya brotherhood. Special ties have also been sought with "moderate" Arab nations, such as Saudi Arabia, that serve as important sources of foreign assistance. Yet despite a willingness to seek closer ties or at the very least maintain a diplomatic dialogue with the so-called radical Arab states, including Algeria, Iran, Iraq, Libya, and the Sudan, a variety of security concerns—most notably a fear of the rise of Islamist movements—has strained relations with several of these nations at different points in time. In January 1984, for example, the Diouf administration expelled Iranian diplomats and broke diplomatic ties amid charges that the Iranian government was illegally funding Islamist movements on Senegalese territory. Regardless of these conflicts, the Diouf administration nonetheless has consistently pursued its policy of dialogue in the hopes of promoting a more moderate brand of Islam, conducive to Senegal's unique stature as a predominantly Muslim country that maintains a constitutionally mandated separation between church and state. In the case of Iran, this policy of dialogue resulted in the renewal of diplomatic links in February 1989.

The fourth concentric circle of Senegalese foreign policy revolves around the pursuit of close ties with the West. Historically speaking, the pursuit of such ties was synonymous with maintaining privileged relations with France. In almost all spheres of foreign policy, the importance attached to maintaining these privileged ties is evident: Senegalese policymakers are among the strongest proponents within the francophone world of la francophonie and the strengthening of Franco-African summits; they favor the continued use of Senegalese territory for French military bases; they strongly support Senegal's continued adherence to the CFA franc zone; and they clearly recognize that France remains the largest foreign aid donor in both Senegal and francophone Africa in general. Perhaps the most poignant reminder of how deeply rooted France remains as an object of foreign policy was demonstrated by the national response—at least among the urbanized elite—to the death of former French President François Mitterrand on 9 January 1996. For an entire week, the front-page headlines of newspapers and the primary story for all newscasts and radio shows revolved around paying homage to a man who was called "a friend of Africa." President Diouf was one of over twenty heads of state who traveled to Paris to pay his last respects to a "personal friend" and "fellow combatant" for socialist ideals in Africa.[52]

The inauguration of the Diouf administration heralded the beginning of a new era of seeking closer ties with the United States and other Western democracies, most notably Japan, that was subsequently reinforced by the end of the Cold War. As is the case in other examples of relatively peaceful transfers of power that primarily have occurred in Africa during the post–Cold War era, the emergence of what I elsewhere have referred to as a "second generation" of African leadership inevitably leads to foreign policies that are much more independent of their former patrons within the international system.[53] Similar to many of his second-generation counterparts, President Diouf is taking advantage of growing economic competition among the industrialized Western democracies in the post–Cold War era to lessen his country's foreign policy dependence on France. In a sharp departure from Senegal's past tendency to provide preferential treatment to French companies within the highly protected oil industry in francophone Africa, President Diouf withstood intense

French pressures and signed contracts with South African and U.S. companies in 1995 to exploit oil fields discovered off the southwestern coast of Senegal.[54]

The Diouf administration's actions in this case are not unique—witness the emergence of Japan as the second major aid giver to Senegal during the 1990s and its growing role in the Senegalese automobile market—but rather indicative of a more open foreign policy that is less reflexive to the foreign policy interests of France. Some French observers might assess the direction of Senegal's foreign policy under Diouf as moving into the U.S. sphere of influence, a development that would be welcomed by Washington policymakers. In keeping with a trend toward "regionalization" in U.S. foreign policy, Senegal's regional position, its deepwater port and international airport, and its respectable democratic practices make the country a likely choice for U.S. recognition as a pivotal state in West Africa, especially given the ongoing problems inside Nigeria.[55]

Conclusion: The Challenges of Democratization and Marginalization

The analysis of Senegalese foreign policy suggests that the dependency, Cold War, or personal rule–oriented explanations of African foreign policies are inadequate and possibly misleading. A more complex and nuanced understanding is clearly in order. At least in the case of Senegal, this must incorporate understandings of the French colonial past, the initial elite acceptance of socialist ideology, the impact of traditional Wolof culture, the economic stagnation and decline, the role of Islam, and a democratic tradition that never experienced military rule.

Senegal's democratic tradition is especially relevant to any understanding of the future evolution of foreign policies in a continent increasingly populated by democratic regimes. In a sense, Senegal's uniqueness is increasingly becoming the norm, with important implications for our understanding of African foreign policy. Specifically, Senegal offers an important case study not only of the continuities and changes in the substance of foreign policy that occur when a peaceful transition of power takes place but also of the evolving role of a variety of official and nonofficial policy actors within a democratic setting.

This study also underscores the importance of the impact of the end of the Cold War on African foreign policies. Whereas conflicts during the 1960s and 1970s often were rooted in ideological differences that formed part of a larger international competition between the superpowers, the 1980s and 1990s have engendered direct challenges to the integrity of the Senegalese nation-state and the rise of regional competition over the management and development of shared border resources. Senegalese policymakers themselves have cited several additional challenges, such as the rise of Islamist movements, the contagion effect of a renewed round of military coups d'état against nascent democracies, the economic impact of devaluation within the CFA franc zone countries, and the marginalization of Africa within the post–Cold War era.

The challenge posed by marginalization—and the response of policymakers—is especially intriguing in that it confounds the classic argument that marginalization (especially in regard to declining levels of foreign assistance) constitutes a negative trend within African international relations. Specifically, as witnessed by the actions (as opposed to the official statements) of Senegalese policymakers, marginalization has reinforced the tendency to look for solutions *within* the West African subregion, particularly among the countries that directly share borders with Senegal. It is therefore plausible to state that marginalization may actually be providing the impetus for greater regional cooperation and development, which were too often lacking when governments could more easily turn to their external benefactors. In essence, marginalization has promoted an African search for African solutions to African problems.

Notes

Research for this chapter was funded by my Fulbright grants to Senegal for the 1994–1995 and 1995–1996 academic years, during which I served as a lecturer in the Faculté de Sciences Juridiques et Politiques at Cheikh Anta Diop University. Research support was provided by Nefertiti Gaye, a graduate student who attained a Diplôme des Etudes Approfondies (DEA) in public law, with a specialization in international relations.

1. The most comprehensive (but now dated) analysis of Senegalese foreign policy remains W.A.E. Skurnik, *The Foreign Policy of Senegal* (Evanston, Ill.: Northwestern University Press, 1972). For an analysis of this policy during the 1970s written by a French scholar, see Pierre Biarnès, "La diplomatie Sénégalais," *Revue Française d'Etudes Politiques Africaines*, 149, 1978, pp. 62–78. For a recent overview focusing on Senegal's regional foreign policy and written primarily by Senegalese scholars, see Momar Coumba Diop (ed.), *Le Sénégal et ses voisins* (Dakar, Senegal: Sociétés-Espaces-Temps, 1994).

2. Stated in Article 1 of the constitution. Six languages—Diola, Malinke, Pulaar, Serer, Soninke, and Wolof—are recognized in the same article as "national" languages.

3. See Sheldon Gellar, *Senegal: An African Nation Between Islam and the West* (2d edition) (Boulder: Westview Press, 1995), p. 39.

4. Doudou Thiam, *The Foreign Policy of African States: Ideological Bases, Present Realities, Future Prospects* (London: Phoenix House, 1965), p. 39.

5. For example, see the special issue of *Le Débat* (26 February 1996), a Senegalese weekly newspaper, devoted to coverage of the 1996 visit to Senegal of Pierre Mauroy, the president of Socialist International.

6. During 16–30 June 1995, for example, the Senegalese government organized a major international conference, "L'AOF: De la Création à la Balkanisation (1895–1960)" (AOF: From Creation to Balkanization [1895–1960]), which heralded the centennial of the creation of the AOF. See also Joseph Roger de Benoist, *L'Afrique Occidentale Française de la Conférence de Brazzaville (1944) à l'indépendance (1960)* (Dakar, Senegal: Les Nouvelles Editions Africaines, 1982).

7. For an overview of Wolof culture, see Abdoulaye-Bara Diop, *La société Wolof: Tradition et changement* (Paris: Editions Karthala, 1981).

8. See Leigh Swigert, "Cultural Creolization and Language Use in Postcolonial Africa: The Case of Senegal," *Africa*, 64(2), 1994, pp. 175–189.

9. See Makhtar Diouf, *Sénégal: Les ethnies et la nation* (Paris: Editions L'Harmattan, 1994).

10. Gellar, *Senegal*, p. 55. For an overview, see Gilles Duruflé, *Le Sénégal peut-il sortir de la crise? Douze ans d'ajustement structurel au Sénégal* (Paris: Editions Karthala, 1994).

11. Gellar, *Senegal*, p. 55.

12. See Momar Coumba Diop and Mamadou Diouf, *Le Sénégal sous Abdou Diouf: Etat et société* (Paris: Editions Karthala, 1990), especially chaps. 5, 9, and 12.

13. Personal interview.

14. For a historical overview, see Martin A. Klein, *Islam and Imperialism in Senegal: Sine-Saloum, 1847–1914* (Stanford: Stanford University Press, 1968).

15. See Leonardo A. Villalón, *Islamic Society and State Power in Senegal: Disciples and Citizens in Fatick* (Cambridge: Cambridge University Press, 1995).

16. For example, see Crawford Young and Babacar Kante, "Governance, Democracy, and the 1988 Senegalese Elections," in Goran Hyden and Michael Bratton (eds.), *Governance and Politics in Africa* (Boulder: Lynne Rienner, 1992), and Leonardo A. Villalón, "Democratizing a (Quasi) Democracy: The Senegalese Elections of 1993," *African Affairs*, 93, 1994, pp. 163–193.

17. Villalón, *Islamic Society and State Power in Senegal*, p. 2.

18. See Zyad Limam, "Afrique cherche porte-parole," *Jeune Afrique*, 1794, 25–31 May 1995, pp. 52–54.

19. Personal interviews.

20. For an overview of the problems associated with such schemes, see Guy Martin, "African Regional Cooperation and Integration: Achievements, Problems and Prospects," in Ann Seidman and Frederick Anang (eds.), *21st Century Africa: Towards A New Vision of Self-Sustainable Development* (Trenton, N.J.: Africa World Press, 1992), pp. 69–100.

21. Gellar, *Senegal*, p. 84.

22. See Peter J. Schraeder, "From Berlin 1884 to 1989: Foreign Assistance and French, American, and Japanese Competition in Francophone Africa," *Journal of Modern African Studies*, 33(4), 1995, p. 548.

23. For example, see Moriba Magassouba, *L'islam au Sénégal: Demain les mollahs?* (Paris: Editions Karthala, 1985).

24. See Diop and Diouf, *Le Sénégal sous Abdou Diouf*, p. 19.

25. Personal interview.

26. Personal interviews.

27. Personal interviews.

28. See François Soudan, "La contagion kaki," *Jeune Afrique*, 1833, 21–27 February 1996, pp. 19–20.

29. See Sennen Andriamirado, "Sénégal: Ça n'arrive qu'aux autres," *Jeune Afrique*, 1833, 21–27 February 1996, p. 23.

30. Ousmane Tanor Dieng, "Exposé sur la Politique Extérieure du Sénégal," p. 7. Speech delivered on 15 September 1989 to a meeting of PS members (text provided by Ministry of Foreign Affairs).

31. Personal interview.

32. See Badara Diouf, "Le nouveau gouvernement: Un nouveau challenge pour Habib Thiam," *Le Soleil*, 16 March 1994, p. 8.

33. Elhadj Mbodj, "Senegal's Foreign Policy," typed notes of a presentation made at the University of Wisconsin, Madison, nd.

34. Ibid.

35. See Momor Coumba Diop and Moussa Paye, "Armée et pouvoir au Sénégal," paper presented at a CODESRIA-sponsored seminar, on "The Military and Militarism in Africa," Accra, Ghana, 21–23 April 1993, pp. 8–9.

36. Ibid.

37. Personal interviews.

38. For example, see Robert A. Mortimer, "Senegal's Role in Ecomog: The Francophone Dimension in the Liberian Crisis," *Journal of Modern African Studies*, 34(2), 1996, pp. 293–306.

39. Quoted in Papa Mor Sylla, "Le travail des députés: Entre les séances-marathon et le repos prolongé," *Le Soleil*, 27 July 1995, p. 5.

40. Ibid.

41. See Abdou Latif Coulibaly, "Rôle de la presse dans la sauvegarde et la consolidation de la démocratie au Sénégal," *Afrique Espoir*, 12 December 1994, pp. 15–19.

42. See the series of articles and op-ed pieces in *Le Soleil*, *Le Sud*, and *Wal Fadjri* during the week of 11–18 March 1996.

43. See Ron Parker, "The Senegal-Mauritania Conflict of 1989," *Journal of Modern African Studies*, 29(1), 1991, pp. 155–171, and Anthony G. Pazzanita, "Mauritania's Foreign Policy: The Search for Protection," *Journal of Modern African Studies*, 30(2), 1992, pp. 281–304.

44. Indeed, other regions (e.g., Latin America and South Asia) are considered important to the future of Senegalese foreign policy, although they are not usually cited when discussing Senegalese foreign policy priorities.

45. Confidential interview.

46. Ibid.

47. See Momar Coumba Diop, "Des équilibres instables," in Diop, *Le Sénégal et ses voisins*, pp. 1–32.

48. See Jean Schmitz, "Hydropolitique du fleuve Sénégal (1975–1991): Problèmes fonciers, frontière et ethnicisation des conflits," in Diop, *Le Sénégal et ses voisins*, pp. 60–81.

49. Diop, "Des équilibres instables," p. 21.

50. Personal interviews.

51. For an overview of Senegalese-Nigerian relations during the Senghor years, see Bamitale Omole, "Bilateral Relations Between Nigeria and Senegal, 1960–1980: Cooperation and Conflicts," *Génève-Afrique*, 25(2), 1987, pp. 80–101.

52. For example, see the coverage of this event in *Le Soleil*, 9–14 January 1996.

53. See Peter J. Schraeder, "Elites as Facilitators or Impediments to Political Development? Lessons from the 'Third Wave' of Democratization in Africa," *Journal of Developing Areas*, 29(1), 1994, pp. 69–90.

54. For a more extended analysis, see Schraeder, "From Berlin 1884 to 1989."

55. For example, see Salih Booker, "Thinking Regionally: Priorities for U.S. Policy Toward Africa," Africa Policy Information Center, Background Paper #5, March 1996.

Select Bibliography

Biarnès, Pierre. "La diplomatie Sénégalais," *Revue Française d'Etudes Politiques Africaines*, 149, 1978, pp. 62–78.

Diop, Momar Coumba. *Le Sénégal et ses voisins* (Dakar, Senegal: Sociétés-Espaces-Temps, 1994).

Diop, Momar Coumba, and Mamadou Diouf. *Le Sénégal sous Abdou Diouf* (Paris: Editions Karthala, 1990).

Gellar, Sheldon. *Senegal: An African Nation Between Islam and the West* (2d edition) (Boulder: Westview Press, 1995).

Klein, Martin A. *Islam and Imperialism in Senegal: Sine-Saloum, 1847–1914* (Stanford: Stanford University Press).

Mortimer, Robert A. "Senegal's Role in Ecomog: The Francophone Dimension in the Liberian Crisis," *Journal of Modern African Studies*, 34(2), 1996, pp. 293–306.

Omole, Bamitale. "Bilateral Relations Between Nigeria and Senegal, 1960–1980: Cooperation and Conflicts," *Génève-Afrique*, 25(2), 1987, pp. 80–101.

Parker, Ron. "The Senegal-Mauritania Conflict of 1989: A Fragile Equilibrium," *Journal of Modern African Studies*, 29(1), 1991, pp. 155–171.

Skurnik, W.A.E. *The Foreign Policy of Senegal* (Evanston, Ill.: Northwestern University Press, 1972).

Villalón, Leonardo A. *Islamic Society and State Power in Senegal: Disciples and Citizens in Fatick* (Cambridge: Cambridge University Press, 1995).

9

The Early Foreign Policy of the Democratic South Africa

PAUL-HENRI BISCHOFF AND
ROGER SOUTHALL

South Africa is presently undergoing an enormously complex transition under the auspices of the Government of National Unity (GNU). The GNU is led by the African National Congress, which is driving a remarkable transformation of South Africa's foreign policy. From defense of the morally indefensible and politically unviable under the old order, the "new South Africa" is elaborating an international role that seeks to unite the moral imperatives deriving from the antiapartheid and prodemocratic struggles of the past with appropriate responses to the awesome challenges posed by an increasingly globalized economy, in which the rest of sub-Saharan Africa participates on ever more unfavorable terms.

This requires an extremely difficult balancing act. On the one hand, there is both international and domestic expectation that SA will emerge as a nonracial African state vigorously engaged in the promotion of peace and human rights at home and abroad. On the other, the deepening of democracy within the country will require the deconstruction of continuing white domination of the economy while simultaneously rendering the latter more globally competitive.

These different agendas are not necessarily contradictory, yet the initial attempt to reconcile them has been uneven. Nonetheless, the level of success that SA achieves in meeting these challenges will prove influential in determining whether the country joins the global "winners" or "losers" during the early decades of the twenty-first century.[1]

Given South Africa's particular inheritance as a (now deracialized) semi-industrialized state and regional power, its government has three particular strategies that it may choose to pursue, separately or in combination. First, it may seek to build upon SA's heritage as a middle power, able to join in shifting alliances with other similarly positioned states that want to shape events either in cooperation or competition with the dominant powers of world politics. Second, it may advocate, in concert with state or nonstate actors, multilateral solutions to individual global issues. And third, it may bid to attract international support for wider African concerns and thereby provide leadership on the African continent.[2]

The Continental and Domestic Setting

The end of the Cold War undercut Pretoria's claim to Western support as an anticommunist ally and simultaneously extinguished any immediate threat of nuclear proliferation in Africa: Indeed, SA's capacity to produce nuclear weapons seems to have been systematically dismantled with the prospect of the ANC gaining power. Even so, the continent remained fractured by enduring civil conflicts in countries as diverse as Sierra Leone, Liberia, Somalia, Rwanda, and Angola. Yet with a post–Cold War, postapartheid "peace dividend" in view, the major preoccupation of governments in sub-Saharan Africa was how they should attempt to grapple with the continent's increasing global marginalization.

As a classically "semiperipheral" economy, SA primarily exports raw and semiprocessed minerals and agricultural products to advanced industrial countries; in return, it imports chemicals, mining and transportation equipment, aircraft, industrial machinery, telecommunication and sound equipment, and computers. Yet with an average per capita income of US$2,530 in 1990 (compared to $647 for the rest of the Southern African region), SA is defined according to World Bank criteria as an upper-middle-income country. Furthermore, with a GDP of $90.720 billion in 1990, more than three times larger than the combined GDPs of all the nine member states of the former SADCC, SA possesses the strongest economy in Africa. Its exports of agricultural, chemical, and industrial goods and services to other parts of Africa rose from $456 million in 1987 to $6.3 billion in 1994, compared to imports that stagnated at an annual average of $1.6 billion.[3] With manufacturing value added of $19.937 billion in 1989 (in contrast to the SADCC countries' combined $3.958 billion), SA stands out as a relatively sophisticated industrial power, and it is widely viewed as the African country most likely to join the ranks of newly industrializing countries such as Hong Kong, Singapore, South Korea, and Malaysia. Against that prospect, any success attained by SA must be earned in the face of a thoroughly formidable unemployment rate of 36 percent.[4]

Under apartheid, SA's economic dominance underwrote attempts to establish regional political and military hegemony. However, the newly liberated SA is no longer regarded by neighboring states as an aggressor;

rather, it is viewed as being able to actively contribute to the peace needed for growth, as well as to provide the markets, investment, and expertise to kick-start development throughout the war-weary, impoverished subcontinent. The ANC is attempting to facilitate that role domestically by balancing the expectations of its mass constituency against an emphasis upon national reconciliation, which is viewed as necessary to keeping and developing skills within the country. Central to its strategy is its Reconstruction and Development Programme (RDP), which is designed to mobilize resources toward the final eradication of apartheid by meeting basic needs, developing human resources, and building an integrated, dynamic economy; a coordinated national public works program that will marry "the leading and enabling role of the state" to "a thriving private sector" is envisaged.[5]

The RDP has enjoyed astonishingly wide support across political parties, business, and labor. The problem, however, is whether agreement can be maintained around a platform that, while addressing inequalities and basic needs, simultaneously stresses fiscal discipline, the phasing out of protective tariffs, containment of state spending, and strict control over budget deficits. Meanwhile, a widespread desire to emulate the fast-growing economies of Asia rather than reproducing African decline is linked to a cautious approach to the IMF, which has provided an $850 million facility in early support of the GNU. Against that, there is criticism that the new government's policies owe more to a neoliberal design to attract international capital than an effort to implement the longer-term developmentalist philosophy of the RDP. Such criticism threatens to undermine any consensus-based strategy for growth.[6]

The Making and Orientation of South African Foreign Policy

Democratic SA's initial posture is one of universalism—of being a friend to all and an enemy to none—and it recognizes all states regardless of their ideological complexion.[7] This position is underscored by the peculiarly internationalist endeavor that supported the struggle against apartheid. Just as the ANC recognizes its debt to a host of nonstate actors (ranging from trade unions through churches and solidarity groups to the African-American community), so it also insists upon its obligations and debts to governments and liberation movements across the ideological spectrum. Yet not all these demands are compatible, and the government is now being called upon to make its choices about where SA stands in world politics.

An initial debate has concerned whether South African policy should be guided more by principles than pragmatism. This debate centers upon an assertion that because the campaign against apartheid was a struggle for the most basic human rights, a new foreign policy should represent a decisive break with the past. In particular, it is proposed that SA should place human rights at the center of its foreign policy, eschew hegemony in favor of a more egalitarian relationship with its immediate region, and forcefully identify with the efforts of the South to strive for a better global deal. In contrast, the counterposition argues that in the "real world" of diplomacy, the simplistic application of human rights principles is mediated by highly complex rules and practices; simultaneously, the domestic demands being placed upon the postapartheid order are so great that a popularly responsive government cannot reasonably be expected to prioritize an international human rights agenda over the urgency of reconstruction and development.[8]

This debate has been fueled by confusion about who is actually "making" foreign policy. At present, this seems to somehow emerge from divergent inputs by President Mandela, Deputy President Thabo Mbeki, the Department of Foreign Affairs (DFA) and Department of Trade and Industry (DTI), parliamentarians, and, to some extent, various organs of civil society. Importantly, too, policy is also now subject to review by a new parliamentary committee on foreign affairs. However, although a new emphasis on consultation and accountability is indeed a tribute to democracy, there has been some cost in clarity and assertiveness. There has been concern that the minister of foreign affairs, Alfred Nzo, and his deputy, Aziz Pahad, have failed to impose themselves upon the management of their department, mostly because its most senior officials, headed by Director-General Rusty Evans, were appointed under the old order. Though some commentators have argued that considerable continuity in policy was to be expected from a national liberation movement assuming the reins of government after the end of the Cold War,[9] others have objected that too little has changed in terms of who is actually conducting foreign policy.[10]

The DFA itself claims to have embraced the move away from apartheid enthusiastically. Under Pik Botha, foreign minister from 1977, it had pushed a "verligte" ("enlightened") line,[11] which surviving officers claim was reinforced by their personal and political isolation when they served on the diplomatic circle overseas. This, they argue, contributed to the department's marginalization during the era of "total strategy," when most key foreign policy decisions were hijacked by security and intelligence agencies. The transition has therefore enabled the DFA to facilitate the desperately needed changes in SA's foreign policy and practice that they had previously been urging upon their erstwhile political masters.

If there is an element of self-exoneration, there is also no doubt that the transition has allowed the DFA to claim back territory that it had previously lost to the generals. Its "verligte" or, perhaps more accurately, its "realist" stance also enabled it to arrive at a degree of consensus with the ANC when, during the transition, a series of joint seminars were held to engage key personnel from the "old" and "new" foreign policy orders in dialogue.[12] (To be sure, important differences did remain; for example, the DFA worked to remove sanctions, and the ANC worked to maintain them.) Subsequently, in response to criticism that it has been too slow in initiating change, the DFA claims to have been severely constrained by terms of the transitional deal, under which—in addition to its accepting recruits from the liberation movements—it was also required to absorb a considerable number of undertrained and largely inexperienced "foreign service" officers from the four former "independent" homelands. Meanwhile, it also pleads the particular difficulties of having to physically establish embassies in numerous countries (mainly in Africa) where it was previously unrepresented.[13]

It may be, as D. O'Meara[14] proposes, that on return from exile, the ANC is no more adequately equipped than the old DFA to think beyond previously rigid, Cold War postures. More particularly, the problem may be that the RDP addresses national rather than regional development needs and was not drawn up to cover foreign relations. Consequently, the DFA has been left to conduct its business in a vacuum. Furthermore, not least because the DFA has been viewed as outside the circuit of the RDP, other foreign policy actors, new and old, official and unofficial, have stepped forward to pursue (proclaimed) RDP objectives via a number of diverse initiatives.

New on the scene are the provincial governments as political players (Western Cape Province is the first to draft its own constitution). Assisted by national government and foreign donors, provinces are establishing clear identities for themselves in their attempt to obtain investment from abroad. Within the broader region, for instance, Mpumalanga (formerly Eastern Transvaal) has taken a key role in promoting a transport corridor to Maputo.[15] Similarly, North-West Province has concluded an agreement with Santiago Province in Cuba that provides for exchanges of personnel, economic links, and cooperation in infrastructure, sport, culture, education, and health. And Gauteng premier Tokyo Sexwale visited the United States to lobby for expertise, assistance, and investment.[16] Again, the Eastern Cape government and the Brittany regional council are establishing trade links and identifying areas of cooperation in agriculture.[17]

Established players are also asserting themselves internationally. The city of Cape Town launched a bid (albeit unsuccessfully) for the 2004 Olympics; Johannesburg hosted a special trade fair for Arab states in 1995; the parastatal Electricity Supply Company (ESKOM) is engaged in actively seeking to expand its role as an electricity supplier throughout the subcontinent; and negotiations by the Transvaal Agricultural Union have prompted the signing of a draft bilateral agreement between the South African and Mozambican governments on the settlement of South African farmers on Mozambican land.

The problem is not that these initiatives are undesirable but rather that the new SA's foreign policy risks becoming uncoordinated. Although the overall impact of such external relations would seem to have directly or indirectly boosted the RDP (though much foreign "aid" promised after Mandela's inauguration has been slow in coming),[18] the lack of an integrated foreign policy framework—which might be better provided by a merger of the DFA with the DTI, as has happened in a number of countries to cope with the globalization of the world economy—suggests that the foreign policymakers of the new SA may face a choice: to stay universalist and as a result turn increasingly reactive or to become more selective, creative, and innovatory.

The Recapture and Redefinition of Middle-Power Status

Middle-power status has traditionally been associated with a country's geopolitical and geostrategic position and aspirations and with the foreign policy resources it is able to expend on *maintaining* its hegemony within a region or *containing* the hegemony of other locally preponderant powers. However, in the more fluid conditions that obtain today, territoriality would seem to be less important than a country's ability to consistently generate successful initiatives at regional, bilateral, and multilateral levels.

Apartheid SA was regularly identified as a "subimperial," "semiperipheral," or regional power. As projected by Kenneth Grundy,[19] the autarkical development fostered in SA by its specific brand of settler colonialism enabled the country to claim an "intermediary" place in the productive and control chain of the "Euro-American" global system. This was founded upon a conflicting yet complementary economic partnership with core countries, with whom SA shared a positive community of security interests. However, as argued by Patrick McGowan, the republic's position in the world declined from the mid-1970s under the impact of domestic and external challenges adverse to white minority power, so much so that unless negative trends are arrested, SA could, within two decades, come to resemble "a big Zimbabwe, at the border between the periphery and the semi-periphery."[20]

The immediate problem for SA is that of discovering a new identity. From being an international pariah, the democratic SA has earned universal international approbation for its bid to be recognized, in Archbishop Desmond Tutu's term, as the "rainbow nation." It is precisely the government's vigorous espousal of national reconciliation, together with its determination to imprint upon the state a representative but nonracial character, that has provided the basis for the initial rapid elevation of its international status. SA has seen its formal diplomatic links with other countries increase from 31 in 1989 to 124 today, and it had joined or been readmitted to some 16 international organizations by 1996 (notably the UN General Assembly, the OAU, the SADC, and the Commonwealth). However, SA has not yet resolved several crucial issues: Can it combine strong connections to the North while also being part of Africa? Can it arrest its decline as a semiperipheral state without harming the region or the rest of the developing South?

Just as the idea of the "rainbow nation" implies a unity of different strands, so must a foreign policy that seeks to deal with these dilemmas be multifaceted. What may appear as ambiguous or contradictory to those who would like SA to belong either to the North or to the South, or to Africa only, or to uncomplicatedly espouse principle, overlooks the country's peculiarly "in-between status," for it straddles the North and South and is very international and developed for an African state. Thus, an approach that puts South Africa at the heart of Africa's international relations is increasingly being paralleled by a "South-South" focus. A coherent strategy to restore the country's position in the international economy must mean engaging the world politically as well as economically. Politically, it makes sense to link up not only with Africa but also with Southern economies in a similar stage of development. Thus, the DFA is identifying strategic partners such as Brazil, Chile, Malaysia, and India as part of a "Southern Hemisphere bloc" in order to increase the lobbying power of medium-sized Southern states.[21] On the economic front, such a strategy requires that SA adopt domestic policies likely to stimulate consistent growth; support industry in terms of research and development and human resource development; and attract new investment, aid, and loans. Under present conditions, this implies prudent management in the deregulation of the economy, planned exposure to global competition by the gradual dismantling of protective trade barriers coupled with strategic support for South African industry exposing itself to an open world market, and the reworking of relationships with the dominant global powers.

Reorienting the Economy

The growth of the economy requires that urgent attention be paid to SA's dwindling share of world trade. Excluding gold, this fell from 1.5 percent of world exports and 1.4 percent of world imports in 1965 to 0.9 percent and 0.6 percent in 1985, respectively.[22] Meanwhile, the country's share of global gold production plunged from 75 percent in 1970 to 31 percent in

1994.[23] Further, whereas between 1980 and 1990 South Korea, Malaysia, and Thailand enjoyed an average annual export growth rate of over 10 percent, SA managed just 1.3 percent.[24] Any attempt to reverse this decline must clearly give immediate priority to increasing trade with old markets and establishing links with new ones. This in turn is closely associated with increasing the inflows of capital, for with a low domestic savings rate of only some 17 percent of GDP, SA is vitally dependent upon external finance to achieve an acceptable minimum rate of growth over a lengthy period.

Hitherto, the GNU has enjoyed relative success. The end to isolation has seen considerable external interest in SA as an emerging market and as a trade partner. Foreign business is taking a hard look at the country as a gateway to Africa, and South African exports are increasingly beginning to penetrate previously closed markets. SA increased its positive trade balance with Central and Eastern Europe from R800 million in 1992 to nearly R1.2bn in 1993; by early 1995, the fastest-growing trade relations were with Iran, Malaysia, India, and Brazil. Meanwhile, trade was also increasing markedly with established partners such as the United States, Germany, Britain, and Japan and growing with Africa dramatically. However, overall, even though imports had risen sharply, the export performance in 1994 was reported as "disappointing." This resulted in the trade balance declining to R11.5bn from R16.4bn in 1993, although subsequently, exports were to increase from 17.7 percent of GDP in 1994 to 20.1 percent in 1995.[25]

After a large outflow of capital in 1994, which depleted net reserves to zero, the GNU has achieved a dramatic turnaround: From 1984 to 1993, SA had to accommodate a net capital outflow of over R50bn, but the second half of 1994 and the first three quarters of 1995 saw net capital inflows of around R9bn and R14bn.[26] This bears testimony to the much greater confidence in the country's postapartheid prospects, but it is also a product of the easing of foreign exchange controls, which took place with the abolition of the financial rand in early 1995.[27]

Nonetheless, although SA has dispatched and received a host of trade missions, its reentry into the world economy has by no means been all plain sailing. For a start, a dramatic 30 percent drop in the value of the rand against the U.S. currency from February to December 1996 showed the extreme jitteriness of the global financial markets about South Africa's stability and pursuit of a globalist economic policy. It also showed the enormous vulnerability of the economy and its exposure to largely short-term, foreign investment on recall and the relative lack of longer-term foreign direct investment (FDI). This development delayed further progress toward the total abolition of exchange controls for which, paradoxically, international capital is looking.[28] Foreign investors complain that the low

productivity of South African industry can only be addressed by a deregulation of the labor market and rapid privatization of parastatal enterprises. However, this approach runs counter to positions adopted by labor, notably the Congress of South African Trade Unions (COSATU),
which argue strongly for raising minimum wages, educating the workforce, and having the government pursue an actively interventionist role
in the economy.

SA and the West

SA's attempt to reverse its decline would face a far more hostile environment were it not that major global players are keen to help South Africa
succeed. As explained by Franklin Sonn, Pretoria's ambassador in Washington, it is scarcely SA's economy—three times smaller than that of
Texas—or Southern Africa's economy—"peanuts" compared to regions
such as Asia or the Pacific Rim—that so attracts official U.S. interest.
Rather, it is because a high value is placed on SA's peaceful transition as a
role model at a time when racial rivalries elsewhere have given rise to
ethnic cleansing and civil war.[29]

This appraisal underlies the establishment of the U.S.–South African Binational Commission. The commission demonstrates the particular importance attached to SA, for Washington has previously established such
bodies only with Russia in 1992 and Egypt more recently. Its purpose, it is
explained, is not to replace the traditional channels of diplomacy but
rather to supplement them by bringing together the most senior decisionmakers and officials from each government so as to develop a familiar,
committed, and enduring mutual relationship. Cochaired by Vice Presidents Al Gore and Thabo Mbeki, the second and third meetings of this
commission in December 1995 and February 1997 involved several cabinet ministers from each country and concluded with the signing of three
agreements concerning increased cooperation in areas of science, technology, the environment, and taxation.[30]

The emergence of a closer working relationship with the United States
is matched by a strengthening connection to the EU. This is of particular
importance not only because the EU is the republic's dominant trading
partner (taking 22.6 percent of exports and supplying 42.8 percent of imports in 1994) but also because the EU accounts for 40 percent of world
trade, a ratio that will increase in concert with the future expansion of the
EU itself.

From the 1970s, the trading connection with the European Union (EU)
was complicated by the EU's growing opposition to apartheid, which culminated in the adoption of (limited) sanctions in the mid-1980s. However,
a lack of unanimity concerning how to respond to Frederik Willem

De Klerk's democratization initiatives then led to some considerable disarray, with individual states unilaterally dropping sanctions before they were officially lifted in September 1993. But thereafter, there was a return to consensus around the need for the EU to provide immediate assistance for SA's transition while simultaneously working toward the drawing up of a comprehensive and long-term trade agreement. Central to the latter was to be the negotiation of improved terms of access for SA to the European market.

The EU's interest in the success of South African democracy was enhanced by worries that, were it to fail, up to 2 million South African residents with claims on European citizenship might leave for member states; moreover, a breakdown of the South African economy would dash hopes for the continent as a whole. However, it was also recognized that the forging of a comprehensive trade agreement would be a highly complex and time-consuming task. Consequently, following a proposal by the European Commission in 1992 that SA be included in its Generalized System of Preferences for developing countries, the EU concluded an interim agreement with Pretoria in October 1994 that offered various concessions and opened the way for SA to obtain loans from the European Investment Bank. It also stressed that EU–South African cooperation should work to promote development throughout the region; this agreement followed a meeting between the EU and SADC (now inclusive of SA) in September 1994 that had underlined the desirability of regional economic integration. The difficulties likely to be encountered in arriving at a long-term treaty were rendered evident by the very considerable opposition to the proposed terms of the interim agreement put up by the French government, which wanted to deny preferential entry to a long list of South African (mainly agricultural) exports that would compete with French products. Subsequently, when the European foreign ministers met to negotiate the mandate for talks with SA concerning longer-term arrangements, which they agreed in principle should incorporate about 90 percent of total mutual trade, the French were joined by various other member countries (notably Germany) in seeking exclusions that would affect up to 40 percent of the republic's agricultural exports to the EU; this prompted serious South African concern about European protectionism.[31] However, by the end of March 1996, the scene was set for substantive negotiations, with SA boosted by Irish leader Mary Robinson declaring to parliament in Cape Town that her country's forthcoming presidency of the EU would be dedicated to securing better access for the republic to the wider European market.[32]

The encounter with Brussels underlines the republic's middle status. Although SA initially forged an agreement with the ACP group of states that called for it to join them as a full member of the Lomé Convention, the EU has insisted that GATT world trade rules do not allow SA to benefit from what would provide its most favorable option.[33] Certainly, too, there is the problem that South African admission might be accomplished at some expense to existing Lomé members with which it might compete, although this problem could have been overcome had the EU been sufficiently flexible.[34] During the negotiations, South Africa had to ultimately give up a key demand, that South African firms be allowed to tender for EU projects on a preferential basis and on par with firms from other ACP member states.[35] There is the danger, too, that even though South African agriculture may be allowed restricted access to the EU, European manufactures may impact disastrously upon SA's long-protected industry. Clearly, South Africa had to prove its capability in politically tough and technically difficult negotiations from 1995 to 1997. However, as a recent detailed study of the negotiations concluded, the longer talks continue and the further South Africa moves away from the popular crest of 1994, the less obligated the EU will feel to arrive at a sympathetic arrangement.[36]

SA has already been honing its bargaining skills in a major disagreement with the United States. The crisis arose over Pretoria's refusal to pay a R37mn fine to the U.S. courts, following the indictment by the U.S. government of Arsmcor (the South African, government-owned arms supplier) for contraventions of U.S. arms export control laws and sanctions against SA. The case arose from the discovery during the Gulf War of U.S. parts in South African artillery shells supplied to Iraq.

The particular problem arose not because the United States was unsympathetic to SA's concern that it should not pay for crimes committed by the previous regime but because Pretoria chose to argue that as a wholly state-owned subsidiary, Armscor should enjoy sovereign immunity from criminal prosecution in U.S. courts, a claim that the U.S. Justice Department was not prepared to allow. The stakes were further raised by a South African threat to make revelations about U.S. complicity in illegal arms deals during the sanctions years and by a further suggestion that even the binational commission was at risk and that diplomatic representation could be downgraded. The crisis only neared resolution following direct contact between Gore and Mbeki. Gore indicated that if Armscor entered a "no contest" plea, admitting its guilt, the defense would be allowed to make a strong plea to the court that the new government should not be unfairly penalized, although Pretoria's hawks continued to insist that there should be no compromise of SA's sovereignty.[37] Similarly, tensions over the possible sale of military technology to Syria and U.S. threats about cutting off aid if such a deal occurred had to be defused in quiet diplomatic moves involving Mbeki and Gore.[38]

The U.S. pullback also overlooked differences with SA over the latter's determined establishment of friendly relations with Cuba (a good friend to the ANC during the liberation struggle), with Iran (which was rapidly emerging as a valuable trading partner), and with Libya (also an erstwhile supporter of the liberation struggle). The pullback was driven in part by recognition that an open breach with President Mandela (who vowed that no one would dictate to South Africa who it should have relations with) could be costly to the Clinton administration before and beyond the 1996 elections, especially among African-American voters. But it was also shaped by the long view that sees SA emerging not just as a growth pole but also as the guarantor of regional peace and security. Simultaneously with the compromise over Armscor, it emerged that the United States was planning to sell five excess C-130 transport planes to the South African Air Force, at one-eighth their market value,[39] and that plans were moving ahead for joint military exercises, cooperation in peacekeeping operations, the exchange of officers, and the sharing of military intelligence.[40] However, although South African brinkmanship may prove to have paid off in this first instance, similar encounters with other great powers could prove costly.

Other Challenges

One foreign policy failing was SA's internationally unsupported attempt to run a Two China policy. At the cost of failing to formalize relations with the PRC, SA continued the apartheid government's diplomatic recognition of Taiwan, in contrast to the position taken by most other countries, which enjoy diplomatic relations with Beijing but only trading relations with Taiwan.

The reasons for this had as much to do with Taiwan's economic presence as it did with Taiwanese diplomacy. Some 350 Taiwanese companies in SA provide some 45,000 jobs, and although it was an ally of Pretoria during the Total Onslaught era, Taipei contributed heavily (R35mn) to the ANC's election campaign in 1994 and has energetically lobbied parliamentarians since.[41] Furthermore, there is wide agreement that SA has more in common with Taiwan, which is now a reforming multiparty democracy with a respectable human rights record, than with the PRC, which remains a highly authoritarian state.

However, given the virulence of the PRC's stance on the issue and the further irony that Taiwan has never actually proclaimed its independence, SA's initiative was always unlikely to fly, as was an offer by Mandela to mediate between Taipei and Beijing. Pretoria therefore was left in the awkward position of having to play for time and wait for international support for the idea of an independent Taiwanese state. When, in the latter part of 1996, China said it would close South Africa's consulate in Hong Kong after July 1997,[42] and further, when it became clear that

Hong Kong and China's combined economic contacts with South Africa's economy were going to exceed those with Taiwan (the PRC had already emerged as SA's primary market for iron ore),[43] the implications for future business and trade prompted Pretoria in December 1996 to abruptly announce its recognition of the PRC in place of the ROC.

Thus Pretoria, in line with Asian states in general, had to recognize China's rising political and economic dominance in world affairs. The switch in relations also aligned the national interest with the inheritance of the national liberation movement-in-government: to affirm those states such as the PRC who in the past supported the forces of liberation.

In the Middle East, the peace process—although troubled—has enabled SA to simultaneously maintain strong support for the Palestinian cause and to strike up good relations with Arab states without disrupting relations with Israel (which in 1995–1996 continued to absorb over half the DFA's budget for that region). Western powers responded quietly to the invitation to visit SA that Mandela extended to Ma'ammar Gadhafi as the ANC's payment for debts it incurred during the struggle years. But the president's profession of willingness to meet a visiting representative of Hamas, which had recently killed more than sixty people in terror bombings in Israel, drew a strongly negative reaction, not least of all from the twelve Arab states represented in Pretoria.[44]

In the few short years since its first democratic election, SA has made considerable strides toward improving its position in the global hierarchy, and it has established itself as an independent foreign policy actor. Yet its nascent stature as a middle power will only be seriously tested as its presently favored international status diminishes, apartheid recedes into the past, and its foreign policy thinkers evolve creative strategies to drive a foreign policy presaged on South Africa as a vibrant democracy and unconventional player in world politics.[45]

South Africa's Emergence as a Multilateral Actor

Multilateral coalition building among state and nonstate actors is becoming increasingly important in a world groping for the reestablishment of order. For world powers, multilateral solutions are a useful cover for the continued pursuit of their own power. For smaller states faced with a decrease in bilateral aid, they remain an opportunity to take advantage of cooperation. In turn, for middle powers, they offer the chance to consolidate status and influence by modifying the agendas of the powerful in favor of the less powerful and for developing their own capacity in particular issue areas.[46]

The new SA claims excellent credentials for contributing to international problem solving. First, it enjoys the advantages of leadership by

Mandela, who is unrivaled in world esteem as a principled democrat and humanist. Second, the ANC's heritage as the key element in the international coalition of forces that displaced apartheid and its proclaimed determination to push Africa upward on the global agenda provide the GNU with moral and political authority to become a multilateral facilitator in world affairs. Third, SA is the only country to have unilaterally divested itself of nuclear weapons and, more recently, to have opted to stop production and destroy its existing stock of land mines.[47] Fourth, as proclaimed by Nzo, the demise of apartheid will now give rein to SA's potential to mediate between the North and the South.[48]

Central to the GNU's early effort to engage in multilateral action has been an attempt to reposition SA away from the previous government's unambiguous identification with the North. Although the basic orientation for the moment is to remain with Europe, North America, and Japan as sources of investment, technology, and aid, there is a growing recognition of the advantages to be gained by building relationships with other actors, not only in Africa but also in Asia and Latin America. Admission to the Non-Aligned Movement in 1994, complemented by readmission to the Commonwealth in the same year, provide the opportunity for SA to forge creative relationships with, notably, the emerging powers of Asia, such as India, Malaysia, Singapore, and Indonesia. Indeed, complementing a present boom in intergovernmental and trade relations with India has been SA's initiation of the idea of an association of Indian Ocean states,[49] which was taken up at two specially convened meetings held in Mauritius and Australia in 1995.[50] Nzo has also mooted an association of South Atlantic rim countries, which would foster cooperation between the likes of Brazil, Uruguay, and Argentina and African counterparts such as Nigeria, Ghana, Namibia, Angola, and SA.[51]

SA and GATT

Much of the impetus behind SA's emergence as a multilateral actor lies with the DTI, which, in seeking to drive a dynamic and full return to the world economy, has moved participation in GATT to the forefront of its list of priorities.

SA had little chance to influence the proceedings of the Uruguay round of talks from 1986 to 1994, which preceded GATT's drawing up of the new agreement. However, as the transition loomed, the then government stepped up its efforts to participate in the new trading order. Critical of a lack of consultation and worried about what commitments the apartheid government might make on behalf of its democratic successor, the ANC and its trade union allies pushed strongly to be included. The result was that the National Economic Forum, a tripartite body linking government, labor, and business, took over responsibility for revising SA's offer. Subsequent support by Mandela (as leader of the ANC) for the bargaining stance taken on the key issue of clothing and textile tariff liberalization provided the background to SA's accession to the Marrakesh Agreement on 13 April 1994.[52]

SA obtained important concessions on the reduction of tariffs in textiles and clothing: Instead of a 30 percent cut in five years, a 45 percent cut is to take effect within twelve years. Similarly, motor manufacturers were given a maximum of eight years to adjust instead of five, with a terminal maximum tariff of 50 percent rather than 30 percent. Nevertheless, overall, the new trading regime (which will see a major reduction of tariff levels and lines over the five-year period) will impose strictures that will be costly in employment terms and will give the industries concerned a relatively short time to measure up against global competition. However, as viewed by Pretoria, if SA fails to make the effort needed to compete in the world economy by the new rules, it will never be able to meet the objectives of the RDP.

SA may prove particularly suited to playing a mediating role between advanced and developing countries with regard to labor and environmental protection. On the one hand, SA has powerful trade unions and other social movements pressing it toward higher standards of behavior in these areas, which competing advanced industrial countries are likely to endorse. On the other hand, enforcement of improved standards could work to disadvantage South African competition against its regional neighbors and many countries in Asia. As argued by A. Hirsch, SA will therefore see "both the necessity for labour and environmental clauses, and the necessity to prevent their becoming protectionist barriers."[53]

SA and Other Multilateral Regimes

Such a mediating role will mean a proffering of moderate solutions to problems, focused not on the moral high ground but rather on the politically possible. SA's role in the early 1995 talks aimed at extending the Nuclear Non-Proliferation Treaty (NNPT) suggests that the lesson has already been absorbed.

The fact that Pretoria had been a nuclear power but had unilaterally disarmed provided SA with both the moral clout and the opportunity to push for adoption of a face-saving formula around which both nuclear and nonnuclear states could rally, allowing for a somewhat conditional renewal of the NNPT. Indeed, SA's part in the deliberations played a key role in bringing two initially polarized sides from the North and the South to an agreement.[54]

Similarly, at the Conference on the Convention on Prohibitions and Restrictions on Certain Conventional Weapons in October 1995, SA initially attempted to steer a middle course between those who wanted a total ban on land mines and those who wished to maintain the largely uncontrolled status quo: Member states should phase out production of existing in favor of "short-life" land mines and limit their use in a number of ways. This solution, argued Foreign Affairs Deputy Director-General Abdul Minty, constituted a practicable way of having more than just a few states agree to the convention,[55] although it was later to draw sharp criticism from Oxfam and antiweapons activists speaking before the parliamentary defense committee.[56] By early 1997, Pretoria unilaterally declared itself ready to stop the production, storage, and export of this weapon—the cause of untold harm during wars in neighboring states, notably Angola and Mozambique.[57]

These successes have earned SA plaudits, but the new government has also learned that assuming a high profile on the international stage can be costly. To be sure, SA declared its formal condemnation of the series of French nuclear tests undertaken in 1995–1996 in the Pacific, yet its credibility as a disarming power was sorely tested when it simultaneously held bilateral discussions with France aimed at signing an umbrella agreement on Franco–South African nuclear cooperation as well as trade.[58] Similarly, despite its good intentions about contributing toward a coalition on human rights in Africa and beyond, its practice has been marred by inconsistencies. Although the establishment of links with Indonesia strengthens the connection to the South, SA's silence on the situation in East Timor has attracted substantial criticism. Establishing diplomatic relations with Sudan amid allegations of genocide being perpetrated against Sudan's southern population seems an example of misapplied universalism.[59] And although the government appointed a commission under Judge Edward Cameron in September 1994 to investigate reports that the illegal sale of weapons by Armscor had helped to fuel civil conflicts in Yemen, Rwanda, Croatia, and Angola, there is concern that the DFA and the Defence Ministry are reluctant to subject arms dealers to anything like adequate accountability.

On a continent tortured by dictatorship, an adherence to an agenda prioritizing democracy and human rights must inevitably complicate SA's relations with many fellow African states. An immediate challenge, therefore, is whether its foreign policy can simultaneously criticize nondemocracies in neighboring states while staking a broader claim to continental leadership.

The Bid for African Leadership

Postapartheid SA sees itself as an integral part of Africa. An ANC-led government, Deputy President Thabo Mbeki holds, must take part in an

African renaissance. Peaceful coexistence, the promotion of democracy, development, and constructive interaction with other governments are all crucial to arresting the continent's alarming decline. Meanwhile, the broad security issues of the post–Cold War era—including economic marginalization, political instability, and diminution of state authority—also draw SA into the maelstrom of African politics.

As indicated by its invitation to address the G7 summit in 1995, where Thabo Mbeki made a plea for Africa to be included in plans for a Global Information Order, SA is well placed to keep Africa on the global agenda and to solicit Northern support for continental development. It can do this by exploiting its prominence in arenas such as the annual Davos World Economic Forum, which provides an important platform on which to present the continent's plight before the world's leaders. However, SA can only bargain credibly on global issues that affect the South if it has Africa's backing, particularly at the UN, and thus, a new connection to the continent must be forged.

The expectation that SA would play an axial role on the continent was initially countered by President Mandela at the 1994 OAU summit in Rabat, when he spelled out SA's modest capacity to respond. Indeed, rather than providing a venue for continental leadership, the OAU has so far not lent itself to more than limited South African participation. To be sure, SA's bid to strengthen relations with francophone nations was initiated by state presidential visits to Mali and Togo in the run-up to the OAU's heads of government's summit in July 1996; furthermore, SA is one of eleven members who have joined the OAU's new Mechanism for Conflict Prevention, Management and Resolution. Nonetheless, OAU membership still has regional rather than continental connotations. In short, foreign policy resources for Africa seemed limited, and the GNU was most heavily committed to the development of the immediate region, especially when South Africa was unexpectedly asked to chair SADC (from 1996 to 1999).

With the advent of the Great Lakes crisis and the questions surrounding the post-Mobutu Congo state, South Africa was forced to adopt a greater leadership role than it had originally sought.

SA and Its Region

In 1994, SA become a member of SADC, which was formed in August 1992 as the successor to SADCC in order to bring about a closer economic union. Aware of how the South African economy was historically built on the contributions of people from the surrounding countries, the new state is taking pains to act cooperatively and ensure that the region obtains a genuinely developmental regime. Meanwhile, SADC has developed protocols on the free movement of persons and free trade, anticipating a single regional market and free trade area by the year 2004 that will make provision for states with developing and least developed economies.[60]

SA chose SADC rather than COMESA (formerly the PTA) as the region's principal vehicle to achieve integration. However, SA also remains part of another regional organization, the South African Customs Union (SACU), whose relationship to SADC remains subject to deliberation.

The future of SACU and its customs union agreement that ties Botswana, Lesotho, Swaziland, and Namibia closely to the South African economy is presently being reevaluated, with discussions revolving around a renegotiation of the 1969 customs formulas. Until recently, SA, as the dominant player in SACU, acted unilaterally in the determination of the common external tariff, but in the future, tariffs will need to be subject to a collective process of negotiation among all member states. However, not least because commitments made under GATT impinge on any extension of SACU membership to other states,[61] SADC will remain the predominant regional body.

Between 1980 and 1992, disengagement from SA provided the rationale for regional integration within SADCC. Nonetheless, this project was always tenuous in that even as Botswana, Lesotho, and Swaziland (and latterly Namibia) remained members of SACU, Zambia, Zimbabwe, Malawi, and Mozambique retained strong bilateral economic ties with the apartheid economy.

With attempts to promote integration between SACU and SADC still in the offing, SA similarly relies on bilateral trade relations. These are underpinned by trade agreements with Malawi, Mozambique, and Mauritius, and similar arrangements have been sought by Kenya, Zimbabwe, and Zambia. However, although trade with the total continent has grown exponentially (by a massive 63 percent during 1994–1995), these bilateral arrangements leave SA open to charges of building hegemony. This is because the drive northward has inevitably been to the detriment of African trade balances with the republic[62] and has led to fears that South African business exports will contribute to the further de-industrialization of the subcontinent, already affected by the various SAPs imposed by the IMF on the region. Furthermore, SA's subscription to the new GATT rules has allowed it to consider any special tariff allowances for non-SACU states in Africa only in terms of timing. Zimbabwe in particular, however, has also faced the imposition of newly protectionist measures: The initial failure of talks on a new trade treaty led to SA requiring Zimbabwean traders to post large financial deposits to move shipments to and from South African ports.[63] (For a Zimbabwean perspective on relations with South Africa, see Chapter 11.)

172 PAUL-HENRI BISCHOFF AND ROGER SOUTHALL

In this environment and given the need to still fully develop an industrial and investment strategy that takes into account the weaker economies of the region, SA's actual commitment to wider African development is viewed by some with skepticism. However, beyond differences over regional development, the major point of tension in SA's emergent relationship with Africa is the focus on human rights.

SA and Human Rights in Africa

SA's stance on human rights has met with a decidedly mixed response in Africa. On the one hand, Pretoria is criticized for its failure, as yet, to sign the African Charter on Human and People's Rights. On the other, SA's policies are widely viewed as too uncomfortably critical and as reflexively reproducing a general Western position. Consequently, securing backing on human rights issues has been difficult.

The resources the GNU is either able or willing to spend in the conduct of its relations with Africa are, as already noted, limited. This has meant that priorities have had to be more clearly identified than elsewhere. Yet human rights and security have forced their way to near the top of the list. All this is fed by the pace of domestic change and the concern that SA should, in Alfred Nzo's words, "lead by example in the region."[64] However, if the government believed that African dictatorships were going to be moved by words of sweet reason, they were soon to be humiliatingly disabused of that idea by General Sani Abacha of Nigeria.

When, in 1995, the military junta in Abuja compounded its previous assaults on the Nigerian prodemocracy movement by securing the death sentencing of writer Ken Saro-Wiwa and eight fellow Ogoni activists, the major world powers looked to the Mandela government to take the lead in exerting pressures to prevent the executions. However, despite warnings by Nigerian exiles and even by Archbishop Desmond Tutu (who had earlier been sent by Mandela to intervene with Abacha to secure the release of imprisoned presidential candidate Moshood Abiola) that the regime would respond to nothing but coercion, the SA government opted instead for quiet diplomacy. Mandela disregarded analyses contending that this was as ineffective and morally spineless as the "constructive engagement" strategy on apartheid that was adopted by Reagan's United States. On his arrival in New Zealand in November for the Commonwealth summit, Mandela announced that, rather than calling for Nigeria's expulsion from that organization, SA would continue with its policy of persuasion. This strategy immediately blew up in his face when the regime then proceeded to hang Saro-Wiwa and his unfortunate companions. (For a discussion of Nigeria, see Chapter 7). The SA government could not hide from its first foreign policy debacle.[65]

To its credit, SA soon switched tracks, recalled its high commissioner to Nigeria, and called for Nigeria's suspension from the Commonwealth and the imposition of an arms embargo, as well as oil and other sanctions by the United States and Britain. However, the moment of opportunity was lost, the West placed its thirst for oil above its concern for Nigerian democracy, and pressure upon Abacha slowly melted away. Not least of the reasons for the junta's minimal discomfort was that SA proved singularly unable to persuade SADC to adopt a collective position of censure in late 1995.[66]

This failure, along with particularly hostile Kenyan resistance to international pressure upon Nigeria,[67] demonstrated the reaction SA could expect to receive from African governments were it to continue to call for their accountability on matters of democracy and human rights. Consequently, although the government did eventually join the international community in censuring Sudan at the UN,[68] SA had in the interim become somewhat more hesitant about taking a strong lead in Africa itself and more cautious about striking out on its own.

SA and Regional Security

If SA's bid for continental leadership depends upon Pretoria's ability to manage differences with other African governments over human rights, it will also require South Africa to make a substantial contribution to the wider conditions within which development may successfully take place. This implies a shift toward an understanding of security that embraces the need for governments to deal with any bundle of political, economic, social, and environmental dangers that give rise to conflict between communities and countries.

Today, with hostilities replaced by goodwill, the major threats to states' stability are increasingly viewed as emanating not from any military quarter but from enemies shared by the region as a whole: poverty, unemployment and massive economic migration southward from a desperate continent, environmental degradation, AIDS, drug running and organized crime, the alarming availability of a massive supply of small arms in the wake of numerous wars, and so on.

The recognition that these are shared difficulties has provided a substantial basis for regional cooperation. For instance, there is increasing awareness of the need for a counteroffensive against the growing influence of international gangsterism, which, riding upon the massive interstate movement of people triggered by the end of apartheid and the rapid expansion of SA's air and trade links, has led to the country being targeted as a major transshipment center for a wide variety of narcotics.[69] Similarly, while acknowledging that the massive number of illegal migrants (up to 8 million) must be controlled, SA realizes that the presence of foreign African communities within its borders may also serve as a major stimulus to regional economic growth. This realization was indicated by Pretoria's decision to allow migrant workers from SADC who have worked in SA continuously for five years to claim permanent residence (although this move has disturbed the government of Lesotho, which depends heavily upon migrants' remittances).

SA has also come to play an increasingly significant role in the reorientation of the region toward "peacemaking." This was prefaced by a commitment made by SADC at its founding to the establishment of a framework and mechanisms to strengthen regional solidarity and provide for mutual peace and security. Consequently, following SA's accession to SADC, it was decided at the SADC summit in August 1994 to disband the Front-Line States—the entente that had served as the effective political arm of SADCC in the struggle against apartheid—and to replace it by a new framework for political and security cooperation. The meeting of SADC foreign ministers that convened in Harare in March 1995 subsequently proposed the establishment of the Association of Southern African States (ASAS), which would become the primary mechanism for dealing with conflict prevention, management, and resolution in Southern Africa.

ASAS changed its name to the Organ on Politics, Defence and Security (OPDS) at Gaberone and was constituted in June 1996. It is meant to complement and not replace OAU mechanisms, and it operates independently from the SADC secretariat. The OPDS, which operates at both a ministerial and a technical level, briefs SADC heads-of-government summits on matters affecting regional security, although its eventual subordination to the SADC summit still remains open to interpretation; this issue was not resolved at the September 1997 summit meeting. OPDS's chair—the first chairperson is Zimbabwe's President Robert Mugabe—rotates among member states, and heads of government constitute its decision-making authority. At the same time, the Inter-State Committee on Security (ISSC), a body held over from the disbanded FLS, is meant to form part of the OPDS, though actual integration is still to be achieved.

The OPDS is to safeguard the region against internal and external instability, but it has yet to begin to operate both effectively and proactively. Some believe that the present apparent preoccupation with traditional security concerns indicates the need to develop a guide on democracy and good governance for this body. On an immediate, practical level, OPDS promotes police, security, and defense cooperation to deal with interborder crime regarding specific issues such as weapons smuggling, drug trafficking, or stock theft. Preventive diplomacy, mediation, arms control, and peacekeeping activities also form part of its brief, and it is recognized that such a multilateral organization ought to be able to provide the intelligence support for preventive diplomacy initiatives. In a somewhat ambitious move, the OPDS has also indicated it wants to bring about an eventual defense pact and thereby create a collective security capacity for itself.

The South African National Defence Force (SANDF)—which is still being forged in the crucible of the integration of apartheid, homeland, and liberation armies—argues that its commitment to the new agenda could be exemplified by its engagement in such major operations as mine clearing in Angola and Mozambique, demobilization and disarmament of paramilitary and irregular forces, and monitoring of peace agreements. It has also been made aware of the immediate region's enormous sensitivity to the South African defense presence, and it recognizes the need to avoid any suggestion that it is attempting to impose a new, even if benevolent, military hegemony.

Within the region, South Africa possesses both "hard power" in terms of its economic and military weight and "soft" power on the basis of its symbolic significance as the postapartheid, "rainbow democracy." Thus, SA is well placed to project its success at internal reconciliation on the African stage and act as a peacemaker (although this will be, to a considerable extent, dependent on resolving the continuing conflict within Kwa-Zulu Natal). If such an intermediary agenda was carefully implemented, it could elaborate the most low-cost, yet high-profile, role South Africa could perform. While maintaining SA's prominent position on the global map, effective peacemaking would exemplify Pretoria's commitment to human rights and could simultaneously generate valuable spin-offs in other aspects of international cooperation, such as aid, trade, tourism, and cultural exchanges.[70]

Hitherto, SA's moves to enact such an agenda have been positive yet cautious. Despite pressures to become more deeply involved, care was taken to avoid insensitive participation by an as yet unstructured SANDF in UN peacekeeping efforts in Rwanda and Angola in 1994. And when tensions in Burundi threatened to erupt into civil war and ethnic slaughter in 1995, Nzo played only a low-key role in OAU efforts to contain confrontation.[71] However, when Lesotho's king (backed by the opposition and a disgruntled army) displaced the government of Ntsu Mokhehle sixteen months after an internationally approved election, Mandela worked closely with Presidents Masire and Mugabe of Botswana and Zimbabwe, as agents of both the FLS and the OAU, to bring about a restoration of democracy through a pragmatic mix of negotiation and coercive persuasion.[72] Similarly, efforts by Thabo Mbeki in particular to mediate the dispute between RENAMO and the National Election Commission on the eve of the Mozambican election were instrumental to a peaceful and favorable outcome. Moreover, SA has strongly supported the latest regional efforts to secure peace in Angola and, as we write, in the Republic of

Congo and in Central Africa.[73] More recently, a personal initiative by Mandela, in collaboration with Masire and Mugabe has brought firm but quiet pressure upon King Mswati of Swaziland to respond positively to swelling demands by trade unions and popularly based movements for a return to democracy.[74]

Whatever the outcome in Swaziland (for the Swazi crisis has yet to be resolved), SA's mediation in this matter was prompted, in part, by COSATU, which pressured the SA government to become involved. COSATU also gave fraternal support to trade unions in Lesotho during that country's own transition to democracy. Likewise, it is prominent among the NGOs that have launched the South Africa Nigeria Democracy Support Group, working in close collaboration with Nigerian exiles and seeking to bring divided opposition forces from that country together.[75]

More than just becoming a magnet for Africa's political refugees, SA's democracy is inviting attention from an increasing number of exiled movements, which take the ANC's past experience as the touchstone for their own present struggles.[76] Yet such attraction can be costly: When Mandela met Anouar Haddam of Algeria's opposition Islamic Salvation Front, Algeria threatened to recall its ambassador and only relented under pressure from fellow Arab states and after face-saving direct contact was made between the two presidents.[77] But if today's most prominent exiles are from Nigeria, Algeria, or former Zaire, tomorrow they may be from Zimbabwe, where Mugabe's rule is becoming increasingly dictatorial and oppressive. Whether and how SA responds to requests from such movements for active assistance, especially where such help might impact adversely upon South African trade, will test Pretoria's diplomatic skills to the limit. Yet only consistent support for democracy abroad, along with the maintenance of democracy at home, will provide a solid foundation for SA's projected continental role.

Conclusion

SA's transformation has attracted worldwide acclaim, and as a result, the country's relations with the international community have expanded rapidly. Not least of the reasons for this has been the hope that a South Africa that has overcome apartheid will hold the key to resolving equally acute conflicts elsewhere. Furthermore, in Nelson Mandela, SA has a leader whose personal stature has made his country a symbol of freedom to the globally dispossessed and a potential player in conflict situations around the world, especially in Africa.

International expectations have had their effect on the content and conduct of SA's foreign policy. The initial response of the ANC-led GNU has been to welcome one and all—past opponents of the apartheid state as well as those who had spurned or opposed the liberation struggle. This policy of universalism has been a natural first response to the world's affirmation of the new SA, and it offers a chance for those who helped sustain apartheid in the past to now make amends. Universalism has also suited the realities of the negotiated settlement. The seeming neutrality of the policy has suited a country that is still feeling its way through a process of nation-building, heavily preoccupied with the search for stability, and deeply engaged in a quest for identity as "the rainbow nation."

On the one hand, there has been no clear break with the past. The DFA, staffed by both old and new political forces, initially subscribed to a pragmatic realism rather than raising matters of principle as many had expected it to do (notwithstanding attempts by the parliamentary Standing Committee on Foreign Affairs to make the department more accountable and foreign policymaking more participatory). On the other hand, the ANC stands for transformation—the deepening of democracy and the practice of human rights at home—and it has begun to concern itself with these issues in its relations with others. Consequently, an effective policy of universalism has been underpinned by a solid commitment to human rights.

The wish to act as a facilitator for democracy and human rights is most readily applicable to an Africa close to home and in the throes of an uneven yet nonetheless widespread struggle against authoritarian rule. SA's brief is to use human rights and the broad security issues associated with poverty and conflict as the means to involve itself as a progressive player in its region and throughout the wider continent. However, as the luster of the transition has begun to recede, SA is being forced to position itself as a middle power and a multilateral actor in world affairs.

In the absence of any considerable foreign policy resources of its own, SA is in the process of learning to build coalitions, both locally and internationally, in order to facilitate cooperation on issues of peace and development that affect the increasingly marginalized, wider continent. However, the priority remains the nature of regional cooperation in Southern Africa.

Alongside the fast-growing countries of Asia and South America, semi-peripheral SA is the only African state with the potential to close the technological gap between North and South. Similarly, as a multilateral actor and middle power in international affairs, it has the potential to act with others to creatively address the political and economic disparities between the countries of the advanced and the developing worlds.

Yet this can only happen if SA can arrest its decline as a semi-industrial power. Considerable new wealth needs to be created at home and in the region (the target set by government for the national economy through 1999 is 6 percent per annum), and it must be more equitably distributed in an economy that hitherto was both structured by apartheid law and practices and crushingly dominant throughout the region.

The challenge is to establish a long-term foreign policy framework that remains true to the ideals espoused in the struggle for national liberation but also balances the costs and opportunities of a period of rapid transition at home, in the region, and throughout the rest of the world at the end of the current millennium.

Notes

1. P. Kennedy, *Preparing for the Twenty-First Century* (London: HarperCollins, 1993).

2. P-H. Bischoff, *Democratic South Africa and the World One Year After: Towards a New Foreign Policy,* Centre for Southern African Studies, University of the Western Cape, Working Paper No. 46.

3. *Sunday Independent,* 4 February 1996.

4. South African Institute of Race Relations, "Unemployment—How Bad Is It?" *Fast Facts,* 4, 1996.

5. African National Congress, *The Reconstruction and Development Programme: A Policy Framework* (Johannesburg: Umanyanano Publications, 1994).

6. V. Padayachee, "Debt, Development and Democracy: The IMF in Democratic South Africa," *Review of African Political Economy,* 62, pp. 485–493.

7. Meeting of the Parliamentary Select Committee on Foreign Affairs, 14 March 1995.

8. C. Landsberg, G. le Pere, and A. van Nieuwkerk, *Mission Imperfect: Redirecting South Africa's Foreign Policy* (Johannesburg: Foundation for Global Dialogue/Centre for Policy Studies).

9. C. Alden, "From Liberation Movement to Political Party: ANC Foreign Policy in Transition," *South African Journal of International Affairs,* 1(1), 1994, pp. 62–81.

10. "Prisoner of the Past? The New South Africa Abroad," *Southern African Report,* 10(5), 1995, pp. 7–10.

11. J. Barber and J. Barratt, *South Africa's Foreign Policy: The Search for Status and Security, 1945–1988* (Cambridge: Cambridge University Press, 1990), p. 213.

12. R. Southall, "The New South Africa in the New World Order: Beyond the Double Whammy," *Third World Quarterly,* 15(1), 1994, pp. 121–137.

13. Under the terms of the preelection negotiation process, the DFA was required to accept as foreign service officers some 140 (later reduced to 120) out of 300 people recommended by the ANC. Additionally, the DFA, whose full staff complement was 1,900, was required to cater for the absorption of a significant number of the 800 (sic!) "foreign service" staff of the four former "independent" homelands. During subsequent rationalization, the experience and qualifications of all staff were assessed and translated into appointments to actual positions, which the Public Service Commission allowed to increase by some 200 posts. The complete restructuring process has seen retrenchment of some 115 staff members—40 of them whites and the rest apparently from the former homelands. In the final analysis, this means that the weight in bodies of the ANC is considerably less than that of personnel from the old DFA and its satellites, although by the end of 1995, four out of the five deputy directors-general had been appointed from the

ranks of the liberation movement. See L. H. Evans, "Preventive Diplomacy in Lesotho and Mozambique," in J. Cilliers and G. Mills (eds.), *Peacekeeping in Africa*, Vol. 2 (Pretoria: Institute of Defence Policy and South African Institute of International Affairs, 1995), pp. 187–198; *Business Day* (Rosebank), 22 December 1995.

14. D. O'Meara, "South African Foreign Policy: What's the Problem?" *Southern African Report*, 11(2), 1996, pp. 25–27.

15. *Mail and Guardian* (Johannesburg), 23–29 February 1996.

16. *Sunday Independent*, 25 February 1996 and 2 March 1996.

17. *Daily Dispatch* (East London, South Africa), 5 April 1996.

18. *Mail and Guardian* (Johannesburg), 15–21 March 1996.

19. Kenneth Grundy, "Intermediary Power and Global Dependency: The Case of South Africa," *International Studies Quarterly*, 20(4), 1976.

20. Patrick McGowan, "The 'New' South Africa: Ascent or Descent in the World System?" *South African Journal of International Affairs*, 1(1), 1993, pp. 58–59.

21. *Sunday Times* (Saxonwold), 23 February 1997.

22. P.D.F. Strydom, "South Africa in World Trade," *South African Journal of Economics*, 55(3), 1987.

23. *Daily Dispatch* (East London, South Africa), 16 March 1996.

24. McGowan, "The 'New' South Africa," p. 57.

25. South African Institute of Race Relations, *Race Relations Survey 1994/5*, p. 395; *Mail and Guardian*(Johannesburg), 15–21 December 1995.

26. *Mail and Guardian* (Johannesburg), 15–21 December 1995.

27. Economist Intelligence Unit, *South Africa*, Country Report (London: Economist Intelligence Unit, 1995–1996), pp. 37–38.

28. *Sunday Independent*, 25 February 1996.

29. *Eastern Province Herald* (Port Elizabeth), 6 December 1995.

30. Ibid., and *Business Day* (Rosebank), 4 November 1996.

31. *Daily Dispatch* (East London, South Africa), 29 February and 25 March 1996; *Business Day* (Rosebank), 22 and 25 March 1996; *Sunday Independent*, 24 March 1996.

32. *Daily Dispatch* (East London, South Africa), 27 March 1996.

33. *Pretoria News*, 10 April 1995.

34. A. Guelke, "The European Union: A Most Important Trading Partner?" in G. Mills, A. Begg, and A. van Nieuwkerk (eds.), *South Africa in the Global Economy* (Johannesburg: South African Institute of International Affairs, 1995), p. 98.

35. *Daily Dispatch* (East London, South Africa), 25 February 1997.

36. P. Cross, "Negotiating a Comprehensive Long-Term Relationship Between South Africa and the European Union: From Free Trade to Trade and Development," Master's thesis, Department of Political Studies, Rhodes University, Grahamstown, South Africa, 1997.

37. *Business Day* (Rosebank), 5, 14, 22, and 28 March 1996.

38. *Neue Zuercher Zeitung*, 15 January 1997; *Daily Dispatch* (East London, South Africa), 12 February 1997.

39. *Business Day* (Rosebank), 22 March 1996.

40. *Sunday Independent*, 24 March 1996.

41. D. Geldenhuys, *South Africa and the China Question*, Working Paper 6, East Asia Project, Department of International Relations, University of the Witwatersrand, 1995.

42. *The Star* (Johannesburg), 19 August 1996.

43. J. Daniel, "One China or Two? South Africa's Foreign Policy Dilemma," Proceedings of the Conference: The Taiwan Experience. Johannesburg: Consulate-General of the Republic of China, pp. 157–175.

44. *Sunday Independent*, 10 March 1996.

45. Peter Vale, *Mail and Guardian* (Johannesburg), 6 February 1997.

46. Robert Keohane, "Cooperation and International Regimes," in R. Little and M. Smith (eds.), *Perspectives on World Politics* (London: Routledge, 1991).

47. *Daily Dispatch* (East London, South Africa), 24 February 1997.

48. *Mail and Guardian* (Johannesburg), 8–16 March 1996.

49. E. Serpa, "India and Africa," *Africa Insight*, 24(3), 1994.

50. P-H. Bischoff, "Opening Perspectives: Democratic South Africa and the States and Regimes of an Emergent Asia-Pacific," Department of Political Studies, Rhodes University, Grahamstown, South Africa, 1995.

51. *Business Day* (Rosebank), 2 April 1996.

52. A. Hirsch, "From GATT to the WTO: The Global Trade Regime and Its Implications for South Africa," in Mills, Begg, and van Nieuwkerk, *South Africa in the Global Economy*.

53. Ibid., p. 54.

54. Bischoff, *Democratic South Africa*; M. Shaker, "The 1995 NPT Conference: A New Beginning," *Disarmament*, 28(3).

55. *Mail and Guardian* (Johannesburg), 29 September–5 October 1995.

56. *Business Day* (Rosebank), 28 March 1996.

57. *Daily Dispatch* (East London, South Africa), 24 February 1997.

58. *Mail and Guardian* (Johannesburg), 29 September–5 October 1996.

59. R. Ajulu, "South Africa and the North/South: Pragmatism Versus principle." in C. Landsberg, G. le Pere, and A. van Nieuwkerk, *Mission Imperfect: Redirecting South Africa's Foreign Policy*.

60. *South Scan*, 16 July 1993.

61. R. Davies, ANC Member of Parliament, Address to Department of Trade and Industry Workshop on a SADC Protocol, 1995.

62. *Business Day* (Rosebank), 22 December 1995.

63. *Daily Dispatch* (East London, South Africa), 22 February 1996.

64. *Hansard, House of Assembly*, No. 4, 8–12 August 1994, p. 916.

65. *Daily Dispatch* (Rosebank), 16 November 1995; *Mail and Guardian* (Johannesburg), 17–23 November 1995.

66. *Mail and Guardian* (Johannesburg), 15–21 December 1995.

67. *Sunday Nation* (Nairobi), 14 January 1996.

68. *Sunday Independent*, 11 February 1996.

69. S. Baynham, "The Fourth Horseman of the Apocalypse: Drug Trafficking in South Africa," *Africa Insight*, 15(3), 1995.

70. J. Van der Westhuizen, "Can the Giant Be Gentle: Peace-Making as South African Foreign Policy," *Politikon*, 22(2), 1995.

71. A. Pahad, "South Africa and Preventive Diplomacy," in J. Cilliers and G. Mills, (eds.), *Peacekeeping in Africa*, Vol. 2 (Johannesburg: Institute of Defence Policy and South African Institute of International Affairs).

72. K. Matlosa, "The Military After the Election: Confronting the New Democracy," in R. Southall and T. Petlane (eds.), *Democratisation and Demilitarisation in Lesotho: The General Election of 1993 and Its Aftermath* (Pretoria: Africa Institute).

73. L. H. Evans, "Preventive Diplomacy in Lesotho and Mozambique," in J. Cilliers and G. Mills (eds.), *Peacekeeping in Africa*.

74. *Mail and Guardian* (Johannesburg), 22–28 March 1996.

75. Federation for Global Dialogue, *Global Dialogue*, 1(1), 1996.

76. *Mail and Guardian* (Johannesburg), 16–21 December 1995.

77. *Mail and Guardian* (Johannesburg), 23–29 February 1996.

10

The Foreign Policy of Tanzania: From Cold War to Post–Cold War

MARIA NZOMO

Even as scholarly perspectives shift to studying the post–Cold War era of globalization, conditionalities, and the emergence of new issues shaping the foreign policies of African states, it should be underscored that this "newest" era is not entirely novel. The role played by the international financial institutions, such as the World Bank and International Monetary Fund, is hardly new. Structural adjustment programs of the 1980s and 1990s and the accompanying conditionalities are part of a long trend of policies imposed upon Africa, often with disastrous results.

The struggles for democratization of political economy and society are also not entirely new phenomena. Internal pressures for democratic reforms were evident long before the global popularization of democracy and human rights was triggered by events in Eastern Europe at the end of the 1980s. What is new, perhaps, is the external pressure for democratization that has become an important aspect of IFI and donor political conditionalities. Because of this, the focus of foreign relations has shifted away from diplomacy and ideological posturing to economic restructuring and globalization.

Against this background, this chapter attempts to reconstruct and reinterpret Tanzania's foreign policy. Although specific issues have changed over time, it is argued that the basic structural conditions and factors that have shaped foreign policy since independence in 1961 have not fundamentally altered. These resilient factors are primarily (1) the colonial legacy, (2) idiosyncratic variables, and (3) the phenomena of economic underdevelopment and external dependence. The basic socioeconomic and political conditions that have influenced foreign policy are examined first, followed by a discussion of trends and changes that have evolved over time.

Colonial Legacy and Foreign Policy

In Tanzania, as elsewhere on the continent, the social, economic, and political structures inherited from colonialism continue to influence the making and implementation of domestic and foreign policy. Tanzania inherited from the colonizers (Germany and Britain) an export-oriented economy geared primarily to the production of a narrow range of primary commodities (coffee, cotton, sisal, and pyrethrum); little concern was given to subsistence production.

Perhaps because of its mixed colonial history, as well as its poor soils and difficult climate, Tanzania turned out to be one of the worst cases of colonial neglect. Only minimal attention was given to the development of productive social forces, such as a commercial class, skilled personnel, and physical infrastructure (transportation, communication, health, education, and urban facilities).[1] At independence, one of the striking features of Tanzania's new government and bureaucracy was the shortage of indigenous technical, managerial, and administrative cadres, which had important implications for postcolonial governance.

At the political level, the colonial state bequeathed highly undemocratic and authoritarian structures of governance. Indigenous organizations had been outlawed until almost the eve of independence, and elections were only held thirty-three months before independence and then not on the basis of universal franchise. Consequently, the political culture inherited from colonialism had all the ingredients of autocracy. This culture was perfected by the postcolonial state, with significant implications for foreign policy, especially in facilitating the dominant role of the president.

Tanzania emerged at independence with weak social and political institutions and with an equally weak, underdeveloped economy. That economy was highly dependent on foreign exchange earned from a few primary commodities whose prices have been, for the most part, on the decline since independence, whereas the costs of manufactured commodities have consistently been on the rise. Consequently, economic and technological dependence on the outside world has largely shaped foreign economic and political relations.

The lack of well-developed class interests and pressure groups and, to some extent, the absence of ethnic and religious tensions at independence provided a rare opportunity for consolidating power and gave President Julius Nyerere a relatively free hand to shape and direct development and foreign policies without being constrained by competing interests.

The Nyerere Factor in Foreign Policy

Although Nyerere's dominant role has been widely acknowledged, there are some who argue that he was only one of several actors in foreign policy, including government ministries, parliament, and the ruling party, Chama cha Mapinduzi (CCM).[2] It is my argument, however, that government and party functions centered upon the president, at least until 1984 when the constitution was amended to provide for separate heads of government and ruling party. Indeed, in Tanzania as elsewhere in Africa, the colonially inherited state-centric and authoritarian political culture ensured that the president and/or the head of state shaped the country's foreign policy objectives, approaches, and strategies. Nyerere's personal philosophy, ideology, principles, and changing perceptions of the domestic and global environments were largely manifested in Tanzania's foreign policy posture for nearly twenty-five years.

Nyerere's dominant role in foreign policy also derived from his charismatic personality and from the circumstances in which he found himself at Tanzania's formal independence, for few others at that time had sufficient knowledge or interest in foreign affairs to influence or contribute to foreign policymaking.[3] Nyerere's initial prominence in foreign affairs was soon augmented by authoritarian and repressive tendencies that were clearly manifested in various policy actions taken between 1964 and 1977. These involved the suppression of critics within the government and the co-optation and elimination of potential sources of political opposition, from civil society groups to opposition political parties.[4] These actions effectively removed alternative actors that could have contributed to foreign policy. Instead, the president's monopoly over policymaking and implementation enabled him, if he so wished, to resist or ignore constraints, domestic and international, and to assert autonomous policies and strategies.[5]

The same colonial legacy that propelled Nyerere to prominence in foreign affairs was also marked by underdevelopment and external dependency, which severely limited the country's choices and its capacity to translate desired foreign policy objectives into practice.

Development and Foreign Relations: 1961–1985

The foreign policy guidelines spelled out by Nyerere in December 1961 remain in force today, although the emphasis and focus have shifted and changed. Between 1961 and 1966, Nyerere naively assumed that Tanzania could pursue its domestic and foreign policy objectives without offending vested interests in the international system. It was wrongly assumed that objectives could be advanced through appeals to reason and humanitarian sentiments alone, without recourse to material or military resources.

This attitude was reinforced by an equally misconceived view that Western donors would be willing to finance up to 78 percent of Tanzania's First Five Year Development Plan and that the procurement of external resources would promote economic growth and/or development within the framework of inherited colonial structures.

Events, both external and internal, in 1964 and 1965 compelled Nyerere to change his perceptions and expectations of the international environment. By 1967, he had come to realize (1) that Tanzania had little influence in international affairs, and (2) that Western "allies," such as Britain and the United States, felt no moral obligation to assist Tanzanian development and foreign policy objectives but wanted to keep Tanzania within their sphere of influence. The major events that triggered this realization included Tanzania's army mutiny, conflict with the United States over expelled diplomats, conflict with West Germany over the "Hallstein doctrine," the Congo crisis, and conflict with Britain over Rhodesia's unilateral declaration of independence (UDI). All these events, well documented elsewhere,[6] basically demonstrated Tanzania's naïveté and powerlessness globally, as well as Nyerere's determination to defend nonalignment and contribute to Africa's liberation.

The government came to realize that repression had to be balanced by some degree of economic growth and that a popular ideology was needed to at least temporarily persuade the disgruntled and impoverished masses that development was taking place, albeit slowly. Some version of "African socialism" that could serve as a unifying ideology had to be devised, and this came in the form of the 1967 Arusha Declaration.[7]

It was the Arusha Declaration, rather than formal independence, that marked the beginning of change in relations with the global political economy. By 1970, Tanzania had significantly diversified its trade and aid links *within* the Western bloc but only marginally outside it. By 1974, a clear preference had emerged regarding the countries from whom assistance should be obtained: These included China, the Scandinavian countries, and Canada, all of which were perceived to be sympathetic to Tanzania's developmental and foreign policy goals and to lack interventionist tendencies. This diversification and other post-Arusha policies may have enhanced the range of choices in development and foreign policy matters and minimized the chance of sabotage by a single donor. But they did not increase effectiveness in implementing chosen goals. Tanzania's relative powerlessness and peripheral position in the global context persisted and was only exacerbated by other crises in the 1970s and 1980s.

These crises included the 1971 coup in Uganda that brought Idi Amin to power and the intensification of liberation wars in Southern Africa, which contributed to Tanzania's economic woes and brought the question of security to the forefront of national and foreign policies—hence, the increased defense expenditure after 1970 and the introduction of a peoples' militia in 1971. The superpowers' military buildup in the Indian Ocean compounded the question of security and pushed Tanzania toward a more activist nonalignment policy.

The 1973–1974 oil crisis also negatively impacted Tanzania, as it did other developing states, by widening the economic gap with industrialized countries. This led to a demand for a fundamental restructuring of the postwar Bretton Woods order. The 1974 UN declaration calling for the establishment of a New International Economic Order marked the beginning of the North-South dialogue for a more equitable order. Tanzania played an active and leading role in lobbying for NIEO, but North-South dialogues did not produce the expected results. Moreover, the alternative proposed by Nyerere and other Third World leaders, namely, the formation of a South-South "Trade Union of the Poor," also did not succeed.

In general, however, Tanzania had, by the 1970s, become less dogmatic and more pragmatic in its pursuit of principles, and it had learned to utilize nonalignment to access development resources from both Cold War blocs. The conception of nonalignment in economic rather than political terms represented an attempt to adapt policy to the changed international system, an adaptation that gradually became accepted by most leaders in the nonaligned movement.[8]

While nonalignment took center stage, the major issues that preoccupied the leadership in the first two decades after Tanzanian independence essentially revolved around the security of the regime and/or state, domestic political "stability," and the search for economic development and growth. Early diplomacy placed a higher premium on political independence than on economic assistance.

Foreign Relations in East and Southern Africa: 1961–1985

At the regional level, Tanzania pursued a policy of good neighborliness and promoted cooperation, liberation, and decolonization. Nyerere's activism and leading role in the OAU was generally accepted. He served as a chairman of the OAU, and Tanzania was the headquarters of the OAU Liberation Committee. With the formation of the Front-Line States in 1975, of which Nyerere became the first chair, Tanzania became active in the liberation of Southern Africa.

Tanzania was also instrumental in the creation of the Southern African Development Coordination Conference, having hosted the 1979 meeting where SADCC was negotiated. SADCC signified a shift away from a total focus on the liberation struggle toward a preoccupation with economic empowerment. Consequently, SADCC members gradually reduced the tempo and rhetoric about liberation, and they became more pragmatic in order to cope with rising domestic pressures for liberalization, democratization, and debt reduction. This, combined with Nyerere's departure, contributed to Tanzania's waning role in Southern Africa from the mid-1980s. Other critical factors were worsening economic crises, IFI demands for the implementation of SAPs, and the Reagan administration's rejection of Tanzania's leadership role in Southern Africa.[9]

Tanzania's relations with Kenya and Uganda went through several cycles of conflict and cooperation, despite the declared policy of good neighborliness. Since independence, the three East African countries have recognized the need for regional integration, but ideological and personal differences, the colonial legacy of economic inequalities between them, and external interference in their affairs have bedeviled all efforts toward economic integration and peaceful coexistence.

During the existence of the East African Community between 1967 and 1977, economic, ideological, and personality differences among the leaders made the community unworkable. Both Tanzania and Uganda felt that Kenya was unfairly benefiting from the EAC. The coming to power of Idi Amin in 1971 compounded the problem, as Nyerere swore that he would never meet with the Ugandan leader.

The closure of the border between Tanzania and Kenya following the collapse of EAC in 1977 forced both countries to look elsewhere for economic and political cooperation. Tanzania turned even more southward. However, Nyerere still had to deal with Amin, whose army invaded and occupied part of Tanzania in October 1978 and declared it to be Ugandan. Nyerere promptly declared war and kept Tanzanian troops in Uganda until after Amin was overthrown and an alternative government was established. This military venture lasted for six years at an exorbitant cost to Tanzania, estimated at over $500 million.[10]

Amin's removal ultimately contributed to improved relations with Uganda and Kenya, as did the death of President Kenyatta in 1978. Tanzania was also in serious economic straits and simply could not afford to keep the border closed. Furthermore, IFIs had made the reopening of the border a condition for further economic assistance to Tanzania. Thus, in November 1983, an agreement was reached between Kenya, Tanzania, and Uganda on the distribution of assets and liabilities of the defunct EAC. The common border was reopened, and bilateral relations were normalized.

Political Economy of Foreign Policy: 1985–1998

Over the years, Nyerere had developed a knack for sensing the right time to change course in national and international affairs. Perceiving himself to be a major obstacle to economic liberalization, he opted to retire in

1985. However, at President Ali Hassan Mwinyi's request, Nyerere retained his powerful post as chairman of CCM, to which he was reelected for a further five-year term in 1987. Recognizing that his presence as chairman of the country's sole party could compromise debate and delay the transition to multipartyism, Nyerere relinquished his post in June 1990, halfway through his new term, shortly after initiating the debate on multipartyism in February 1990.

The transition from Nyerere to Mwinyi had its own dynamics not only because of the idiosyncratic differences of the leaders but also because it coincided with other domestic changes, as well as shifts in regional and global political economies. Therefore, there has been debate as to whether Nyerere's departure brought real change in development and foreign relations. Some have argued that it did, whereas others contend that the changes, if any, have been superficial at best. Mwinyi himself subscribed to this latter view when he stated: "We are just carrying on from where [Nyerere] left off, because after all, I don't think my government can reverse party policies. . . . There is no change whatsoever. There may be changes in style, but no change in policy matters."[11]

The CCM party program drawn up in 1987 did, however, shift the emphasis from political to economic development as a priority area of foreign policy. The party noted that although Nyerere's government had succeeded in laying a strong political foundation, the economic aspect had remained weak and should become the major focus in foreign policy: "A weak national economy is detrimental to a country's foreign policy, since it leads to failure by the country to make independent decisions and hence failing to achieve its aims in foreign policy. It is for this reason, therefore, that CCM has to see to it that national investments during this period are aimed at strengthening national economy for a stronger foreign policy."[12]

One indication of this shift has been the cutback in the number and size of foreign missions since 1992. Out of Tanzania's twenty-eight foreign embassies and high commissions in 1992, at least six had been closed by 1995, and the number of personnel in the remaining offices was reduced.[13]

It was not until 1994 that the Ministry of Foreign Affairs formally undertook a review of foreign policy in the light of post–Cold War developments. Mwinyi, who participated in the May 1994 foreign policy review workshop, noted in his opening statement that the "new" foreign policy must take into account new issues, new actors, and a radically changed external environment. In regard to new actors, he stated that "as we go forward into the next century, a realistic foreign policy for our country must be one that is broad-based; one that is not the preserve of a few mysterious diplomats but one that truly seeks to take into account the interests of all the sectors of the nation."[14]

Concerning new issues in a changed environment, he noted:

> We are heading for the 21st century in an amoral pursuit of national interests . . . back to the era of "realpolitik" where big powers pursue their security and commercial interests abroad with renewed vigor, characterised by double standards and hypocrisy. . . . We have no option but to take into account this emerging phenomena on the international scene, and to reorient our foreign policy accordingly. . . . Beyond the core interests of survival and sovereignty, we have to put emphasis on the promotion and protection of our commercial interests abroad. . . . We can only enter the 21st century as a respectable state, with some influence on the international scene, if we improve the socio-economic situation in our country.[15]

The transition from Nyerere to Mwinyi occurred during a challenging period. The implementation of the Economic Recovery Program (ERP), adopted in 1986 as part of SAP implementation, resulted in some improvement in food production; industrial output increased by 4.2 percent in 1987 and by 5.4 percent in 1988; and the rate of inflation declined from 43 percent before the ERP to an average of 23 percent in 1989. Furthermore, GDP improved from its negative trend and grew by 4.1 percent in 1989.[16]

But the Mwinyi regime employed an autocratic style of governance and resisted power sharing and popular participation. Despite the reintroduction of multipartyism in 1992, the incumbent and still undemocratic state continued to control the democratic transition—albeit ineffectively. The transitional government seemed determined to control the pace and direction of political change and ensure CCM's electoral victory: "CCM will not agree to supervise the loss of its 30 year grip on power and has therefore decided to be member of team, captain, referee and linesman all in one."[17] The more than a dozen opposition parties initially threatened to boycott the elections, but they ultimately participated in October 1995 despite the government's refusal to respond to their electoral demands.

The political landscape did begin to change in March 1995 when former cabinet member Augustine Mrema, whom Mwinyi had sacked in February 1995 for criticizing government corruption, defected to a major opposition party—NCCR Mageuzi (National Convention for Construction and Reform). He soon became the party chair and a presidential candidate. Mrema, a populist and a crowd puller, significantly tilted the political balance in favor of the opposition parties.[18] Meanwhile, Nyerere, who had criticized governmental corruption in his 1994 book *Uongozi na Hatima ya Tanzania (Our Leadership and the Future of Tanzania)*, made another scathing attack on the corruption in Mwinyi's government that echoed the sentiments expressed by Mrema.

Corroborating Nyerere's concern, the March 1995 economic report of the Bank of Tanzania indicated that the economy continued to decline. Inflation was up to 42 percent in March 1995, and the government lacked revenue due to widespread tax exemptions, rampant evasions, and improper monitoring of external trade transactions.[19] Furthermore, at the time, CCM was split on the issue of its presidential candidate, with Nyerere and Mwinyi having different preferences. Nyerere finally prevailed with the nomination of Benjamin Mkapa,[20] who went on to win the presidential election at the end of 1995.

Adjustment, Globalization, and the Post–Cold War Era: 1980–1998

Tanzania has had to adjust to global economic changes since the 1980s, including the rising debt burden and the conditionalities of IFIs. During the 1960s and 1970s, it had acquired a status beyond its meager resources and capability. Tanzania exploited nonalignment to attract economic resources from both Cold War blocs, but the resources procured were increasingly inadequate—hence the search for additional resources from the IMF and World Bank. Nyerere viewed IFI conditionalities as an insult and as another conspiracy by international capitalism to undermine sovereignty and nonalignment. Consequently, between 1980 and 1985, Tanzania played cat-and-mouse games with IFIs, while remaining basically intransigent on SAPs. In the meantime, the country's economy continued to deteriorate.[21] The breakthrough in this economic standoff came shortly after Nyerere's resignation.[22] Mwinyi appeared more pragmatic and less idealistic, and he agreed to the conditionalities implemented through the 1986 ERP.

The point to be underscored here is that Tanzania continued to be structurally dependent on the international capitalist system, having very little power to influence events or resist conditionalities. It continued its nonaligned posture, but it became more preoccupied with economic relations with bilateral and multilateral donors. It also adopted a low-profile and nonconfrontational approach to most issues—a stance that was somewhat similar to Kenya's "quiet diplomacy" of the 1960s and 1970s (see Chapter 6). Even in the absence of SAPs and economic crisis, Tanzania's external role was bound to diminish with the attainment of Southern African liberation and the end of the Cold War. Thus, by 1990, there was no international conflict about which it could be nonaligned, and external actors proved more interested in enforcing liberalization than in global diplomatic posturing.

Democratic pluralism was as much a response to domestic pressures as it was a reaction to external pressure from international donor countries and institutions. Although the government conceded to multipartyism, the state continued to demonstrate a reluctance to democratize the institutions of governance and to facilitate fair elections. Today, donors and many Tanzanians alike continue to be concerned with the rampant misuse of the state machinery for the personal acquisition of wealth by leading members of the political elite and their families. In 1991, Sweden, one of the major aid donors, reduced its assistance to $10 million to protest the corruption and inadequate accountability in the civil service.[23] Other donors have since taken the cue from Sweden and have, during various periods since 1993, held back economic aid. In November 1994, for example, Norway withheld $35 million in balance-of-payments aid amid reports that over a one-year period, the Tanzanian government had mysteriously lost $125 million.[24] After Mkapa came to office, IMF credits did begin again, and a November 1996 investors' forum produced plans for $786 million of projects.

At the regional level, much of Tanzania's preoccupation with Kenya and Uganda has focused on another attempt at integration, essentially to resuscitate the defunct EAC in a transformed format. In 1987, the Tripartite Commission was established to coordinate cooperation and integration in transport and communications, scientific research, and commerce and industry. After a series of meetings between government officials, the presidents finally signed an agreement expressing the intention to establish a community. This was followed in November 1994 by the establishment of the Permanent Tripartite Commission on East African Cooperation, whose headquarters were to be in Arusha, Tanzania. The commission took off slowly, each country blaming the others for the delay, but increasingly, Tanzania and Uganda bonded together against Kenya.

Impediments to integration include the presidents' idiosyncratic differences, which worsened in 1995 as Kenyan president Moi and Ugandan president Museveni traded accusations supporting each other's dissidents. Another factor has been Ugandan and Tanzanian participation, since March 1995, in a joint venture with South Africa to form a regional airline. Kenya views this as backtracking on protocols related to civil aviation cooperation and the emergence of a joint East African airline.[25]

It could also be argued that these countries are biting off more than they can chew in their involvement with competing integration initiatives, including SADC, COMESA, the East African Tripartite Commission, and, at the continental level, the AEC. The region, which has lacked the capacity to manage and sustain even one grouping, may benefit more from a single large common market than many smaller groupings. An important precondition for integration is democracy, ensuring that the principal participants are "people" and not politicians. According to M. Nyirabu: "African economic cooperation is a long term matter. The principal agents of such a long term project ought not to be politicians, lest it be trivialised and overshadowed by their mundane culture, ceremonial, whiny rhetoric, manipulation, intrigue, etc. . . . When conflict breaks out between two or more African political leaders, one of the areas that suffer is economic cooperation."[26]

This view echoes the sentiments expressed by Mwinyi on the signing of the Tripartite Agreement: "The People of East Africa had always been ahead of the leadership . . . even animals and fish cooperate while political leadership continued to delay cooperation.[27] The fact is that all three countries are operating under the dictates of IFIs that stress single-country economic policies, often incongruent with regional integration. Consequently, attempts toward integration under present structural conditions will entail high costs for implementation and enforcement, and they will have a high risk of failure.

Tanzania has a serious problem with refugees from war-torn Rwanda and Burundi. The influx of 700,000 refugees in 1995, for example, caused severe economic and security problems. Some Tanzanian MPs suggested that Tanzania should simply annex Rwanda and Burundi, since the two were historically part of Tanganyika. This idea came in the wake of Ali Mazrui's "recolonization theory" for beleaguered states,[28] and it does not appear to have the support of government, which also must resolve the problematic question of union between Tanganyika and Zanzibar.[29]

Tanzania's diminished role in Southern Africa has been manifested in a number of ways. For instance, it had only a marginal role in the negotiations leading to Namibia's independence in 1990. It also succumbed to IMF pressure and recalled 3,000 troops sent to Mozambique after 1986 to support the government against the South African–supported Mozambique National Resistance (MNR) rebel forces. Furthermore, between 1990 and 1993, South African liberation movements based in Dar es Salaam were relocated to South Africa. Finally, the elections in South Africa in April 1994 marked the end of Tanzania's active involvement in the liberation of Southern Africa. Tanzania remains active in SADC, but it is increasingly redirecting its attention toward its East African neighbors.

New Issues and Actors in Tanzania's Foreign Relations

The state has long ceased to be the only actor in international relations. Many interactions are now carried out by nonstate actors, mainly intergovernmental organizations (IGOs), nongovernmental organizations, and multinational corporations. These have been joined in the post–Cold War era by additional nonstate actors, and new issues, including democracy, human rights, gender, drug trafficking, and corruption, have come to the fore.

NGOs are now said to have their own foreign policies. Timothy Shaw has argued that the state's role in foreign relations will continue to shrink and that foreign relations will increasingly include nonstate actors.[30] Shaw further projects that the external relations of African states may be more and more limited to SAP negotiations. But even in regard to SAPs, the state has lost its power to the World Bank and the IMF, which not only control local currencies and macroeconomic policies but also determine foreign policy to a greater extent that in the past. The indebted African state is left with little more than responsibility for judicial functions and the maintenance of public order.[31]

The preceding arguments notwithstanding, in most African countries, as in Tanzania, the resilience of the state and its determination to control and manage change remains phenomenal. Indeed, many setbacks and reversals in countries that have returned to pluralism precisely reflect the resilience of the authoritarian and unyielding state. This persistence suggests (1) that it is not enough for the state to withdraw from the economy and to legalize political parties without democratizing the entire system of governance and (2) that the emergent civil society is not yet strong enough to prevail upon the state to govern democratically.[32]

The hope inherent in democratization has given rise to a resurgence of civil society, best manifested by the mushrooming of NGOs, women's groups, youth groups, religious groups, and professional organizations involved in promoting human rights and democracy. These groups seek to redefine their role in the emerging order, devise novel strategies of social struggle, augment popular participation, and assert local control over the seemingly remote forces of globalization.[33] The emerging NGOs also seek to improve the lives of those people who otherwise would not benefit from government programs.[34]

Part of this NGO phenomenon in Tanzania has been manifested in the global expansion of the women's movement and specifically women's human rights and empowerment NGOs, whose voices can no longer be ignored at international conferences.[35] A case in point is the fourth women's global conference, held in Beijing in September 1995. The conference brought together over 50,000 female representatives from around the world, displaying women's increasing presence as actors in global affairs. Today, women are actively lobbying and negotiating with key international actors, including donor agencies, IFIs, UN agencies, the Vatican, heads of state, and governments. The infiltration of women into the previously male-dominated international scene has given credence to gender as an important element of international relations and diplomacy.[36] More broadly, there is need to restructure the new international division of power and labor that to date has contributed to disempowerment and marginalization of the female gender in private and public life.[37]

The return to pluralism has at least created some political space for articulating gender interests and lobbying for gender-sensitive democratic development and foreign relations.[38] Until the mid-1980s, Tanzanian women had only marginally participated in this kind of activism, despite the UN women's decade. The situation has changed significantly since 1992. With the reemergence and redynamization of civil society groups, new forms of women's organizations are emerging.[39] They seek to transcend class, religious, racial, ethnic, and other social divides and focus on issues that unite, such as the impact of SAPs on women, gender violence, and women's marginalization in strategic decisionmaking positions. An example of these new forms of organization is the national women's NGO known as Baraza Ya Wanawake wa Tanzania (BAWATA), launched in May 1995 to coordinate and promote women's rights in the emerging democratic environment. Although it is still too early to predict its performance, it would seem that BAWATA has the potential to galvanize Tanzanian women to become influential actors in future development and foreign relations.

Pluralism has also energized a number of longer-established women's organizations, such as the Tanzania Media Women's Association (TAMWA), Tanzania Gender Networking Programme (TGNP), Tanzanian Women's Lawyers Association, and university women research groups. At a global level, Tanzanian women have already made an impact: For example, Gertrude Mongella served as the Tanzanian secretary-general for the 1995 Women's Beijing conference. As international donors become disenchanted with the Tanzanian state, they are increasingly turning to women NGOs as more reliable actors for promoting development and democracy. This new partnership puts women among the most significant "new" actors in Tanzania's foreign relations.

Drug trafficking is another security issue that has acquired prominence. Some argue that drug trafficking, along with the spread of AIDS, has resulted from the increase in poverty globally and more so in the South. Drug trafficking became a concern in Tanzania only in the early 1990s after the arrangement whereby drugs were smuggled into Western Europe and North America via Eastern Europe collapsed with communism. Tanzania, with its coastal capital of Dar es Salaam and an apparent lack of drug-detection equipment, was an attractive new transit route for narcotics traffickers. Consequently, Tanzania became a major transit route, playing a role comparable to other drug centers such as Nigeria, Kenya, and South Africa.

Corruption, like drug trafficking, is a global phenomenon that reflects the failure of states to meet social demands and control social action and crime. Unbridled corruption can become a major obstacle to democratic development and international transactions, as it discourages foreign investment and creates political instability and insecurity. In Tanzania, corruption gained recognition as an issue of concern only in the 1990s, partly due to the anticorruption campaign spearheaded by Nyerere. The government's immediate response was to take action against key officials accused of corruption in Nyerere's 1994 book.[40] However, international donors appeared unimpressed with Tanzania's official action.

Conclusion

This chapter has examined, reconstructed, and reinterpreted the trends in Tanzania's foreign relations and diplomacy since independence. Foreign policy has been located within a global political economy that has, for the most part, influenced choices and constrained the attainment of desired goals. Until the mid-1980s, there were more continuities than discontinuities in that policy, but with the emergence of the NIDL and NIDP in the post–Cold War era, Tanzania, like most other African states, has been forced to rethink its foreign policy. Earlier, the focus was on defense and nonalignment, but in the post–Cold War era, such posturing has ceased to be relevant, as has nonalignment itself.

Before the end of the Cold War, Tanzania had developed an inflated international status built around its commitment to nonalignment and its leadership of the NAM, the Group of 77, and the North-South lobby. But it found itself without these portfolios in the post–Cold War era. Tanzania's loss in international status coincided with a similar decline in its status within Africa, especially in regard to its leadership in FLS and the African liberation movement.

By 1998, the focus of Tanzania's foreign relations had shifted. Under President Mkapa, rhetoric and a preoccupation with diplomacy were supplanted by a more pragmatic emphasis on economic survival under the weight of debt, SAPs, NIDL, and NIDP.[41] The current tendency is toward strengthening national economic structures and resources and building regional economic alliances in Southern and Eastern Africa. Furthermore, although the traditional issues of security and sovereignty remain fundamental pillars of foreign relations (including increasing secessionist pressures within Zanzibar), they have been redefined so that security concerns are less militaristic and more focused on food security, drug trafficking, refugees, migration, and ecology.

Economic and political liberalization have generated new issues and actors, notably NGOs. Corporatism that had prevailed for over thirty years has weakened considerably, but authoritarian structures of governance remain in place. In the meantime, a civil society that had been muzzled is finally reasserting itself by consolidating organizational structures and strengthening capacities. In particular, since 1994, the dynamic and

flourishing independent media have kept up the pressure for change by
forcing transparency and accountability in governance, thereby contributing to the empowerment of other sectors of the civil society. And as
international donors become disenchanted with the Tanzanian state as a
reliable partner, they are increasingly enhancing partnerships with development and human rights NGOs.

As the twenty-first century approaches, sustainable and viable foreign
relations for Tanzania and other countries in the South are unlikely to develop without a strong and empowered civil society. In this regard, there
is hope yet for Tanzania.

NOTES

1. Brian Cooksey, David Court, and Ben Makav, "Education for Self-Reliance
and Harambee," in J. D. Barkan (ed.), *Beyond Capitalism vs. Socialism in Kenya and
Tanzania* (Boulder: Lynne Rienner, 1994), pp. 201–233.

2. K. Matthews and S. Mushi (eds.), *Foreign Policy of Tanzania: A Reader* (Dar es
Salaam: Tanzania Publishing House, 1981), pp. 3–23, and M. Hodd (ed.), *Tanzania
After Nyerere* (London: Pinter, 1988).

3. O. Nnoli, *Self-Reliance and Foreign Policy in Tanzania: The Dynamics of the Diplomacy of a New State, 1961–1971* (New York: NOK, 1978), p. 35.

4. G. K. Munishi, "Politics and Competition at the Crossroads of Liberalization
and Democratic Transition in Tanzania," paper presented at the First Regional
Conference on Law, Politics and Multiparty Democracy in East Africa, Dar es
Salaam, October 1993; R. F. Hopkins, *Political Roles in a New State: Tanzania's First
Decade* (New Haven: Yale University Press, 1971); and Nnoli, *Self-Reliance and For-
eign Policy in Tanzania.*

5. Jon Kraus, "The Political Economy of African Foreign Policies: Marginality
and Dependency, Realism and Choice," in Timothy M. Shaw and Julius Emeka
Okolo (eds.), *The Political Economy of Foreign Policy in ECOWAS* (London: Macmillan, 1994), p. 262.

6. Maria Nzomo, "Foreign Policy of Kenya and Tanzania: The Impact of Dependence and Underdevelopment," Ph.D. dissertation, Dalhousie University,
Canada, 1991; Matthews and Mushi, *Foreign Policy of Tanzania*; Nnoli, *Self-Reliance
and Foreign Policy in Tanzania.*

7. C. Pratt, *The Critical Phase in Tanzania, 1945–1968* (Cambridge: Cambridge
University Press, 1976), p. 28.

8. Julius Nyerere, *Freedom and Development* (Dar es Salaam: Oxford University
Press, 1973), and Matthews and Mushi, *Foreign Policy of Tanzania*, pp. 219–266.

9. A. H. Omari, "The Rise and Decline of the Front-Line States (FLS) Alliance in
Southern Africa: 1975–1990," Ph.D. dissertation, Dalhousie University, Canada,
1991.

10. D. F. Gordon, "International Economic Relations, Regional Cooperation and
Foreign Policy," in Barkan (ed)., *Beyond Capitalism vs. Socialism in Kenya and Tanzania*, p. 246.

11. *Africa Report*, 33, January-February 1988, p. 27. For these discussions, see Hodd, *Tanzania After Nyerere*.

12. Chama cha Mapinduzi, "CCM Party Programme: 1987–2001," Dodoma, 1987, p. 99.

13. Information obtained from the 1992 Tanzania Diplomatic List and from an interview with a Tanzanian official, Nairobi, June 1995.

14. H. A. Mwinyi, "Official Opening Statement of the National Foreign Policy Review Workshop," Zanzibar, 12 May 1994, p. 5.

15. Ibid., p. 6.

16. *Africa Report*, September-October 1990, pp. 26–27.

17. *The East African*, 12–18 June 1995, p. 9.

18. *The East African*, 13–19 March 1995, p. 1.

19. *The East African*, 1–7 May 1995, pp. 1 and 3.

20. *The Weekly Review* (Nairobi), 28 July 1995, p. 28.

21. W. Biermann and J. H. Wagao, "The IMF and Economic Policy in Tanzania: 1980–84," *Journal of African Studies*, 14(3), Fall 1987, pp. 118–126.

22. D. L. Horne, "Passing the Baton: The Presidential Legacy of Julius K. Nyerere," *Journal of African Studies*, 14(3), 1987, pp. 89–94; B. L. Obichere, "Tanzania at the Crossroads: From Nyerere to Mwinyi," *Journal of African Studies*, 14(3), 1987, pp. 84–88.

23. B. Sorokin, "End of an Affair," *Africa Events*, January 1992, pp. 22–23.

24. *The East African*, 20–26 February 1995.

25. *The East African*, 27 February–5 March 1995, pp. 5 and 19.

26. M. Nyirabu, "East African Cooperation: A Path Strewn with Obstacles," paper presented at the Foreign Policy Review Workshop, Zanzibar, May 1994.

27. Mwinyi, "Official Opening Statement," p. 14.

28. *Sunday Nation* (Nairobi), 5 February 1995, p. 7.

29. A. Jumbe, *The Partnership: Tanganyika Zanzibar Union: 30 Turbulent Years* (Dar es Salaam: Amana Publishers, 1994).

30. Timothy M. Shaw, "Globalisation, Regionalism and the South in the 1990s: Towards a New Political Economy of Development," paper presented at the International Political Science Association conference, Berlin, August 1994.

31. Adebayo Adedeji (ed.), *Africa Within the World: Beyond Dispossession and Dependence* (London: Zed, 1993).

32. John Harbeson and Donald Rothchild (eds.), *Africa in World Politics* (Boulder: Westview Press, 1995); John Harbeson, Donald Rothchild, and Naomi Chazan (eds.), *Civil Society and the State in Africa* (Boulder: Lynne Rienner, 1994).

33. James Mittelman, "The End of a Millennium: Changing Structures of World Order and the Post Cold War Division of Labour," in Larry Swatuk and Timothy Shaw (eds.), *The South at the End of the Twentieth Century* (London: Macmillan, 1994), pp. 15–27.

34. Julius Nyang'oro, "Reflections on the State, Democracy and NGOs in Africa," in Swatuk and Shaw (eds.), *The South at the End of the Twentieth Century*, pp. 130–137.

35. J. Peters and A. Wolper (eds.), *Women's Rights, Human Rights: International Feminist Perspectives* (New York: Routledge, 1995).

36. H. Pietila and J. Vickers, *Making Women Matter: The Role of the United Nations* (London: Zed, 1994); N. Funk and G. Mueller (eds.), *Gender Politics and Post Com-*

munism: Reflections from Eastern Europe and the Former Soviet Union (London: Routledge, 1993); "Feminists Write International Relations," *Alternatives*, Special Issue, 18(1), Winter 1993; R. Grant and U. Newland (eds.), *Gender and International Relations* (Buckingham, England: Open University Press, 1991).

37. P. Sparr (ed.), *Mortgaging Women's Lives: Feminist Critiques of SAPs* (London: Zed, 1994); United Nations, *Women in Politics and Public Decision-Making in the Late Twentieth Century* (New York: United Nations, 1994); Maria Nzomo, "Beyond Structural Adjustment Programs: Democracy, Gender Equity and Development in Africa," in Julius Nyang'oro and Timothy Shaw (eds.), *Beyond Structural Adjustment in Africa: The Political Economy of Sustainable Democratic Development* (New York: Praeger, 1992); L. Beneria and S. Feldman (eds.), *Unequal Burden: Economic Crises, Persistent Poverty, and Women's Work* (Boulder: Westview Press, 1992).

38. Maria Nzomo and M. Halfani, *Toward a Reconstruction of State-Society Relations: Democracy and Human Rights in Tanzania* (Montreal: International Centre for Human Rights and Democratic Development, 1995); Maria Nzomo, "Women in Politics and Public Decision Making," in Ulf Himmelstrand et al. (eds.), *In Search of a New Paradigm for the Study of African Development* (London: James Currey, 1994).

39. R. Meena, "Do Women Have an Agenda in the Democratisation Process?" paper presented at a TGNP Gender and Development Series, Dar es Salaam, July 1994.

40. *The East African*, 6–12 March 1995.

41. Harvey Glickman, "Tanzania: From Disillusionment to Guarded Optimism," *Current History*, 96(610), May 1997, pp. 217–221.

11

Zimbabwe's Foreign Policy

SOLOMON M. NKIWANE

During the Cold War era, the single most absorbing preoccupation of small states tended to be their survival as independent sovereign entities. This was because world politics had degenerated into a hostile arena in which only the superpowers, traditional great powers, and middle powers had any meaningful activities beyond their borders. In such an environment, there seemed to be little room for small states to engage in or make any meaningful input or contribution to international affairs.

This study examines the foreign policy of one of the smallest states in the world, Zimbabwe. It seeks to show that, unlike the foreign relations of many other small states, Zimbabwe's external relations have been robust, active, and daring. During the eighteen years of its sovereign existence since 1980, Zimbabwe's foreign policy has reflected or encompassed regional and global considerations—proving that some small states have the capacity to play a constructive role in world affairs.

Zimbabwe, like many other states in sub-Saharan Africa, is bracing itself for the turn of the century. It is not that there is anything magical about the year 2000. Rather, there is a sense and hope in government circles, as well as in the population at large, that the start of the twenty-first century will mark a fresh beginning in national and international affairs.

For Zimbabwe, an analysis of the period from 1980 to 2000 is crucial in attempting to understand, if not to project, the nature of its future involvement in international affairs. During this twenty-year period, Zimbabwe will have emerged from a state of colonial subjugation to sovereign independence; shifted from being a Marxist-Leninist, one-party state to a multiparty and market-oriented state; and moved from being a leading member of the Front-Line States in confrontation with apartheid

South Africa to being a partner with the Republic of South Africa in strengthening regional security and economic cooperation.

Within Zimbabwe itself, besides the diverse domestic and external factors influencing foreign policy, it is imperative to consider the historical background of the country before its independence in 1980. This is because the historical legacy, especially that associated with settler colonialism and the subsequent liberation struggle, continues to cast a shadow over contemporary affairs.

However, before proceeding, it is necessary to comment briefly on foreign policy generally, in order to throw some light on the theoretical underpinnings of this study.

A Theoretical Framework

Generally, foreign policy refers to the behavior or activities of a state, normally beyond its national borders, that bring the state into direct or indirect interaction with other states in the international system.[1] Small states' foreign policies have generally been aimed at ensuring that their sovereignty and independence are respected. This has often taken the form of supporting the UN and other international institutions that recognize and uphold those principles that favor the small powers' existence and heighten their status. Because they are militarily weak, economically underdeveloped, and sometimes politically unstable, small states have tended to be inward-looking, passive, and often preoccupied with fears of internal disintegration.

Africa's small states have the added problem of being relatively newly independent, after centuries of European colonization. Their survival was threatened more by internal conditions, such as political instability due to ethnic or tribal conflicts, economic weakness and underdevelopment, and by other negative factors emanating from the legacies of colonial exploitation and deprivation. That is, that the newly independent states of SSA have been the least capable of developing truly independent foreign policies. It is interesting, then, that Zimbabwe, encumbered and burdened by a similar colonial legacy, has carved out an activist, externally oriented, and robust foreign policy. This study shows why Zimbabwe's policy has not followed the pattern of most small states and why being small need not be a hindrance to participating fully and actively in the international system.

A fundamental feature of the contemporary international system is the interrelatedness and growing mutual dependence of its units, particularly the states. Increasingly, the viability of the state is measured less in terms of power and self-reliance and more as a function of the degree of cooperation and mutual assistance established with other states and nonstate actors. Even without the handicap of being landlocked, Zimbabwe's survival and development cannot be sustained without the participation and contribution of other states, especially its immediate neighbors in the region.

However, the contemporary international system, rightly or wrongly, is generally understood to be inhospitable to small states. Like its neighbors, Zimbabwe is a small power on the world political scene. But this smallness can be partially compensated for by cooperation or even integration with other states. This is one lesson that stands out prominently in the experiences of the EU. The small states of Southern Africa, as others elsewhere, need to work together rather than at cross purposes in order to survive and develop. This lesson has been driven home in the emerging environment of the post–Cold War era, in which regional economic and peacekeeping endeavors gather pace.

Within the relatively short span of time since independence, Zimbabwe has penetrated the international system and established itself as a voice to be heard. Under normal circumstances, one would have expected a small and landlocked country like Zimbabwe to be inward-looking and insular. But for a number of reasons, amplified later in this analysis, Zimbabwe's thrust in foreign relations has been activist.[2]

Nonetheless, being hemmed in and restricted by its borders is a serious handicap for Zimbabwe in its international activist role. Its borders with its neighbors must be rationalized and stabilized if it is to have sufficient space in which to pursue its internationalist role, without handicaps or hindrances. Preoccupation with immediate border conflicts and other border issues can have a deadening effect on the state's other policies. It would also be in the interests of all Southern African Development Community member states if border issues were dealt with sooner rather than later in order to create a wholesome environment in the region, which would contribute to political stability and development.

Zimbabwe's External Relations Before Independence

Zimbabwe became an independent state only in 1980, but that did not mean that its predecessor, colonial Zimbabwe (Southern Rhodesia), had no relations or experiences with the external world. As a matter of fact, the colony of Southern Rhodesia under the British crown controlled much of its internal affairs and enjoyed some autonomy in conducting aspects of its external affairs, such as trade and commerce. Because of that autonomy, Rhodesia had trade missions in London and Washington, D.C.

There is no question, however, that Southern Rhodesia was a dependent territory and had no formal foreign policy of its own. Its policy was that dictated and implemented by the British government. Consequently, one is hard put to imagine or trace any element of continuity between the foreign policy of independent Zimbabwe and that of the British government as applied to Southern Rhodesia.

This is an important consideration in the analysis of the foreign policy of a newly independent state. After all, it does not necessarily follow that independence for a former colony amounts to a complete break with its past in every sense. A certain degree of continuity can be assumed in most cases, especially if political independence was preceded by a harmonious transfer of power or, at least, by some form of negotiations between the colonizer and the colonized.

However, in the case of Southern Rhodesia, even its participation in the Commonwealth was strictly as an appendage of the British Foreign Office, not as an independent political entity like Australia and South Africa at the time. Also, as the following brief historical section will indicate, the African population was systematically denied any meaningful contact with the outside world, underlining the point that continuity in foreign policy behavior between Southern Rhodesia and independent Zimbabwe cannot be assumed, if it exists at all.

Before 1980, colonial Zimbabwe had only limited contacts with the outside world. In Africa, it had links in the form of governors' conferences with such colonies as the Gold Coast (Ghana) and Kenya. For geographical and historical reasons, Southern Rhodesia had closer links with South Africa, despite the fact that it refused to become part of South Africa in 1923.[3] After 1923, the prime minister of Southern Rhodesia was often invited to the Commonwealth prime ministers' conferences.

Between 1953 and 1963, Southern Rhodesia became part of a federation with Northern Rhodesia and Nyasaland.[4] This linkage brought Southern Rhodesia directly into an organic relationship with the two central African territories. In the ten years of the existence of the Central African Federation, Southern Rhodesia played a central role in its affairs,[5] perhaps because of its relatively larger white population in comparison to the other two. Salisbury, the capital of Southern Rhodesia, also became the capital of the federation, and Southern Rhodesia controlled the crucial sectors of the armed forces, the transportation industry, agriculture, and manufacturing. The federation had no independent foreign policy of its own except that exercised by the United Kingdom.

After the breakup of the federation in 1963 and through the unilateral declaration of independence (UDI) period (in Southern Rhodesia) until 1975, Southern Rhodesia lost its links with the rest of Africa, except for South Africa, Angola, and Mozambique. With the independence of Angola and Mozambique in 1975, all physical links with the rest of Africa came to an end. In reality, therefore, Zimbabwe had little contact with the rest of the world before 1980, except indirectly through the Colonial Office in London. In Africa, Zimbabwe's very localized links were with the Central African Federation and South Africa.

The seriousness of this situation becomes obvious if one realizes that before 1980, only white Rhodesians actually participated in official contacts with the outside world. During the colonial period, no black Zimbabweans took part in the trade missions in London and Washington, and even during the years of the federation, Southern Rhodesia Africans were really not involved except in token terms. Until independence, no serious effort was made to involve Zimbabwean Africans in the government's civil service, let alone in the diplomatic service.

It is in this context that one must try to understand and appreciate Zimbabwe's role in international affairs. Like South African blacks until recently, the Africans of Zimbabwe until 1980 were denied not only the right to participate in the governance of their country but also the training necessary to cope with the multiple and complex issues of international life. It seems that this suppression only helped to whet appetites of Africans for self-education and self-improvement. Many Zimbabweans dispersed themselves to the corners of the world to acquire the skills that had been denied them at home, and many became refugees in African states.

Thus, when independence came in 1980, the returning Zimbabweans, including the present leaders, had become familiar with the African diplomatic scene. This familiarity and in particular the acquaintances these individuals had cultivated made it possible for Zimbabwe to quickly find its place in African circles. As refugees and guests of several independent African states, Zimbabweans had ample time and opportunity to observe firsthand how the affairs of state were being handled in their adopted countries. Inevitably, they brought with them both positive and negative experiences when they returned at independence, some of which would be reflected in the country's foreign policy behavior.

The protracted liberation struggle began in earnest at about the time the European powers gave in to African demands elsewhere for independence. The founding of the African National Congress of Southern Rhodesia in 1957 coincided with the granting of independence to Ghana.[6] Significantly, the establishment of the external wings of the Zimbabwe African National Union (ZANU) and the Zimbabwe African People's Union (ZAPU) occurred in the same year that the Organization of African Unity was founded, 1963, about three years after the majority of African territories had been granted political independence. These events affected the external behavior of both liberation movements, which they would later bring with them in an independent Zimbabwe.

For a state of its size, Zimbabwe has played an active role in world politics, at both regional and continental levels, since 1980. Zimbabwe's voice has also been heard at the global level in the NAM and in the UN. In December 1990, President Robert Mugabe had this to say in a state of the nation address: "I wish briefly to report the record of success and positive contributions we have made in this challenging field. Zimbabwe, as a member of various international and regional organizations, has actively continued to follow developments affecting not only our region and the African continent, but the world at large."[7]

Given its short history as a sovereign state, its inexperience in international affairs, and the fact that it is small and weak even by African standard, Zimbabwe might have been expected to take its time before casting itself into the hurly-burly of world politics. In fact, one would have expected the state to spend the first few years putting its house in order and attending to the immediate problems of reconstruction, reconciliation, and nation-building as a prelude to the task of economic development.

Instead, Zimbabwe has featured prominently in the politics of Southern Africa, the OAU, the UN, the Commonwealth, and the NAM. How does one account for this active role given the above constraints? What are the dominant issues and problems in Zimbabwe's development of foreign policy? And what are the expectations and future prospects for Zimbabwe in international affairs?

The Context of Zimbabwe's Foreign Policy

The issues that have been crucial to the development and context of Zimbabwe's foreign policy include: the decolonization and liberation of the African continent; the adherence to the principles of sovereignty and equality of states; the underdevelopment and economic plight of Third World states; South Africa's apartheid policy and racism in general; and the question of socialism versus capitalism. Zimbabwe's perspective on the international scene in 1980 and its involvement since then have largely been informed and guided by this cluster of issues.

Having just emerged from ninety years of British colonialism, it is not surprising that Zimbabwe's thrust in international affairs began with a strong commitment to the total liberation of the African continent. In fact, one of the first sovereign decisions was to recognize the Saharawa Liberation Front as the legitimate government, though in exile, of the Saharan People's Republic. Even at that early stage, Zimbabwe was willing to incur the displeasure of Morocco by supporting the guerrillas of Western Sahara who were fighting against Morocco's occupation of their territory. To Zimbabwe, Morocco was nothing less than "expansionist."

Zimbabwe joined forces with the FLS and the OAU in support of the peoples of Namibia and South Africa working to liberate their countries.

After all, Zimbabwe became independent partly because of the tremendous support of the FLS.[8] The concrete manifestation of this commitment has been demonstrated in its assistance to liberation movements elsewhere in Africa. Thus, in its external relations and interactions, Zimbabwe has strongly promoted the nonnegotiable principle of self-determination for all the peoples of Africa. This policy was not changed by the Unity Accord between ZANU-PF (the ZANU-Patriotic Front) and ZAPU-PF (the ZAPU-Patriotic Front), for under the leadership of Joshua Nkomo, ZAPU-PF has always been equally committed to the liberation of the African continent.[9]

As a small state, Zimbabwe is fully committed to the principles of sovereignty and equality of states. The Mugabe government has been consistent in its condemnation of acts by more powerful states that have tended to trample on the sovereignty of others. For instance, Zimbabwe was uncompromising in its condemnation of U.S. intervention in Grenada and Panama in the 1980s, and it equally condemned the USSR in its intervention in Afghanistan. And Zimbabwe did not mince words in its condemnation of a fellow nonaligned state, Iraq, when it invaded Kuwait in August 1990. As Mugabe commented: "The Iraq invasion and subsequent annexation of Kuwait have shattered the peaceful atmosphere the international community had just started to enjoy. Zimbabwe joined the international community in condemning the act of aggression which threatens international peace and security."[10]

The 1979 Lancaster Conference between Britain, the two Zimbabwean liberation organizations (ZANU and ZAPU), and the Muzorewa government of Zimbabwe-Rhodesia created a political constitutional framework that would be utilized for ten years, in clear recognition of the socioeconomic reality of the country. Zimbabwe's social and economic climate in this period resembled that of Kenya some twenty years earlier (see Chapter 6).

First, Zimbabwe had a sizable minority of whites who, for historical reasons, constituted the mainstay of both the skilled workforce of the relatively sophisticated economy and the civil service. It was feared that without some constitutional provision or guarantee, Zimbabwe's economy would be crippled by a sudden loss of thousands of skilled white personnel. Second, at independence, Zimbabwe's economy was essentially controlled by this minority, which in turn was controlled by or directly related to the multinational corporations. Prudence dictated that the newly elected government of Zimbabwe should not frighten this important sector of the economy. It was therefore important that the private sector and the MNCs be assured not only of their profits but also of the country's long-term political stability. The one assurance that commanded respect in this regard was that provided for by the constitution.

The Conduct of Zimbabwe's External Relations

Zimbabwe entered the international diplomatic community with a zeal characterized by the proverbial "new broom sweeping clean." It was not too long before the newly independent state was heard in world forums. Its first executive president, Robert Mugabe, became the chairman of the NAM for three years from 1985 to 1988.

Overall, one can argue that Zimbabwe has been a positive and uniting force in the tottering OAU councils. Except in a very few instances, Zimbabwe has tried to avoid taking sides on African issues. It has given unequivocal support to the principles enshrined in the OAU charter, including the adherence to nonalignment. In this regard, it has strongly criticized continued imperialism, colonialism, and superpower hegemony and meddling in African affairs. Nonalignment means commitment to Third World causes and pragmatism in dealing with the North, both socialist and nonsocialist. As Mugabe said in 1988: "We remain strictly non-aligned and refuse to auction our national sovereignty for a bag of foreign currency. . . . Our sovereignty has never been and can never in future be for sale. It just is not a negotiable commodity! . . . It is a supreme phenomenon of our national being which gives us the absolute right to determine the direction of our policies and infuses us with courage to stand firm on matters of principle."[11]

Contrary to expectations given the dramatic changes in the structure of the post–Cold War international system, which has left the United States as the sole superpower, the Zimbabwean government has continued to espouse socialism or Marxist-Leninism. It has been less than enthusiastic in embracing market-oriented economic strategies, and only circumstances beyond its control have forced the state to adopt the IMF–World Bank's SAPs.[12] Despite the democratization trends of the 1990s, which have been sweeping across the African continent, the Zimbabwean political elite has maintained its one-party political stance, only paying lip service to multiparty democracy. In other words, foreign policy has continued to be dictated by the ideas that emerged from the liberation struggle and has proved resistant to pressures from other sectors of the society.

Zimbabwe occupies an important strategic position in Southern Africa, whether from the point of view of outside powers or that of the OAU. For instance, Zimbabwe was seen as a key state in the U.S. "constructive engagement" policy during the 1980s,[13] which was an attempt to encourage dialogue between South Africa and its neighbors and thereby foster a positive political climate and, presumably, stability in the region. In that eventuality, U.S. investments in South Africa would be protected.[14]

In the case of Zimbabwe, it was presumed that the prospect of a truly multiracial society being created next to South Africa would encourage the latter to soften, if not to abandon, apartheid. Further, with its relatively sophisticated economic and industrial base, Zimbabwe could serve as springboard for increased U.S. investments in the whole region.

As things stand today, however, it would appear that business circles in the United States and Europe find South Africa more attractive than Zimbabwe in economic terms (see Chapter 9 on South Africa). For one thing, it is more advanced industrially and technologically, and its economic infrastructure is much more developed and sophisticated. South Africa now is the role model for positive integration, and so it garners more outside support than Zimbabwe. Nelson Mandela also is a more appealing political figure than Robert Mugabe. In these ways, Zimbabwe is likely to lose out in the competition.[15]

Zimbabwe would probably have become an important base in the region for the USSR in the 1980s had the latter not supported Joshua Nkomo's ZAPU-PF in the contest for power. The ruling party, Mugabe's ZANU-PF, could not have been expected to forget that "betrayal" quickly, although one sensed that relations were warming up between the two governments prior to the collapse of the USSR.[16] This is as it should be. Enlightened leaders should know very well that in international relations, there are no permanent enemies, only permanent interests.

Zimbabwe and Africa

To understand Zimbabwe's position in African affairs, it is important to note that the new nation inherited a relatively sound economic base from the former racist regime of Ian Smith. This quickly made Zimbabwe an economic leader in all parts of Southern Africa outside South Africa. Indeed, there were hopes and expectations during the 1980s that Zimbabwe would gradually replace South Africa as the economic anchor of the Southern African region. SADCC had two principal goals: (1) to reduce the dependence of member states on South Africa, and (2) to so isolate the apartheid regime from the international community that South Africa would either unconditionally abandoned its evil apartheid policy or see its whole political system crumble and give way to a new political dispensation.

There are two central reasons why Zimbabwe was considered an important player in this last battle against racism in South Africa. First, many eyes were turned to Zimbabwe to see whether the feared reverse racism would materialize there. But in fact, not only had the Africans of Zimbabwe taken over all political power from the white minority, it seemed that the Rhodesian version of white racism had disappeared as well, at least officially. All Zimbabweans, black and white, seemed to be going about the business of living without the ghosts of inferiority and superiority dogging their daily lives. The myths of white superiority and black inferiority had been given the kiss of death in Zimbabwe's independence.

Second, since all Africa rallied behind Zimbabwe's nationalists in the struggle for liberation, independent Zimbabwe was conscious of its indebtedness for that support. Thus, Zimbabwe saw itself as having an important responsibility in continuing the struggle for the total liberation of Africa as an expression of its gratitude for the invaluable support it received from the rest of the continent. States like Zambia and Mozambique actually incurred the wrath of Ian Smith by supporting the Rhodesian nationalists, to the extent that their economic infrastructures were wrecked by Rhodesian attacks. And Zimbabwean guerrillas used the neighboring countries as sanctuaries and staging bases, thus exposing those countries to the retaliation of the Rhodesian Air Force.[17]

In return for the help they gave, all the FLS expected from Zimbabwe was that it be truly independent, that it develop in line with its neighbors, and that the majority government act as a natural ally. The logical expectation was that the real task of economic development in the frontline region would resume in earnest, with Zimbabwe playing a pivotal role by using its more developed economy to stimulate the economies of the other states. To date, though, this particular expectation has really not materialized.

Destabilization and Apartheid in Southern Africa

Zimbabwe's prominence in African affairs is primarily due to the fact that it shares a border with South Africa. It is interesting to see how Zimbabwe's role in African affairs was conditioned by its continued economic ties with South Africa, while at the same time it advocated the downfall of the apartheid regime. Here is what the Zimbabwean's foreign minister said: "We shall not establish diplomatic ties with that country [South Africa]. But of course there is no way we can cut off our economic ties at this stage, and South Africa herself had acknowledged that we have to keep those ties on a reciprocal basis."[18]

Zimbabwe's independence was the real trigger for South Africa's policy of destabilization in Southern Africa. Until then, it was not so obvious to South Africa that its isolation in the region was imminent, for Ian Smith's Rhodesia continued to offer possibilities for stemming the southward tide of African liberation.

However, in the late 1970s and 1980s, South Africa let loose its unneighborly policy of destabilization. This was not solely in reaction to the forthcoming independence of Zimbabwe or to its loss as a friend. Rather, destabilization was a preemptive response to the anticipated developments in Zimbabwe and in Southern Africa as a whole,[19] and it reflected concern in South Africa that the implications of Zimbabwe's independence would not serve the interests of apartheid.

Certainly, South Africa feared the example of a successful multiracial society on its immediate border. Zimbabwe not only had a sizable white community, it also had been very close to and had deep roots in South Africa. It was estimated then that 60 percent of Rhodesian whites were either South African or had South African roots. If this white community in Rhodesia accepted living under a black government and learned to live harmoniously with black people, that would be a terrible blow to South Africa's apartheid policy. Developments have demonstrated that as many as 175,000 (out of 300,000) whites chose to remain in Zimbabwe rather than leave, as had been gloomily predicted.

Rather than countenance the successful development of a multiracial society in Zimbabwe, South Africa chose to try to prevent such a development by its policy of destabilization. South Africa's objective in destabilization was twofold. First, it wanted life to be very uncomfortable for the whites, so that they would leave and thus frustrate the efforts to create a multiracial society. Second, South Africa's destabilization was meant to slow down economic development and to force the government to divert its attention and resources from internal socioeconomic development.[20]

It was evident that South Africa detested the idea of a one-party Marxist Zimbabwe as a neighbor and was concerned that the revolutionary ideology could easily and quickly spill across its border to the disgruntled black majority. This seemed possible because, for instance, the ANC and the Pan-Africanist Congress (PAC) had both been given sanctuary in Zimbabwe. Consequently, South Africa attempted to stem this revolutionary tide by destabilizing the country. Zimbabwe was also a problem to South Africa because of its determination to lead the fight for the liberation of Namibia and the downfall of apartheid. Its determination was taken seriously by South Africa's apartheid government because it was a historical fact that Zimbabwe's economy was very much dependent on South Africa.

South Africa's response was not to seek understanding and dialogue with its neighbor but to create chaos and instability, hoping to add so many problems that the government would not have time and energy to devote to external concerns. Unfortunately for South Africa, its strategy failed, as developments have shown. The more South Africa intensified its attacks on Zimbabwe, the more convinced Zimbabwe was that the South African regime had to go, together with its apartheid system. Not long before, Ian Smith's Rhodesia had pursued a policy similar to South Africa's against its neighbors, especially Zambia and Mozambique. In the years between 1965 and 1979, in a desperate attempt to stave off the liberation that was fast closing in on them, the Rhodesians unleashed savage attacks against Zambia and Mozambique to discourage these states from giving sanctuary to the Rhodesian freedom fighters and to prevent the use of their territories as staging grounds for the liberation of Rhodesia.

Under these circumstances, Zambia and Mozambique chose to go all out on the side of ZAPU and ZANU, rather than to allow themselves to be bullied into submission by Rhodesia's superior military machine. They had determined that their own independence was meaningless as long as the racist regime continued to exist. And so, Rhodesia's strategy boomeranged against itself, just as South Africa's strategy against Zimbabwe would do years later.

Yet another fact about Zimbabwe made it the target for South Africa's destabilization. During the 1980s, it had become a pivotal state in the regional grouping SADCC. All the other members of the group looked upon Zimbabwe as the organization's economic center. Its industrial, manufacturing, and agricultural infrastructure placed it in the unique position of possibly replacing South Africa as the region's economic magnet. The other states that had depended upon South Africa economically had been a source of cheap labor for its gold mines and a vast market for its manufacturing goods. The creation of SADCC served not only to pool the resources of the member states and create a strong economic union for mutual benefit but also to reduce their economic dependence on an isolated South Africa.

It seemed logical, therefore, to assume that South Africa would take strong measures to protect its traditional position as the industrial, commercial, and transportation power of the region. Its attempts to destabilize Zimbabwe were a direct result of the threat posed to its economic dominance. However, Zimbabwe could not achieve its economic objectives in the region as long as most, if not all, SADCC members continued their heavy dependence on South Africa.

Finally, South Africa had to cope with a Zimbabwe that was assuming a leading role in African politics in general and in the OAU in particular, which had much to do with its close proximity to South Africa. The rest of Africa, in its collective opposition to South Africa on apartheid and Namibia, had to rely increasingly on Zimbabwe. Meanwhile, Zimbabwe found it necessary to mobilize the whole OAU membership in its campaign to put pressure on South Africa. Thus, South Africa's destabilization had the unintended effect of enhancing Zimbabwe's stature and support in African affairs.

Following several important changes in the international system in the late 1980s and early 1990s, it was only a matter of time before South Africa's destabilization in the region would be neutralized. These developments included the dramatic changes in the Soviet empire that eventually resulted in the collapse of the Soviet state itself in 1991. For Zimbabwe, this occurrence was especially significant because of its close relationship with the USSR as a fellow socialist state. The disintegration of the USSR removed the moral and diplomatic anchor for Zimbabwe's strong socialist thrust in foreign affairs. Only Cuba and North Korea remained as Zimbabwe's staunch friends.

The other major change taking place at about the same time was the dramatic shift in the leadership of the National Party of South Africa, whereby F. W. de Klerk replaced P. W. Botha as the head of that party, as well as president of South Africa, in the late 1980s. De Klerk not only moved fast in dismantling apartheid in South Africa but also decided to change the direction of South Africa's foreign policy. Instead of confrontation, de Klerk chose to develop cooperative arrangements with neighboring states.

Of course, not long after that, in 1994, South Africa further surprised the world by electing a majority black government, led by Nelson Mandela of the ANC. For all practical purposes, this formally ended the policy of destabilization in Southern Africa. In all this, Zimbabwe was able to play a pivotal role, but with the end of destabilization and apartheid, Zimbabwe's foreign policy was to undergo a drastic change.

Some Lessons and Questions

The development of Zimbabwean foreign policy since 1980 offers several general lessons that may be particularly relevant for other states in Southern Africa.

First, no small state in this day and age can afford isolation. Solidarity with the FLS, the OAU, and the NAM has been a major boost to Zimbabwe's stature in international politics. In marked contrast, South Africa under apartheid made itself a pariah in the international community, much as Rhodesia had been during the UDI period.

The broader lesson here is that emphasis should be placed on cooperation rather than confrontation in developing foreign relations with other states. Although Zimbabwe is decidedly small, weak, and underdeveloped in comparison to South Africa, from 1980 to 1994 the country's progressive foreign policy and cooperation with the international community in the fight against apartheid greatly enhanced its stature in the world.

Second, it can be disastrous to choose friends and foes in the international system based on an emotional commitment to some ideology. In the case of Zimbabwe, adherence to socialism and the one-party state has, as a result of developments in the former USSR and Eastern Europe, left it not only ideologically bankrupt but in desperate need of friends.

Third, flexibility is critical in the development of domestic and foreign policy. While other African states are undergoing major political changes

in the post–Cold War era, such as attempts at democratization and graduating from one-partyism to multipartyism, Zimbabwe has generally remained uncomfortably rigid. The irony of all this is that Zimbabwe ad-
heres to the ideology of nonalignment, which should engender flexibility.
However, one can discern some cracks in this ideological rigidity.

Fourth, foreign policy should reflect some national consensus. At a minimum, greater consideration should be given to all sectors of the civil society. It is also true that Zimbabwe's foreign policy has been a creature of the
ruling party. Thus, the policy is, by and large, ZANU-PF's foreign policy.
Diplomatic personnel in the different missions are members of ZANU-PF.
The overwhelming volume of contacts between Zimbabwe and other countries, besides economic relations, have revolved around ZANU-PF's relations with political and other ideologically similar interest groups in those
countries. This is a development that should be avoided.

The challenges facing the country as it approaches the twenty-first century are daunting. The first challenge relates to a reorientation of its policy in view of the end of the Cold War and the disintegration of the USSR.
The second involves the country's economic thrust in the next decade in
the wake of the World Bank's SAPs, which Zimbabwe has decided to embrace, and the challenges posed by the emerging global economy and the
increasing marginalization of Zimbabwe and other African states. Finally,
with the welcome democratic change in South Africa, Zimbabwe's role in
the region is bound to be drastically affected and challenged, leading to
new issues of regional peacekeeping and security and the eclipse of Zimbabwe's star in the shadow of South Africa's.

The foreign policies of African states—and Zimbabwe is no exception—have tended to emphasize relations with extracontinental powers;
sometimes one cannot help suspecting that this behavior is a form of es-
capism from national problems. Zimbabwe's foreign policy in the late
1990s is emphasizing regional and bilateral cooperation to a greater degree than in the past. Eighteen years, though a short time in the lifespan
of states, is long enough for nationals to expect some results from their
rulers. The next five years should be crucial in the further reshaping of
Zimbabwe's foreign policy and its domestic politics in general.

NOTES

1. An authoritative study on foreign policy, especially with reference to the major powers, is Roy Macridis (ed.), *Foreign Policy and World Politics* (Englewood
Cliffs, N.J.: Prentice-Hall, 1992).

2. This is the thrust of the latest study by Solomon M. Nkiwane (ed.), *Zimbabwe's International Borders: A Study in National and Regional Development in Southern Africa* (Harare: University of Zimbabwe Publications, 1997).

3. In a referendum conducted by the Colonial Office in 1923, white settlers in Rhodesia were asked to choose between making up the fifth province of the Union of South Africa or becoming a colony of Great Britain directly under the Colonial Office. The settlers chose the latter. See also Ronald Hyam, *The Failure of South African Expansion, 1908–1948* (New York: Africana, 1972).

4. The federal scheme was hatched in Southern Rhodesia by the white community, ostensibly to thwart or slow the wave of liberation and independence sweeping throughout the African continent. It was presented to Great Britain as primarily an economic union. Thus, Great Britain had no problem in going along with the scheme.

5. Although the Federation of Rhodesia and Nyasaland was totally opposed and deemed unacceptable by the Africans of the three territories on political grounds, Great Britain believed it made much sense on economic grounds. Ironically, in the case of SADC today, economic cooperation, if not economic integration, is freely espoused and envisaged by the same African communities that had vehemently opposed the idea of the Central African Federation.

6. Ghana (the former Gold Coast) has the reputation of being the first sub-Saharan territory to attain political independence in Africa. However, eight other African countries were already independent: Ethiopia (3000 B.C.), Liberia (1847), South Africa (1910), Egypt (1936), Libya (1952), Sudan (1956), Morocco (1956), and Tunisia (1956).

7. *The Herald* (Harare), 13 December 1990, p. 1.

8. See Carol B. Thompson, *Challenge to Imperialism: The Frontline States in the Liberation of Zimbabwe* (Harare: Zimbabwe Publishing House, 1985).

9. Robert Mugabe's ZANU-PF and Joshua Nkomo's ZAPU-PF signed a Unity Accord on 10 December 1987 after a brutal but inconclusive genocidal attack on Matebeleland, ZAPU-PF's stronghold.

10. *The Herald* (Harare), 15 October 1992, p. 1.

11. See Ulf Engel, "The Foreign Policy of the Republic of Zimbabwe (1980–92)," Ph.D. dissertation, University of Hamburg, Germany, 1993, p. 59.

12. Zimbabwe adopted the IMF–World Bank's structural adjustment program in 1991. It appears that the country is preparing to enter into an agreement for a second five-year program.

13. See James Stuart, "Reagan's Policy of Constructive Engagement in Southern Africa," in Hans Kochler (ed.), *The Reagan Administration's Foreign Policy* (Vienna: International Progress Organization, 1984), pp. 272–287.

14. Turkkaaya Ataov, "President Reagan's Policy in Respect to South Africa," in Kochler (ed.), *The Reagan Administration's Foreign Policy*, pp. 288–311.

15. See G. Linington, "Zimbabwean–South African Relations," in Nkiwane (ed.), *Zimbabwe's International Borders*, pp. 42–71.

16. From 1963 and throughout the liberation struggle in Zimbabwe, Joshua Nkomo's ZAPU was supported by the Soviet Union; Robert Mugabe's ZANU was supported by China. It was, therefore, understandable that the power that supported the losing party in the Zimbabwean elections would not enjoy the best of relations with the winning party. See Engel, "The Foreign Policy of the Republic of Zimbabwe," pp. 64–67.

17. See Solomon M. Nkiwane, *Destabilization in Southern Africa: A Historical Perspective*, Dalhousie African Working Papers, No. 13, Dalhousie University, Canada, July 1988.

18. Foreign Minister A. Mangwende in a media statement on 15 May 1982.

19. Nkiwane, *Destabilization in Southern Africa*.

20. Nkiwane, *Zimbabwe's International Borders*, pp. 25–28.

SELECT BIBLIOGRAPHY

Calvert, Peter. *The Foreign Policy of New States* (Brighton, England: Wheatsheaf, 1986).

Cefkin, Leo J. "The Rhodesian Question at the United Nations," *International Organization*, 22, 1968, pp. 649–669.

Chan, Steven, et al. *Exporting Apartheid: Foreign Politics in Southern Africa: 1978–1990* (London: Macmillan, 1990).

Chimanikire, Donald P. *South Africa's Destabilization Policy: The Zimbabwe Experience* (Harare: Zimbabwe Institute of Developing Studies, Research Paper No. 2, 1990).

Davidow, Jeffrey, *A Peace in Southern Africa: The Lancaster House Conference on Rhodesia* (Boulder: Westview Press, 1984).

Good, Robert C., *UDI: The International Politics of the Rhodesian Rebellion* (Princeton: Princeton University Press, 1973).

Gregory, Christopher I., "The Impact of Ideology on Zimbabwe's Foreign Relations (1980–1987)," Master's dissertation, University of the Witwatersrand, South Africa, 1988.

Hull, Richard W., "Overcoming Zimbabwe's Vulnerabilities," *Current History*, 87(529), 1988, pp. 197–200 and 233–239.

Klotz, Audie, "Race and Nationalism in Zimbabwean Foreign Policy," *The Round Table*, 327, 1993, pp. 255–279.

Liebenow, Gus J., "Zimbabwe: A Political Balance Sheet, Part 2: Party Politics and Foreign Affairs," American Universities Field Staff Report No. 15, Hanover, N.H., 1981.

Martin, David, and Phyllis Johnson, *The Struggle for Zimbabwe: The Chimurenga War* (London: Faber and Faber, 1981).

Nkiwane, Solomon M., "Development of Zimbabwe's Foreign Relations, 1980–90," *The Round Table*, 326, 1993, pp. 199–216.

———, *Zimbabwe's International Borders: A Study in National and Regional Development* (Harare: University of Zimbabwe Publications, 1997).

Patel, Hasu H. "No Master, No Mortgage, No Sale: The Foreign Policy of Zimbabwe." Nairobi, Kenya: Centre for Research, Documentation and University Exchange, Paper No. 2.

Thompson, Carol B., *Challenge to Imperialism: The Frontline States in the Liberation of Zimbabwe* (Harare: Zimbabwe Publishing House, 1985).

Weiss, Thomas G., and James G. Bright (eds.), *The Suffering Grass: Superpowers and Regional Conflict in Southern Africa and the Caribbean* (Boulder: Westview Press, 1992).

Windrich, Elaine, "Zimbabwe: Towards Socialism and Non-Alignment," in Stephen Wright and Janice Brownfoot (eds.), *Africa in World Politics: Changing Perspectives* (London: Macmillan, 1987), pp. 120–125.

12

Regionalism and African Foreign Policies

Olufemi A. Babarinde

Much has been written on regionalism in Africa,[1] just as there is a growing body of work on African foreign policies.[2] Unfortunately, little existing scholarship has explicitly examined the connection between regional integration and foreign policy in Africa. If these two issues are linked and/or studied at all, the attention is relatively peripheral and terse at best.[3]

The scholarly discourse on African foreign policy has primarily been at the state level, analyzing the policy of a particular government. Occasionally, scholars modify this conventional approach by comparing and contrasting the foreign policies of two countries or, at times, a handful of countries.[4] Comparative studies of the foreign policies of African states, according to Timothy Shaw, remain essentially "embryonic."[5] In short, most existing studies have not approached foreign policy from the supranational or regional level of analysis, perhaps because doing so is rather challenging. A handful of plausible explanations for this are advanced here.

First, it is argued that whereas Africa is not devoid of regional groupings, especially in the postcolonial era, the life span of some of these entities is often too short to allow for any discernible foreign policy, let alone any meaningful study of the policies. Admittedly, some organizations have existed for a decade or more, but they have been somnolent during much of their existence or have drifted to the brink of disintegration.

Second, to the extent that African states have been preoccupied, inter alia, with nation-building, improving their tenuous legitimacy at home, enhancing their relative autonomy in the global capitalist system, and establishing their own visibility in the international arena since attaining independence, it is conceivable that the pursuit of foreign policy at the regional level was a low priority. Besides, the formulation and implementation of foreign policies are traditionally jealously guarded by national foreign ministries as sacred areas of their sovereignty. In other words, governments have been less inclined to preoccupy themselves with a subcontinental foreign policy, given their predisposition to savor their autonomy.

Third, if the OAU—an august body in which all but one of the continent's states are members—already pursues a continental foreign policy, an issue that will be revisited later, why duplicate the effort at the subcontinental level? Further, is it not enough that the OAU is a pan-African manifestation of national foreign policies? It is thus arguable that African governments are wary of a parallel undertaking at the subregional level, especially given the likelihood that duplication could amount to wasting scarce resources. Besides, it might be equally difficult to establish whether the thrusts for a particular country's foreign policy are essentially pan-African or subregional.

Fourth, to the degree that most of these regional arrangements have an economic underpinning, it may be difficult to discern their foreign policy initiatives, particularly if foreign policy is not one of their explicit mandates, as is the case with many regional groupings. To the extent that a bureaucracy is typically charged with the task of developing and implementing a foreign policy, there may be no comparable agencies at the subcontinental level, especially if member states jealously guard foreign policy as their exclusive domain.

Fifth, given the perennially anemic state of African economies, resource constraints, and the nagging challenges of development, to distinctly pursue an independent foreign policy at the subcontinental level could be overstretching an already overtasked national ministry of external affairs. To be sure, the argument here is not that this is an impossible task for African civil services but that they would have to assume these additional responsibilities with the same or dwindling resources. In fact, most African countries do not even maintain embassies in all the other states of their subregion, largely because of budgetary constraints. All told, the range of foreign policy choices of regional groupings may, after all, be limited.

These reasons notwithstanding, this chapter will delve into how regional integration impacts African foreign policies. The analysis will illuminate the extent to which regional organizations are, if at all, independently developing their own distinct foreign policy initiatives. It will probe the importance of regional policies to participating states. It will also speculate on how the proposed African Economic Community, a pan-African supranational scheme, will impact foreign policy. Of related interest is how foreign policies need to be coordinated in order to realize the AEC.

I will first review regionalism in Africa, considering only the principal and most enduring groupings. In the subsequent section, I will examine evidence of subregional African groups pursuing seemingly autonomous foreign policies. Then I will assess the strength of the linkages between regionalism and foreign policy initiatives and address whether the pursuit of an ostensibly independent foreign policy by regional organizations is desirable and/or advisable, given the balkanization of the continent and the severe constraints on its meager resources. Similarly, I will address the issue of whether subcontinental foreign policy initiatives, where they exist, have been beneficial to the region, its member states, and Africa as a whole. In the succeeding section, I will discuss the Lomé Convention as a case study to illustrate how a group of primarily African countries have attempted a collective foreign economic policy with Europe. The final section concludes with some observations and suggestions with a view to the future.

Regional Groupings in Africa

Regionalism is employed in this chapter to encompass transnational cooperation and integration by sovereign states. Both *regional integration* and *regional cooperation* are employed interchangeably. To demonstrate the similarities between the two—cooperation and integration—and thus to justify using them synonymously, a brief theoretical explanation is offered.

Regional cooperation typically implies collective state action within defined confines controlled by participating governments. Collective state action in this respect is not meant to usurp national authority or to displace sovereignty. Functional cooperation by member states entails minimal regional bureaucracy at best, and national governments are the gatekeepers between the national and regional levels and, thus, can slow down or completely halt the construction of a regional political order.[6]

By contrast, regional integration connotes a process of creating a larger political entity, whose institutions possess or demand jurisdiction over preexisting national ones.[7] Regional integration can be intentional by governmental agents to forge the "rules of the game" and the modus operandi, thus implying the eradication of, usually, economic barriers. This construct of regionalism can also emanate from interaction between socioeconomic actors across national boundaries.

In either manifestation of regionalism, however, states potentially cede some of their sovereignty. However, the levers of power reside with the state, and it may decide not to participate in a joint exercise to maintain sovereignty. Theoretically, no sovereign state could be coerced into collective joint action without, at the very minimum, its acquiescence or its interests being overtly or otherwise served. In any case, this broad interpretation of regional collective action will be applied to the ensuing discussion of regionalism. Regionalism will be used to imply integration and cooperation, especially since existing regional schemes in Africa, such as the AEC, generously employ both concepts synonymously.

Regional cooperation and integration initiatives are not postcolonial phenomena in Africa.[8] They appealed to many leaders of the independence movements and were viewed as a mechanism for countervailing the balkanization of the continent. Notable among those who espoused pan-African cooperation were Kwame Nkrumah, Leopold Senghor, Julius Nyerere, Kenneth Kaunda, and Modibo Keita.[9] They held the view that regional cooperation/integration was necessary to stimulate economic growth and development via industrialization, factor mobility, and economic independence. In response to their campaign for regionalism during the early 1960s, groupings were established, some of which were stillborn (the 1965 nine-member Maghreb Permanent Consultative Committee) and short-lived (the 1959 Union Douanière de l'Afrique de l'Ouest).[10]

These initial attempts failed for the same reasons that current schemes are struggling, namely, that the initiatives were misconceived with regard to their raison d'être. Decisionmaking was often paralyzed because of vendettas between leaders of participating states.[11] Efforts also failed because of nationalism. It was extremely difficult to convince a people just liberated from colonialism, plagued by ethnic-based allegiances, and in search of a national identity of the virtues of supranational collective action. Besides, many postcolonial economic orders were continuations of colonial systems, profoundly influencing consumption patterns and external orientation. Almost four decades after independence, an analysis of trade, direct foreign investment, and economic assistance reveals a lingering colonial legacy and Africa's subordination within the global economy.[12]

Subcontinental Arrangements

Between the 1960s—the decade of African independence—and 1991—when the Treaty of Abuja was signed to create the AEC—there was a proliferation of subcontinental regional arrangements in Africa. Since 1991, in a developing post–Cold War environment, two noteworthy efforts have emerged: first, the 1994 attempt to revive the defunct East African Community and, second, the renaming and reorganizing of the Preferential Trade Area and the Southern African Development Coordination Conference. Despite problems, the spirit of regional cooperation/integration in Africa remains upbeat. All told, it is estimated that there are in excess of 200 regional arrangements in Africa, and about 40 such groupings are located in West Africa alone.[13] Inevitably, countries participate in several regional groupings, and tasks overlap.

West Africa. The Economic Community of West African States was founded in May 1975 to promote cooperation and development in economic, social, and cultural activity. The Treaty of Lagos also set out to raise the standard of living of its citizens, increase and maintain economic stability in the region, coordinate external tariff and macroeconomic policies, improve relations among member states, and contribute to the development of the continent. The community was also charged with the task of creating a common market by 1990, thus enabling trade liberalization and factor mobility, though this did not occur. To assure an equitable distribution of the benefits that accrue from the undertaking, the Fund for Cooperation, Compensation, and Development was set up, to which Nigeria contributes the lion's share of 32 percent and both Côte d'Ivoire and Ghana contribute 13 percent each. Currently, there are sixteen participating countries, with a combined population of about 198 million and an estimated GDP of $71 billion.[14]

East/Southern Africa. The Common Market for Eastern and Southern Africa was established in November 1993 to replace the PTA, which had been created in 1981 at the behest of the UN's Economic Commission for Africa (UNECA), and entered into force in July 1984. COMESA exemplifies the UNECA's urging for an introverted free-trade area, which currently traverses twenty-three Eastern and Southern African states. Presently, it boasts a total population of roughly 300 million and about $120 billion in GDP. Its stated goal is the improvement of commercial and economic cooperation in the region, as well as the transformation of the production structure of participating countries. It is designed to transcend both the economic dominance of the Republic of South Africa and Western capitalism. The Southern Africa Development Community, by contrast, was created by ten Southern African states to defuse the economic threat from a powerful postapartheid South Africa, though South Africa (and Mauritius) joined in 1994 and Seychelles and the Democratic Republic of the Congo joined in 1997.[15] SADC has an estimated combined population of 170 million and a GDP of over $200 billion. Finally, the on-off EAC is on again,[16] as it was revived in late 1994.[17] Although some issues have yet to be resolved by the group—Kenya, Tanzania, and Uganda—the countries recently took a major step toward closer regional integration by agreeing to make their currencies fully convertible.[18]

Central Africa. The Economic Community of Central African States (ECCAS) was set up in October 1983. It is an arrangement between eleven countries that aspire to promote financial and commercial cooperation, by eliminating internal trade barriers and adopting a common external tariff, and eventually create a common market. Its total population is roughly 80 million, and its GDP is about $30 billion.

Northern Africa. A major regional grouping north of the Sahara is the Arab Maghreb Union (AMU), established in 1989 to foster cooperation and integration between Algeria, Libya, Mauritania, Morocco, and Tunisia, as well as better regional linkages with the European Union. The AMU has an estimated total population of 68 million and about $120 billion in GDP.

Constraints of Regionalism

A relevant issue is how these myriad regional arrangements have fared vis-à-vis their stated objectives. At the risk of overgeneralizing, arrangements have either not lived up to potential or have been outright disappointing. One problem is overlapping membership and divided allegiance, for example between COMESA and SADC. Multiple membership also means additional strains on the limited resources of member states. In the same vein, there are linguistic and bureaucratic hurdles to surmount, especially by ECOWAS and COMESA because of the sheer size of their membership and their colonial linguistic inheritance.

Some arrangements, ironically, are still dependent on the largesse of extra-African benefactors. Such was the case with SADCC, which depended on the generosity of the EU. Similarly, all African states are in one North-South dialogue or another with the EU, the most renowned of which is the Lomé Convention. Whereas these North-South arrangements are meant to provide concessions to and facilitate the development of African countries, there is always the possibility that these accords could be competing with Africa's regional groupings for loyalty. Indeed, there is evidence that North-South arrangements such as Lomé or extra-African aid linkages have hindered South-South trade and cooperation and also undermined the goals and cohesion of Africa's regional groups.[19] There were other significant developments, such as the prolonged drought in Southern Africa during the early 1990s; continuing civil wars in Angola, Liberia, Mozambique, and Sudan; the implementation of structural adjustment programs; currency devaluation/depreciation; and other externally prescribed conditionalities, notably by the International Monetary Fund, the World Bank, and other international creditors. Undoubtedly, these factors have constrained viable and credible (sub)continental African foreign policies.

Efforts must be commended at least for some intangible results. ECOWAS, for example, has proven its resiliency, despite coming close to disintegration several times. Moreover, the community recently called for the creation of a single currency. Admittedly, the group may not be close to adopting a single currency any time soon, but the mere fact that its members agreed to do so at this time, calculated posturing or not, must not be easily dismissed. In addition, with the end of the civil wars in Southern Africa, the fall of apartheid, and the end of the Cold War, SADC may be poised for "takeoff."

There is a steadily growing literature on the efficacy of Africa's regional groupings, and the various analyses will not be repeated here.[20] Most analysts seem to believe that these arrangements are more symbolic than real, with respect to bona fide regional cooperation and integration. The profound economic crises of the continent tell the sad story of how ineffective these regional arrangements have been in alleviating underdevelopment burdens of African societies.

Pan-African Arrangements

The OAU is the premier continental postcolonial grouping. Established in 1963, its raison d'être, according to its charter, is to foster peace, security, unity, and development throughout the continent. Article III of the charter comes closest to spelling out a foreign policy mandate, calling on members to respect the territorial integrity of member states, peacefully settle disputes, complete the political emancipation of the continent, and espouse nonalignment. The consensus is that although the OAU has performed admirably in some areas, such as coordinating policies toward extra-African actors and collectively fighting colonial and race domination, it has fallen short of many of its stated goals, especially in moving beyond symbolism to reality and implementation.[21] More than three decades after its inauguration, Africa still has the unenviable distinction of being the least developed continent, which means that the OAU has to work toward improving the socioeconomic development of the continent and its people.

Thus, at its annual meeting in Abuja in June 1991, the OAU formally established the pan-African Economic Community. The event was preceded, a decade earlier, by the OAU's adoption of the Lagos Plan of Action and the Final Act of Lagos.[22] The endorsement of the LPA in April 1980 acknowledged that development would entail some sort of pan-African strategy, which would address the continent's incorporation into the global economy. In order to transform the status quo, African countries would have to reduce their dependence on the North and their susceptibility to external shocks over which they have very little, if any, control. To that end, the UNECA prescribed self-reliance via subregional cooperation as the pathway to development, albeit with some external assistance.[23] Accordingly, the LPA was "the first comprehensive, continent-wide effort to formulate an African-led policy strategy for the economic development of the continent,"[24] and its overall purpose was "not only to promote the development of nations and peoples of Africa, but also their progressive integration over great regional areas; and its ultimate goal is to set up an African Economic Community by the end of the century."[25]

The signing of the AEC treaty in June 1991 must, therefore, be seen as an attempt by the OAU to resuscitate the LPA and as a reaffirmation that regional cooperation and integration are essential to the continent's development strategies. A perusal of the articles of the treaty strongly suggests that its architects patterned the AEC after the EU. Article 4, Chapter 2 of the Treaty of Abuja outlined four main objectives: to promote economic, social, and cultural development and the integration of African economies; to establish a framework for the development, mobilization, and utilization of Africa's human and nonhuman resources; to promote cooperation in all fields of human endeavor so as to raise the continent's living standards; and to coordinate and harmonize policies among existing and future economic communities. Another notable element of the treaty is contained in Article 6, Chapter 2, where signatories committed to a 34- to 40-year timetable for the completion of the AEC. The pan-African integration process was intended to be implemented in six phases, culminating in the functioning of, among other entities, a pan-African economic and monetary union, an African central bank, a single African currency, and a pan-African parliament. To say the least, these were rather ambitious goals for a continent with very discouraging national records when it comes to respect for government accountability and transparency, majority rule and minority rights, and so forth.[26]

In any case, regional integration and cooperation have become the buzzwords of the 1990s. A prevailing view is that in order for Africa to avoid further marginalization, regional cooperation and integration are needed. The emergence of regional trading blocs in different parts of the world provides another rationale for Africa to embrace regionalism more seriously as a strategy to meet development aspirations. Africa has no choice but to be fully integrated in order to enhance its leverage as a viable economic power in the international arena and to enable the continent to adapt better to external shocks.

Regional Groupings and the Pursuit of Independent Foreign Policy

There are several fitting questions to ask in regard to the foreign policies of regional groupings. Do such autonomously developed policies exist? How are they developed and implemented? And how successful are they?

Africa's regional organizations generally exist for the primary purpose of collectively advancing their level of development, irrespective of whether, as insinuated in some quarters, African countries join the integration bandwagon because it is fashionable to do so. A perusal of the treaties and charters of integration schemes would reveal an economic leitmotiv and raison d'être. Arguably, these countries, as is typical of regional integration in general, come together in their subcontinental and continental frameworks with the hopes of using them to forge a better economic environment for their respective societies. The texts of the agreements are often replete with references to such issues as the free movement of people, capital, services, and goods; the coordination of macroeconomic policies; the coordination or joint ownership of production and distribution facilities; and the need for collective security.

The very implementation of "common market" agendas by these groups inevitably connotes the existence of a foreign policy.[27] One reason is that these organizations are still often dependent on extra-African sources for financial, technical, and other assistance. Ironically, therefore, before the groups can achieve relative economic interdependence with the outside world, they must first accommodate those extraneous interests. To that end, the behavior of Africa's regional organizations has to be cognizant of external forces and entities and their policies. For example, the EU and its member states have been instrumental in the creation of many regional cooperation or integration arrangements on the continent, such as the defunct SADCC, or have provided moral and other kinds of support to ECOWAS and others. Given this situation, it would be very difficult for these regional entities to ignore the preferences of external forces or to assume positions that are profoundly confrontational.

This begs the question of what unique types of foreign policy behavior have been exhibited by regional groupings. To the extent that subcontinental challenges are also typically pan-African, it may be difficult to ascertain which foreign policy behavior is unique to subregional entities. Nonetheless, some examples exist.

Perhaps a beginning point is the foreign policy behavior of the Front-Line States, embodied in the policy of SADCC toward SA during the apartheid era. It is well-known that the FLS/SADCC group's subcontinental strategy was to mitigate the effects of the apartheid structure on their members' economies and to transcend the hegemonic status of SA. Several points come to mind here. First, SADCC was constrained by its limited economic capabilities with respect to what policies it could pursue independent of SA. Second, despite ideological differences between SADCC countries and SA, the former managed to accommodate the latter, with respect to trade, shipment of goods across SA, and so forth. Third, although a primary goal of the FLS was the liberation of Rhodesia-Zimbabwe from Ian Smith and his cohorts and, subsequently with SADCC, the ending of the apartheid system in SA, this policy was not peculiarly the FLS's or SADCC's. It was also an OAU policy and, for that matter, the tacit policy of other regional structures in Africa. Nevertheless, SADCC was concerned with counteracting the SA juggernaut, which was a primary reason for its creation in the first place. In the same vein, COMESA was set up primarily to serve an economic purpose.

Were these examples of foreign policy by SADC and COMESA peculiar to the region and independent of policies elsewhere on the continent? To the extent that geographical proximity to SA is a factor, the concerns and the calculated responses were essentially subcontinental. However, because the other regional groupings in the continent could afford to react to SA dominance differently, they were nonetheless engaged on the issue, and this was reflected in the collective actions of their member states, save one or two.[28] The final point here is that neither SADC nor COMESA has an elaborate bureaucracy with which to conduct foreign policy. The staff for both regional frameworks was and is deliberately kept small,[29] which means that whatever independent foreign policy existed for the two almost had to have been an amalgamation of the foreign policies of member states.

ECOWAS, conversely, has a relatively large bureaucracy with which it potentially could develop and implement a foreign policy if it chose to do so. However, the 1975 treaty does not include the pursuit of a foreign policy as an explicit goal. Still, many seemingly economic activities of ECOWAS have external implications or foreign policy connotations. Take, for instance, the recent call to adopt a single currency, which ineluctably affects the CFA franc zone and the age-old privileged relationship between the zone countries of ECOWAS and France. Even though the decision to adopt a single currency, although it may never happen, is intended to facilitate the common market agenda of the group and ultimately facilitate the development of its member states, it poignantly has ramifications that transcend the West African region. France is not the only external entity that would be affected by the realization of this policy; the rest of the EU and other African countries would be affected as well.

Another important ECOWAS policy that contained foreign policy implications was the group's decision to intervene in the mayhem in one of its member states—Liberia—in 1992, two years after the crisis commenced, even though the establishing treaty says nothing about intervening in the "internal affairs" of members. Indeed, it eschews such involvement. There is, however, a quasi-collective security provision that calls for members to come to the rescue of another member in the event of an external threat. Reluctantly and due to pressure from within Africa and from outside (primarily the UN),[30] ECOWAS established a peace enforcement monitoring group, popularly known as ECOMOG.[31] ECOWAS found itself thrust into this role largely because the Cold War was over and because Liberia, like the entire continent of Africa according to the calculus of the major actors, was of practically no geostrategic value (this was a logic behind the later involvement in Sierra Leone as well). The United States was unwilling to directly intervene, especially given its commitment elsewhere in the world at the time (the 1991 Gulf War), and the UN was overstretched. In any case, ECOMOG under Nigerian stewardship (see Chapter 7) stepped in, and the war was brought to a precarious truce. The decision to form ECOMOG had foreign policy implications for ECOWAS because the symptoms of the war spilled over into neighboring countries and because the selfish interests of ECOWAS were involved, not the least of which was how to conduct itself on the world stage. ECOWAS either had to rise to the occasion or risk sanctioning an already battered image of the continent and the OAU as a collective of incompetents.

In 1994, the British government floated a proposal to create a regional peacekeeping organization for Africa in the fashion of the Organization for Security and Cooperation in Europe (OSCE).[32] Several factors accounted for the timing of the proposal, notably the Liberian crisis, the mayhem in Rwanda, the tenuous order in neighboring Burundi, the cessation of hostility in Mozambique, and the fragile cease-fire in Angola. In all these places, blue helmet peacekeeping and/or peace-enforcement missions have been needed. In other parts of the world, such as Bosnia, Haiti, and so forth, the services of UN troops have been required, thereby stretching the capacity of the UN. (Unfortunately, the UN has had to cut back because of dwindling financial support from the richest member states.) In addition, Africa's marginalization has become more apparent in the post–Cold War era, and it is believed that the continent must bear more of the burden, especially given the seeming apathy of the OAU during the Rwandan crisis. It is also believed that SA has the moral, financial, and human capacities to provide leadership and support as a peacekeeper in Africa, although Nelson Mandela has attempted to deflate such expectations (see Chapter 9). So far, little action has occurred on the British proposal.

Briefly, both ECCAS and AMU have also pursued internal policies that have foreign policy connotations. ECCAS, for example, in pursuing its aspiration for a common market, has been trying to coordinate fiscal and tariff policies, with the hope of ultimately eradicating them. These activities not only affect other states, particularly their neighbors, but are also aimed at attracting foreign investment into the region. As in other African countries and subregional groupings, such undertakings are meant to enhance the economic capacity of member states through collective action, thereby stimulating their development. Once again, internal as these endeavors may appear, they elicit some reaction in the international domain. Furthermore, ECCAS has attempted to respond to the internal crises of some of its members, most notably Burundi, Rwanda, and Congo-Zaire.

Because of its geography, AMU is largely preoccupied with Europe and the Middle East in its foreign policy, although it is also concerned with development issues. It should come as no surprise that the group is interested in such things as the EU's Mediterranean policy, the behavior of European Mediterranean states, and the Arab League (to which its members belong). These AMU interests are arguably unique to the area.[33]

Assessing the Linkage Between
Regionalism and Foreign Policy

The task in this section is to address two sets of germane questions. First, when is foreign policy likely to be pursued at the subcontinental level, which countries are likely to push for such a policy, and why? Second, has the pursuit of an autonomous foreign policy by Africa's regional schemes been beneficial to members states, to the group, and to the continent?

If we accept the premise that foreign policy is inextricably linked with domestic policy, then there is ample evidence that African countries have either initiated or supported foreign policy enterprises at the subcontinental regional level. The rule of thumb is that states participate in a collective exercise because their interests are somehow served, not for altruism. Thus, when they participate in foreign policy enterprises within the framework of regional integration/cooperation, they do so because their interests are directly or otherwise involved. Furthermore, if foreign policy is a function of, among other things, domestic economic capacity and population and to the degree that regional integration typically encompasses unequally endowed participating states, it would be in the interest of some states to pursue foreign policy initiatives at the subregional level. To that end, we can conceive of three categories of states and their preference for using the regional integration stage to pursue some of their foreign policies.

At one end of the spectrum are the weak/weakest member states. For them, since they do not have the economic wherewithal and/or the population size to independently pursue a credible foreign policy, they may find it in their interest to pursue some or all of their foreign policy through regionalism.[34]

At the polar opposite are countries that would prefer to autonomously develop and implement their foreign policy at the state level, largely because of their relative dominance and because the state level is where they expect optimum impact or results. However, because of their sheer population size or regional hegemonic status, they may find it prudent to selectively use the subregional stage to pursue their foreign policy agendas.[35]

The third group of states is composed of the medium-sized countries. They belong somewhere along the continuum with regard to their preference for the optimal location for conducting foreign policy.[36]

Each of these categories of countries would have to find its best location in terms of a predisposition for either a more *unilateral* national approach or a more *multilateral* regional emphasis, a decision that would primarily depend on the country and the issue in question. In these scenarios, all members of a regional structure are likely to use the framework for their foreign policy when it serves their interests. In all three instances, members would be availing themselves of the leverage that usually accompanies true regionalism and collective action.

Now, I will attempt to apply that general theoretical framework. Given the economic and military profile of Africa, there are no economic superpowers on the continent; South Africa could possibly be regarded as a subregional power. In any case, countries range from the poorest and weakest to a few medium-sized countries. Against this background, Africa's weak states, which constitute the vast majority, are likely to conduct their foreign policy at the subregional level; the remaining countries are likely to utilize an optimal mix of national and regional approaches. Some examples are illustrative.

First, it is doubtful that countries such as Lesotho or Swaziland, both weak in economic and military capabilities, could have pursued a foreign policy that significantly influenced apartheid SA to change its policies. However, their membership in PTA, SADCC, and the OAU (and UN) gave them some leverage. It would be easier for them to hide behind the cloak of collective action than to unilaterally conduct a foreign policy toward South Africa, especially a confrontational one. Hence, even though PTA and SADCC were relatively loose regional arrangements designed to reduce the dependence of participating states on SA (which might coincidentally have been in the interests of Lesotho and Swaziland), both countries enjoyed not only moral support but also the fortitude and leverage to conduct such a policy. Medium-sized countries, such as Botswana, Tanzania, Zimbabwe, and so forth, also benefited, as can be seen in the respective chapters of this volume.

In ECOWAS, where most members are essentially militarily and economically weak, the countries directly or indirectly benefited from the ECOMOG peace enforcement operation in Liberia, for no one member was strong enough to unilaterally shoulder the burden. Initially, member states, while their leaders traded accusations, seemed to have ignored the problem until pressure to do something mounted, especially from outside the continent. The cessation of hostilities was trumpeted as a foreign policy triumph by the medium-sized participating states, especially Nigeria, although they used the ECOWAS stage to conduct that policy.

As argued earlier, when it suits the interests of medium-sized states, they can avail themselves of the leverage associated with regional integration/cooperation. The propensity for this to happen is perhaps greater when those states either are regional hegemons or have powerful leaderships. In West Africa, for instance, where Nigeria is somewhat of a hegemon largely because of sheer population size, Nigeria's relative prowess may be deemed intimidating or viewed with serious concern by other members. Consequently, a country in, say, Nigeria's position or SA's position may find it prudent, when convenient, to join forces with other member states within the subregional framework, if doing so would assuage skeptical neighbors about its true intentions for the region. Nigeria or SA may not want to be deemed a subregional bully but would prefer to be seen as providing subregional leadership. Thus, a regional group such as ECOWAS or SADC may provide a convenient avenue to flaunt its "team-player," cooperative credentials.[37] Conversely, when a country or a regional group has a charismatic and powerful leader, it is likely that the individual will use the regional cooperation stage to pursue certain foreign policy initiatives. This was the case, as lucidly argued by Daniel Bach, with Côte d'Ivoire's Houphouet-Boigny and his frequent attempts to use francophone regional organizations to conduct his country's foreign policy in West Africa.[38]

Next, I will attempt to answer the question of whether the conduct of an autonomously developed and implemented foreign policy at the subregional level has been beneficial to member states, the regional group, and Africa. Although one could cite an array of regional policies with foreign policy connotations or implications, only a few cases will be mentioned here. Based on these cases, it is obvious that, at least for the poorest and weakest member states, collective action has brought some visibility and the satisfaction of knowing that they mattered. In terms of SADCC policies toward SA, countries such as Lesotho and Swaziland feel reassured that they contributed toward an effective policy by virtue of their membership and participation. Likewise, in the ECOMOG operation in Liberia, the poorer countries could also find some vicarious satisfaction in the dubious success of ECOWAS. In essence, therefore, member countries are likely to benefit from a regional foreign policy success, even if they themselves abstained. It is unlikely that states would endorse or acquiesce to a regional policy incompatible with their interests.

On the question of whether regional organizations benefit when foreign policies are conducted at that level, the answer is a qualified yes. On the one hand, conducting policy for the collective at this level may enhance solidarity; on the other, it potentially may exacerbate friction among them, which could paralyze morale and decisionmaking and possibly lead to disintegration. If a foreign policy succeeds at this level, it bodes well for the organization, but if the reverse is the case, it may cause or aggravate friction, especially if some members had opposed the policy or its conduct in the first place. Finally, on the question of whether Africa benefits when foreign policies are developed and implemented at the regional level, the answer is yes if the policy succeeds and promotes solidarity. If, however, the policy fails, then the continent, which is used to being viewed in a negative light to begin with, provides more ammunition to skeptics and critics, internal and external alike.

African Regional Groupings and the Lomé Convention

The purpose of this section is to examine an age-old and encompassing North-South arrangement, the Lomé Convention, as a case study of regionalism and African foreign policies. Although, as mentioned earlier, the EU also maintains relationships with North African countries under the auspices of the Maghreb and Mashreq agreements, the Lomé Convention is selected here for the following reasons. First, it is widely regarded as the most elaborate of EU relations with the South and as a model for North-South relations. Second, of the EU's existing arrangements with Africa, not only is it the one to which most of the African countries belong, it is also the one with the longest history.[39] Third, the convention presently links the 15 members of the EU to 71 African, Caribbean, and Pacific countries, roughly two-thirds of which are sub-Saharan African.

By the early 1970s, the environment within which the EU was conducting its policies had changed profoundly. Most notable was the first enlargement of the EU, which took place in 1973 with the addition of Denmark, Ireland, and the UK. With the arrival of the UK, the EU extended an open invitation (Protocol 22), primarily to African, Caribbean, and Pacific Commonwealth countries, to consider three possible agreements with the EU.[40] The first official response from the Commonwealth group soon followed, and it was unified and critical. Led by the African countries, the group unequivocally rejected all three alternative arrangements contained in the invitation, contending that several aspects of them smacked of neoimperialism and that they were, thus, incompatible with the group's development aspirations. For example, the group found the "reverse preference" clause in one of the three alternative arrangements objectionable.

Meanwhile, the eighteen-member francophone African Associate States and Malagasy (AASM) of the Yaoundé Convention were concerned that the invitation to the Commonwealth group would chip away at the group's privileges with the EU. The group soon issued a communiqué in which it expressed its desire to maintain its long-standing relations with the EU. That meant retaining the "associate" status of its members and maintaining the reciprocal trade arrangements.

In light of the diametrically opposed positions held by the francophone and anglophone African countries, the OAU and the UNECA soon intervened to bridge the lacuna. In essence, the OAU and UNECA tried to impress upon both groups, particularly the AASM, that they stood a better chance of getting a very good deal from the EU if they collaborated and presented the European Commission with a united front. Following a series of political maneuverings, the AASM group subsequently abandoned its previous position and joined its anglophone counterpart to negotiate an entirely new agreement with the European countries. It was a rare form of "unity" among the mostly SSA countries. Led by Nigeria in July 1974, trade ministers from forty-six ACP countries commenced bloc-to-bloc negotiations with the European Commission on a new convention to replace Yaoundé.[41] The negotiations coincided with the call by the Group of 77 for a New International Economic Order, and they took place in the aftermath of the first energy crisis of the 1970s. Thus, the ACP group presented the European Commission with a laundry list of requests and concessions. For example, the primarily African group requested an automatic mechanism to both stabilize their export earnings against adverse fluctuations and assure specific prices for their commodities.

The eighteen-month negotiation and conclusion of the Lomé Convention was both a victory for and a manifestation of African regional foreign economic policies by Africans on the continent and in the diaspora. The product of the negotiation was a convention that contained an array of economic concessions for the ACP group, which, more than two decades later, still characterize it. The Lomé Convention, named after the capital of Togo where the first and subsequent conventions were signed, has basically included the following concessions, among others: a nonreciprocal trade preference; an economic assistance program; an industrial and technical cooperation program; two insurance schemes for commodities; and separate (sugar, bananas, rum, veal, and so on) protocols. The main rationale of the Lomé Convention is to enable the ACP states to avail themselves of the concessions to facilitate their own development.

Since its inception, however, the Lomé Convention has been criticized by observers for failing to advance the development of the ACP countries as a group. Although some member countries have experienced a degree of economic improvement, the same cannot be said for the majority. The disparity in economic development has created a chasm between members of the ACP group over the years with regard to the renegotiation of Lomé. Although the renegotiation process of the convention has become ritualized and the concomitant outcomes have become predictable, the cohesion of the ACP group has weakened. In the negotiation of the second and subsequent Lomé agreements, the African-dominated group has been less cohesive in presenting the European Commission with a "common agenda."

Apart from the growing economic disparity, other factors account for the disintegrating unity. Foremost among these is the fact that the size of the ACP group has swollen from forty-six in 1975 to seventy-one at present. In addition, there is an absence of leadership. Nowadays, unlike the mid-1970s, Nigeria no longer enjoys an almost unrivaled economic affluence and hegemony.[42] The only other country in SSA that has both the *capacity* and the *willingness* to play the role of a leader in negotiations with the EU, the Republic of South Africa, has battled with the EU to let it into the ACP fold. Simultaneously, both the international political economy (IPE) and the EU have undergone profound changes since 1975, prompting many to wonder about the importance of the convention in the EU's foreign policy enterprise. On the one hand, the current membership of the EU has almost doubled since 1975 and is composed of countries such as Finland and Austria, which historically did not enjoy any ties with Africa in particular and hence are unlikely to be as sympathetic as, say, France or Belgium. On the other hand, new economic opportunities and challenges have sprung up elsewhere in the IPE and have captured the imagination of the EU and its members. For example, the 1989–1990 revolution in Eastern Europe was too close to home for the EU to simply dismiss; it must address the urgent needs of its neighbors.

In short, given the absence of leadership, the poor economic performance within the ACP group, and the profoundly altered IPE, it is arguable that the ACP countries have lost their leverage and are thus no longer in a position to dictate the terms of their foreign economic policies to the EU. Today, the ACP group finds itself in a take-it-or-leave-it dependent relationship with the EU. That is, the EU-ACP relationship of the late 1990s is diametrically opposed to the situation in the mid-1970s. The EU is more confident, more affluent, larger in population and economic size, and confronted by more global challenges (among which Africa is only one). Conversely, the African group is less assured today and less cohesive after almost four decades of postcolonial economic mismanagement, soaring debt, and misfortunes.

Against this backdrop, the African group's foreign policy vis-à-vis the EU seems to be characterized by a more unequal exchange and a more dependent relationship than the "equal partnership" relationship of the 1970s. Some analysts have even argued that the only reason why the EU still maintains its relationship with the ACP countries is because of the latter's "collective weakness."[43] In any case, by the time the fourth Lomé Convention was negotiated and put into force and by the time of its midterm review (1994–1995), it had become evident that though the group was no longer as united as in 1974, it still preferred to negotiate a collective agreement with the EU. Indeed, as the expiration of Lomé IV approaches, talks about the future of the convention have abounded. One school of thought says there will be no Lomé Convention beyond 2000, when the fourth convention expires. Another school of thought states that if there is a Lomé Convention in the next millennium, it will be radically different in structure. In either case, many ACP countries, especially the African ones, have expressed their preference to preserve their privileged collective relationship with the EU.

This decision by the ACP countries might have been inspired by several factors. First, it is plausible that in the calculus of the ACP countries, alternative arrangements with the North did not exist or, if they did, they were not as alluring, especially in light of Africa's weakening position in the IPE. Second, the ACP countries might have also come to the realization that to maximize the benefits of their relationship with the EU, their most valuable asset was perhaps their large size, particularly if they were to effectively counteract a new international division of labor and power. Third, it is also quite possible that the ACP group's decision to stay together in the Euro-African relations could be attributed to the spirit of African solidarity, that is, the need to join forces and heighten the visibility of the continent against the background of the globalization of international capital. In any case, it is ironic that the prospect of losing the privileged arrangement with the EU has reinvigorated the "unity" of the African-dominated group, despite all their differences.[44]

Conclusion

All told, preparing the analysis presented in this chapter has been rather challenging in light of limited amount of previous scholarship specifically on the subject. This undertaking has been approached with an exploratory mind-set, and other portentous areas have been omitted due to space constraints. Future research should address more closely, for example, whether the types of political regimes represented in a regional organization make a difference in terms of the group's decisionmaking on developing and/or implementing foreign policy at that level. For instance, does it matter if some of the members operate under a military dictatorship, such as in ECOWAS, or if the vast majority of participating countries subscribe to a pluralist model, such as SADC? Future research should also probe deeper into the potential effects of the AEC on the foreign policies of states and regions. It would also be interesting to study how, if at all, the continent's regional organizations are using their collective leverage to pursue economic policies in the global system.

Some suggestions are in order. Regional entities in Africa should be utilizing frameworks simultaneously at the subcontinental and continental levels to present their cases to the international financial community on issues such as debt rescheduling. Furthermore, they should be using their collective strength to explore and exploit opportunities in the New International Division of Labor in order to promote their own development. They should also be more aggressive in using the regional stage to win concessions, as in their negotiations with the EU over Lomé and the proposed EU-Maghreb free trade area, in the World Trade Organization, and in other global forums. Frankly, given the economic weakness of these countries, they had better join forces and harness scarce resources if they hope to stem or reverse their marginalization in the global economy. Admittedly, this is easier said than done. After all, despite its forty-plus years of history, the EU still has a long way to go in coordinating foreign policy and presenting a unified front to the outside world. However, that does not preclude Africa from achieving such a feat on a consistent basis.

NOTES

1. See, among others, the volumes by Julius Emeka Okolo and Stephen Wright (eds.), *West African Regional Cooperation and Development* (Boulder: Westview Press, 1990), and Domenico Mazzeo (ed.), *African Regional Organizations* (Cambridge: Cambridge University Press, 1984).

2. See, for example, the extensive surveys in Timothy M. Shaw and Olajide Aluko (eds.), *The Political Economy of African Foreign Policy* (New York: St. Martin's, 1984); Michael B. Dolan, Brian W. Tomlin, Maureen Appel Molot, and Harold Von Riekhoff, "Foreign Policies of African States in Asymmetrical Dyads," *International Studies Quarterly* 24 (3), 1980, pp. 415–454; and Olajide Aluko (ed.), *The Foreign Policies of African States* (London: Hodder and Stoughton, 1977).

3. This was the case in the passing references made to regional groupings and the pursuit of foreign policies in the discussions by Timothy M. Shaw, "Regionalism and the African Crisis: Towards a Political Economy of ECOWAS and SADCC," in Okolo and Wright (eds.), *West African Regional Cooperation and Development*, pp. 115–145, and in Timothy Shaw and Olajide Aluko's "Introduction: Towards a Political Economy of African Foreign Policy," in their *Political Economy of African Foreign Policy*, pp. 1–24.

4. The bibliography in Shaw and Aluko, *The Political Economy of African Foreign Policy*, is replete with examples of such studies.

5. Shaw, "Regionalism and the African Crisis," p. 123. See also Shaw and Aluko, "Introduction: Towards a Political Economy of African Foreign Policy," p. 4.

6. Stanley Hoffman, "Reflections on the Nation State in Western Europe Today," *Journal of Common Market Studies* 21, September-December 1982, pp. 21–37.

7. See Karl Deutsch, *The Analysis of International Relations* (Englewood Cliffs, N.J.: Prentice-Hall, 1968), p. 158, and Ernst B. Haas, *The Uniting of Europe: Political, Social, and Economic Forces, 1950–1957* (Stanford: Stanford University Press, 1958), p. 16.

8. Prior to the independence era, there were indigenous movements for African unity, some of which evolved into pan-African arrangements. For details, see Olatunde Ojo, "Regional Co-operation and Integration," in Olatunde J.C.B. Ojo, D.K. Orwa, and C.M.B. Utete, *African International Relations* (London: Longman, 1985), and Isebill Gruhn, *Regionalism Reconsidered: The Economic Commission for Africa* (Boulder: Westview Press, 1979), pp. 137–142.

9. See, for example, Kwame Nkrumah, *Africa Must Unite* (New York: Praeger, 1963); Julius Nyerere, "A United States of Africa," *Journal of Modern African Studies*, 1(1), 1963, pp. 1–16; and Gruhn, *Regionalism Reconsidered*.

10. R. H. Green and K.G.V. Krishna, *Economic Cooperation in Africa: Retrospect and Prospect* (London: Oxford University Press, 1967).

11. Daniel Bach, "Francophone Regional Organizations and ECOWAS," in Okolo and Wright (eds.), *West African Regional Cooperation and Development*, p. 54.

12. The EU and the United States account for roughly three-fourths of Africa's contemporary total trade. Similarly, the bulk of the continent's economic assistance and foreign investment comes from the same sources.

13. See, for example, Bach, "Francophone Regional Organizations and ECOWAS."

14. The reported figures for ECOWAS and other regional associations, which are discussed below, were for 1993, and the World Bank, *World Tables* (Baltimore: Johns Hopkins University Press: 1995) was used for calculating the population and GDP estimates. To supplement those publications, *Africa South of the Sahara, 1995*, and *The Middle East and North Africa, 1995*, published by EUROPA, were employed.

15. SADCC, formed in 1980, was replaced by SADC in August 1992. For details, see "African Leaders Sign Treaty," *Financial Times* (London), 18 August 1992, p. 3. "Southern Africa Urged to Integrate," *Financial Times* (London), 29 August 1995, p. 4.

16. The EAC has a population of about 71 million and a GDP of $11 billion.

17. See "East Africa Born Again," *New African* (London), February 1995, pp. 24–25.

18. See "East Africa Stopped at the Start," *New African* (London), May 1995, pp. 24–25; "E. African Leaders to Co-Operate," *Financial Times* (London), 26 January 1996, p. 6; and "East Africa Trio in Currency Link to Help Business," *Financial Times* (London), 2 July 1996, p. 4.

19. The activities pursued by certain Northern actors to sow seeds of discord within and between some of Africa's regional groups are well documented. For example, see Thomas S. Cox, "Northern Actors in a South-South Setting: External Aid and East African Integration," *Journal of Common Market Studies*, 21(3), 1983, pp. 283–312, and Sam Olofin, "ECOWAS and the Lomé Convention: An Experiment in Complementarity or Conflicting Customs Union Arrangements," *Journal of Common Market Studies* 16(1), 1977, pp. 53–72.

20. See, among others, Guy Martin, "African Regional Cooperation and Integration: Achievements, Problems, and Prospects," in Ann Seidman and Frederick Anang (eds.), *Twenty-First Century Africa: Towards a New Vision of Self-Sustainable Development* (Trenton, N.J.: Africa World Press, 1992), and Okolo and Wright (eds.), *West African Regional Cooperation and Development*.

21. See, particularly, John Ravenhill's analysis on "The OAU and Economic Cooperation: Irresolute Resolutions," in Yassin El-Ayouty and I. William Zartman (eds.), *The OAU After Twenty Years* (New York: Praeger, 1984), pp. 173–192.

22. The precursors of the LPA included the 1968 Algiers Declaration, the 1970 and 1973 Addis Ababa Declarations, the 1977 Libreville Declaration, and the 1979 Monrovia Declaration by the OAU to establish continental economic integration and collective self-reliance.

23. See, for example, Aderemi Oyewumi, "The Plan of Plans," *Africa Forum*, 1(4), 1992, pp. 45–48.

24. Robert Cummings, "A Historical Perspective on the Lagos Plan of Action," in Julius E. Nyang'oro and Timothy M. Shaw (eds.), *Beyond Structural Adjustment in Africa: The Political Economy of Sustainable and Democratic Development* (New York: Praeger, 1992), p. 29.

25. Organization of African Unity, *Lagos Plan of Action for the Economic Development of Africa, 1980–2000* (Geneva: International Institute for Labour Studies, 1982), sect. 4.

26. For an in-depth analysis of the AEC, see Jonathan Derrick, "En Route to Integration," *Africa Forum* 1(4), 1992, pp. 39–42.

27. Common market regional arrangements, after all, typically obligate participating member states to pursue, inter alia, a common external tariff and a common commercial policy toward third countries, based on uniform principles. When Africa's regional groups pursue such "common" policies, they are, in effect, engaging in foreign policies.

28. It is a well-known fact that on the issue of SA and the apartheid system, the late president of Côte d'Ivoire, Houphouët-Boigny, pursued a policy that was slightly different from the stances of ECOWAS and the OAU.

29. See, for example, Bach, "Francophone Regional Organizations and ECOWAS," p. 64.

30. Initially, the UN resisted involvement in the Liberian crisis, citing a provision in its charter that required (sub)regional groups to try to resolve disputes before UN intervention.

31. The bases of ECOMOG were the Yamoussoukro (Côte d'Ivoire) Initiative and the Cotonou (Benin) Accord, both of which were negotiated by ECOWAS.

32. See "UK Calls for African Peacekeeping Body," *Financial Times* (London), 21 September 1994, p. 4.

33. For more on this observation, see "Euro-Med Conference Breaks New Ground," *Eurecom*, 7(11), 1995, pp. 1–2.

34. In the context of the EU—the most sophisticated regional integration to date—it could be argued that a country such as Luxembourg, because of its tiny population, is an example.

35. Still in the EU context, the UK, Germany, France, and Italy (and possibly Spain) would be examples.

36. The remaining nine or ten states in the EU would fall into this category.

37. Such a rationale might have informed the Babangida military regime's insistence that other member countries, such as Ghana and Senegal, had to contribute military personnel for the ECOMOG operation.

38. Bach, "Francophone Regional Organizations and ECOWAS," pp. 53–65.

39. The history of the Lomé Convention can be traced to the inception of European cooperation in the Treaty of Rome in 1957. Initially, the EU maintained relations with 18 francophone members of the AASM. The relationship was later replaced by a negotiated agreement between the two groups of countries in what was otherwise known as the Yaoundé Convention. The convention went into force in 1963 and was renewed in 1969.

40. One alternative was a Yaoundé-type association agreement, which would cover trade, economic aid, and so forth. Another was the conclusion of a special convention, covering reciprocal trade agreements, and the third option was the conclusion of a simple commercial agreement with the invited Commonwealth states. Interested Commonwealth countries were obligated to specify which of the three alternatives they preferred.

41. It was its wealth and population that enabled Nigeria to provide leadership at the negotiations. Being an oil-rich country, it had benefited immensely from the 1973–1974 oil crisis.

42. Its economy followed a downward spiral during much of the continent's "lost decade" of the 1980s, a misfortune from which it has yet to recover. Hence, even if Nigeria had the willingness, it lacks the economic capacity to play the role of a hegemon within the ACP group.

43. See, particularly, John Ravenhill, "When Weakness Is Strength: The Lomé IV Negotiations," in William Zartman (ed.), *Europe and Africa: The New Phase* (Boulder: Lynne Rienner, 1993), and Ravenhill, "The Lomé Convention: An Aging Dinosaur in the European Union's Foreign Policy Enterprise?" in C. Rhodes and S. Mazey (eds.), *The State of the European Union*, Vol. 3 (Boulder: Lynne Rienner, 1995).

44. See, for example, "Joint Assembly in Gaborone," *The Courier*, No. 139, May-June 1993 and "Spotlight on Lomé IV Mid-Term Review," *The Courier*, No. 144, March-April 1994.

13

Conclusion: African Foreign Policies and the Next Millennium: Alternative Perspectives, Practices, and Possibilities

Timothy M. Shaw and Julius E. Nyang'oro

This concluding chapter seeks to extract salient lessons from the preceding case studies and then suggest comparative insights for at least the medium term, that is, into the first decade of the twenty-first century. We seek to advance the somewhat underdeveloped field of comparative foreign policy on the continent and elsewhere, especially in the South,[1] in part by incorporating promising perspectives from parallel fields, such as comparative, development, environmental, feminist, political economy, regional, and security (now including "peacekeeping") studies. We conclude by indicating some possible future directions for both policy and analysis into the next millennium. The chapter is thus both retrospective and prospective but also self-critical, given deficiencies in a number of previous inquiries, including our own.[2]

"Foreign policy" in Africa has evolved from its initial, energetic, and optimistic postindependence period (see, for example, Chapters 7, 10, and 11) to a more sober, realistic mood in the current, postbipolar era dominated by preoccupation with structural change and adjustment.[3] It has thus shifted in terms of actors (from states and presidents to multiple players, especially economic ones), issues (from diplomatic and strategic to economic), and levels (from national to regional and global). Thus, instead of focusing on classic external relations of "national security" and "high politics," it now concentrates on two relatively novel nexuses: almost continuous negotiations over debt and conditionalities, on the one hand, and increasingly regular rounds of peacekeeping/peacemaking, on the other.[4]

The significance and substance of Africa's belated transformation became undeniable with the sequence of dramatic events around the civil conflicts, peacekeeping challenges, and political changes in Central Africa in the mid- to late 1990s—from ethnic genocide and humanitarian interventions to antiregime movements in Rwanda, Burundi, and Zaire, which themselves were impacted by spillover from long-running civil wars in southern Sudan and Angola. The traumas of Rwanda were thus superseded by the triumphs of Congo. The gaping doughnut hole in the middle of the continent that had become the focus of considerable apprehension was transformed into a symbol of the hope that fundamental change could yet occur—that the cornucopia of Zaire might help revive rather than corrupt or corrode the continent. The post-Amin/Obote transformation of Uganda under President Museveni may yet constitute an alternative, indigenous model instead of the ubiquitous, undifferentiated hegemony of SAP: Will there be a post–Cold War alliance of African developmental states? In short, as suggested in the penultimate section of this chapter, the Congo of the Berlin Treaty may, in the post–Berlin Wall era, symbolize the possibility of transformed regimes, borders, and relationships: Will a new regionalism emerge for the new century, in which state and nonstate, local and global actors cooperate for sustainable human development and human security?

Such preoccupations mark a further transition in the contents and impacts of foreign policies/relations on the continent, constituting another stage or period in contrast to those already identified by Stephen Wright in the first chapter; that is, contents and constituencies as well as contexts and constraints have evolved since the early- and late-independence eras. Thus, we need a more nuanced, flexible notion of "African foreign policy" for the turn of the century, one that not only incorporates and distinguishes among levels, regions, and regimes but also includes nonstate "transnational" relations among multinational corporations, civil societies, and so forth. In particular, taking possible implications for comparative Africa/Third World/global foreign policy studies into account,[5] we would start by privileging nine central syndromes at the end of the century:

1. the (in)compatibility of economic, political, and other liberalization conditionalities, including downsizing of the state and the military, reinforcing of formal multiparty democracy and informal civil society, and so on (see especially Chapter 8);
2. the apparent marginalization versus novel forms of centrality, such as the ubiquitous peacekeeping nexus; the roles of interna-

tional nongovernmental organizations (INGOs); biodiversity/ bioengineering (especially around the remaining rain forests); proliferation of mines and corporate alliances for gold, diamonds, petroleum; and other environmental concerns;

3. the proliferation of "new" foreign policy issues to which both state and nonstate actors alike need to respond in the late twentieth century, from globalization and regionalization to drugs, ecology, migrations, and viruses; these issues also include a range of "human security" issues in addition to those identified above, such as community, economic, and gender (in)security;[6]

4. the foreign policies of "new" states, as both sources and targets (that is, not just African but also myriad new sovereigns in Eastern Europe and Central Asia), whether of new regimes (e.g., postapartheid South Africa) or new actors (e.g., Eritrea) (contrast Chapters 5 and 9)—or even would-be, formally unrecognized states such as Somaliland. Alas, it is not clear to what extent the 1960s new states literature informs either the states' practice or analysis in the late 1990s, although it could usefully be recalled and revised for the late twentieth century;[7]

5. the new inequalities among as well as within African states as a few prosper (e.g., Botswana and Mauritius) while the majority lag, some into the unenviable category of "collapsed" or "failed" states, others merely as (un)successful adjusters or (non)sustained democracies (contrast Chapters 2 and 10 with Chapters 4 and 11);[8]

6. the rise and fall of regional "powers" or regional hegemons, in part because of changing extracontinental pressures, economic and political, such as the erosion of Nigeria's effective leverage in ECOWAS or Kenya's increasingly ambiguous place in Eastern Africa versus the revival of South Africa's potential role postapartheid, albeit in terms of civil society, communications, economics, infrastructures, technologies, and mediation/peace building rather than dominance through destabilization (contrast Chapters 6, 7, and 9);

7. the new varieties of regionalism, not only formal and interstate but also informal and nonstate, including informal trade and regional civil societies (e.g., culture, ecology, ethnicity, language, media, sports, and so forth) (compare to Chapter 12): the development of more flexible, "open" regionalisms, not all of which coincide with formal state boundaries, as well as cooperative and competitive patterns of interregionalism, such as between continental groupings (e.g., COMESA and SADC) and extracontinental (e.g., African Economic Community and/or EU and/or NAFTA and/or APEC, and so on);[9]

8. the NICs and near-NICs as partners and/or models in contrast to inherited Eurocentric North-South links and hegemonic neoliberalism; rather than indicating state shrinkage, East Asian political economies indicate the continued salience of internal dirigisme and external niches, including novel postbipolar/postindustrialization South-South links, especially as resource depletion and environmental regulation compel many Asian MNCs to seek raw materials elsewhere; and finally,

9. Africa's contribution to comparative foreign policy (and established development and embryonic peacekeeping) studies in terms of small, marginal political economies/cultures, as indicated in the introduction, Clapham's own bilateral comparative inquiry (Chapter 5) into Ethiopia and Eritrea, Heilbrunn's analysis of two highly unequal West African states (Chapter 3), and Bischoff and Southall's work (Chapter 9) on the "new" South Africa's reluctance to exert regional dominance. Yet though, taken together, the previous dozen chapters indicate the range of issues and actors, the difficulties of how to rank/explain/predict remain over particular factors/relations at particular times (see especially Chapter 8 as well as those already identified in this list).

We return to such fundamental issues or limitations at the end of this chapter, particularly in the final section on the novel yet already almost ubiquitous peacekeeping syndrome. But we turn first to global and continental contexts at the end of the twentieth century.[10]

Global Contexts

Whether it is always admitted by analysts and practitioners alike, the content and intent of "foreign policy" are changing everywhere at the end of the twentieth century, nowhere more than Africa. This is so for five interrelated reasons.

1. globalization of the world economy, polity, and society;[11]
2. termination of the bipolar Cold War and the South's related response of nonalignment;
3. hegemony of neoliberalism, translated in Africa as ubiquitous structural adjustment programs with their proliferating range of policy conditionalities;
4. rise of "new" security issues, many of which affect Africa directly, from crime, drugs, peacekeeping, and refugees to ecology, gender, and viruses;[12] and

5. new acceptability, even legitimacy, of democratization, in both formal interparty and informal civil society, leading to a new openness in debates and decisions, including foreign relations.

So, African "foreign policy" in the late 1990s is no longer so exclusively state- or strategic-centric. Rather, it has become more open in terms of both focus and process; it encompasses a range of nonsecurity issues, especially of concern to nonstate, transnational actors. Indeed, now more than ever, after a decade and a half of neoliberalism and half a decade of postbipolarity, the discredited and diminished African state has no monopoly over foreign relations, which are increasingly economic in content and transnational in character.[13]

Unhappily, not all students of international relations on and off the continent recognize this as yet; thus, the field is lagging behind some of the revisionist perspectives of comparative politics, development studies, (international) political economy, and even security studies, not to mention environmental, gender, peacekeeping, or refugee studies. Hence, this volume, which attempts to review and advance the field just before the turn of the millennium, is especially timely. The very marginalization of the continent may explain the fact that it has not paid serious attention to some of the salient elements in its own demise, but if it is ever to transcend its own underdevelopment, appreciation of transformations in the global political economy may be especially helpful.[14] Indeed, if outdated, "realist" assumptions are discarded, then the continent's presumed peripheralization may turn out to be something of a myth or overstatement. In particular, its stereotyping by Robert Kaplan may be readily exposed: Is it not so much the "coming anarchy" or conflict but the coming democracy and/or corporatism?[15]

Continental Features

Thus, any "new" approaches to foreign policy in Africa should at least begin to treat the following central contextual features, as, happily, some of the preceding chapters do:

1. *the transformed global system,* if not a "new world order," particularly the proliferation of states, especially in regions of the former Soviet Union such as the Baltic and Turkic states but also including Eritrea and Somaliland in Eastern Africa (see Clapham's Chapter 5);
2. *the transformed states,* especially in regard to state-economy/state-society relations in both North and South given ten to fifteen years of neoliberalism in ideology and praxis, with profound im-

plications for civil society, class, ethnicity, gender, religion, and so forth;

3. *the transformed capitalisms,* now centered upon the Pacific as well as the Atlantic Rims, including novel features such as deindustrialization, flexibilization, feminization, service sectors, and post-Fordism, among others;[16]

4. *the changed agendas,* moving away from interstate conflicts to a broad range of multilateral, "functional" issues such as droughts, emergencies, energy, gangs and guns, global warming, migrations, oceans, and ozone depletion;

5. *the novel relations and institutions,* such as transnationalization among civil societies and multinational companies, sometimes leading to "mixed-actor," "tier-two" arrangements; the rise of a diverse range of middle powers, such as the NICs, and the decline of the Fourth and Fifth Worlds; the emergence of G-7, G-15, and G-24, as well as G-77, especially;[17]

6. *the emergence of "new" regionalism,* not just formal intergovernmental economic and/or strategic groupings but also some "informal" or civil society or ecological "communities" that may have rather different boundaries than those established by interstate organizations such as COMESA, ECOWAS, or SADC;[18] finally, together these factors should lead to

7. *new approaches to practice and analysis* to take such changes into account in the making and explaining of foreign policy in the late 1990s.

National Responses

Given the above configurations, we can privilege nine "foreign policy" issues on the continent today that are apparent from this volume's case studies and related analyses. Their order of importance varies over time and between analytic perspectives; that is, distinct regimes, pressures, and approaches would rank them differently:

1. African responses to exponential "interventions," from adjustment conditionalities and peacekeeping to election monitoring and ecological requirements for commodity exports;[19]

2. increasing inequalities both between and within states, exacerbated by structural adjustment conditionalities and pressures of globalization;

3. growing regional tensions over formal interstate cooperation and transnational factors, such as civil society, crime, drugs, ecology, migration, and weapons;

4. exponential attention to civil strife and a related range of peace-keeping/peacemaking/peacebuilding responses in a growing number of instances, from Angola and Mozambique to Liberia and Somalia and now Rwanda, Burundi, and Zaire (see the concluding section of this chapter);[20]

5. continued preoccupation with endless bilateral negotiations over debt and structural adjustment conditionalities with IFIs and donors, plus (I)NGOs, leading to crucial foreign policy roles for national central banks and financial agencies, along with security/intelligence forces (both national and regional, official and private) and NGOs in peacekeeping coalitions;

6. growing foreign policy involvement for African armies, mainly in peacekeeping activities but also in anticrime roles; that is, novel "security" agendas;

7. endless demands for African participation in international conferences and negotiations over a range of "new" global issues, such as children, disarmament, environment, gender, habitat, land mines, social development, trade, oceans, ozone, and population;[21]

8. increasing domestic pressures for participation in "foreign policy" decisions, given democratic processes around political parties, civil society, ethnic and religious groups, national movements, and NGOs encouraged by global transitions and communication (see Chapter 8 by Schraeder); and

9. implications for continental and regional organizations due to an increase in the numbers of members, from newly liberated Namibia and South Africa to newly independent Eritrea and Somaliland.

Happily, many of the preceding chapters and cases contribute relevant, original, and comparative insights to such analyses and debates, with their policy and predictive potentials. We will take them in the order in which they appear in this collection following the editor's most useful conceptual overview (Chapter 1)—that is, alphabetically by country. In Chapter 2, Malaquias examines the external relations of a highly problematic state, Angola, which really has had two parallel regimes and foreign policies since before formal independence. In Chapter 3, Heilbrunn contrasts the microstate of Benin with the relative regional giant Nigeria, a case of external policy essentially being confined to the region of ECOWAS. By contrast, Zaffiro's examination of another ministate, Botswana, offers a nice comparison with the erstwhile Asian (near-?)NICs, along with a treatment of the role of the military. Then, Clapham's chapter on Ethiopia and Eritrea constitutes a welcome comparative analysis of old and new states. In Chapter 6, Rono offers a defensive explication of contemporary Kenya under an increasingly manipulative and repressive Moi regime. By contrast, Wright and Okolo (Chapter 7) are quite harsh in their judgment of Nigeria's successive and largely military regimes, not only in terms of foreign policy but also in terms of economic strategy and human rights record. Schraeder, in Chapter 8, then emphasizes the domestic aspects of Senegal's series of attempts to deal with liberalization and marginalization. In Chapter 9, Bischoff and Southall offer insights into the "new" foreign policy norms and roles of postapartheid South Africa. Nzomo, writing on Tanzania in Chapter 10, treats a range of interrelated issues, including gender, NGOs, SAPs, and regime change. In the last of the case studies, presented in Chapter 11, Nkiwane's perspective on the Mugabe era in Zimbabwe reminds us how foreign policy used to be dominated by one supposedly great man in each African kingdom. And in the final thematic chapter, Babarinde revisits the lackluster interstate record on regionalism.

Before we turn, in conclusion, to suggest possible analytic and diplomatic syntheses as embodied in possible futures, we will make an initial attempt to treat/integrate the burgeoning policies and practices of the wide-ranging peacekeeping nexus in the interrelated contexts of this collection and field.

Peacekeeping Nexus

With the demise of bipolarity and the rise of civil strife, African foreign policies have rapidly had to refocus on a range of peacekeeping crises and responses even if, regrettably, these have featured unevenly in this collection. The continent may be "marginal" in the contemporary global economy, but its impact on state and nonstate policies toward the peacekeeping syndrome is considerable. This nexus extends from preconflict preventative and confidence-building measures through active peacemaking/peacebuilding to postconflict reintegration, reconciliation, and reconstruction, with variable mixes of policies and partners at each stage. As a recent World Bank analysis indicates,

> civil wars have destroyed African lives, skills and assets, undermined institutional competence and accountability, caused incalculable personal dislocation and suffering, and intensified ethnic hostilities. In sum, internal strife has wrought havoc on civil society throughout much of the region. There is now little doubt, from the Horn to the Cape, that development in SSA cannot be sustained without political stability and underlying security.[22]

Any contemporary analysis of this ubiquitous peacekeeping syndrome needs to focus on five overlooked elements: (1) the disaggregation of the peacekeeping syndrome itself, from prevention through active peace-building to reconciliation; (2) the comparative foreign policies of all involved actors, intra- and extracontinental; (3) the examination of "mixed-actor" peacekeeping coalitions at each stage; (4) the focus on implications at the regional level, given characteristic spillover (compare to the treatment of sequential, interrelated Great Lakes crises in the first section above); and (5) the comparison of local and global peacekeeping responses with those over other contemporary foreign policy issues and processes, as outlined above.

Any such analysis should advance the transformation of comparative foreign policy studies in Africa and elsewhere. It would have to incorporate evolving state-economy/state-society relations in several parts of the continent at the end of the century, in particular the salience of civil society/(I)NGOs in the continuously evolving range of peacekeeping activities. "Humanitarian interventions" constitute medium-term responses to "complex emergencies," which are exacerbated by unsatisfactory levels of development. But their sustainability is quite problematic given the continuing evolution in global and strategic contexts. Such emerging mixed-actor coalitions reflect the transformed nature of foreign policy in the direction of human security.

Given redefinitions of security and instability, a nuanced, interdisciplinary perspective on African foreign policy at the end of the millennium should contribute not only to comparative foreign and development policy but also to studies of international organization/law and of human security, as well as embryonic peacekeeping studies.[23] It should juxtapose insights drawn from several fields to illuminate how both state and nonstate foreign policy at the "margins" affects analysis and praxis elsewhere. In short, the imperative of an enhanced understanding of the peacekeeping syndrome is, then, but the latest challenge to come out of Africa.

Future Scenarios

Meanwhile, more formal "futures" studies of the continent have not been overly successful or useful, although the UNDP has been persistent in its current quest.[24] Nevertheless, given the range of novel issues facing Africa as sketched above, particularly the peacekeeping syndrome, some sense of possible directions is necessary, in terms of both policy and praxis. Given the continent's inheritance and intensification of dependence and marginalization, any such previews are in some measure a function of global as well as local and national trends: economic, political, and strategic but also environmental, ideological, and technological.

Given the case studies and comparative analyses in this volume, a trio of alternative futures can be identified: from the more optimistic to the more pessimistic, the more to less self-reliant/sustainable, the more to less pacific. The dominant divergence is between the IFIs' confidence in the efficacy of market forces and African communities' skepticism, even opposition to market economies. The former's persistence with structural adjustment (at least until the late 1990s) has served to transform political economies, along with foreign policies—the "official" *optimistic* preview. The latter's resistance may yet lead toward self-reliance, as even antici-pated or favored by the *Economist* in "Africa for the Africans,"[25] and/or anarchy. The first of these more indigenous proposals is somewhat *idealis-tic*, given pressures toward globalization. By contrast, the second is decid-edly *pessimistic* or, some would argue, brutally *realistic*. Both would al-most certainly lead toward a revival of "ethnic," religious, and other identities, which in turn might lead to novel constitutional and confi-dence-building arrangements, possibly escalating to peacekeeping/ peacemaking, as sketched in the preceding section.

In addition to these "megatrends," two important "meso" prospects can also be abstracted, reflective of the New International Division of La-bor and New International Division of Power and fifteen years of liberal-izations. Such middle-level *mixed scenarios* would include (1) a range of authoritarian and corporatist responses, particularly from beleaguered regimes, and (2) several "new regionalisms," such as civil society or infor-mal sector-based regional institutions and/or regional hegemons no longer constrained by great power alignments or restrictions, possibly us-ing the cover of "new interventionisms" or peacekeeping/peacebuilding. We would label the first of these two mixed scenarios fairly realistic and the second set somewhat idealistic; both are preferable to the alternative, somewhat stereotypical pessimistic possibilities.

In reality, of course, as the continent anticipates the next century, some mix or sequence of these rather ideal-type scenarios is likely to come to pass. Moreover, some regions may be closer to the idealistic pole (South-ern Africa?) and others toward the more pessimistic (Central and possibly West Africa). Given their continuing, albeit "new," "security" salience, both North and Eastern Africa may expect to experience more realistic conditions. Such divergencies, reinforced by ethnic and religious divi-sions, may further undermine any prospects for continental economic and/or political cooperation in the new millennium despite global pres-sures, including those from Africa's diasporas throughout the North At-lantic area.

Finally, then, as in the nationalist/independence era of the 1960s, African studies contain lessons for the world, especially in terms of "new" foreign policy issues of human security/humanitarian interven-tions. The widespread assumption that the continent is marginal—that is, unimportant and/or uninteresting—could not be further from the truth.

Rather, research on and in today's periphery can illuminate emerging issues for comparative studies of the foreign policy of both state and nonstate actors and in the North as well as the South. In short, for reasons of both causality and efficacy, African foreign policy needs to be brought back into several interrelated fields as the new millennium approaches.

NOTES

1. See Amitav Acharya and Larry A. Swatuk, *Reordering the Periphery: The Third World and North-South Relations After the Cold War* (London: Macmillan, 1998), and Larry A. Swatuk and Timothy M. Shaw (eds.), *The South at the End of the Twentieth Century: Rethinking the Political Economy of Foreign Policy in Africa, Asia, the Caribbean and Latin America* (London: Macmillan, 1994).

2. Ralph I. Onwuka and Timothy M. Shaw (eds.), *Africa in World Politics: Into the 1990s* (London: Macmillan, 1989); Timothy M. Shaw and Olajide Aluko (eds.), *The Political Economy of African Foreign Policies: Comparative Analysis* (Aldershot, England: Gower, 1984); and Timothy M. Shaw, *Reformism and Revisionism in Africa's Political Economy in the 1990s: Beyond Structural Adjustment* (London: Macmillan, 1993).

3. Julius E. Nyang'oro and Timothy M. Shaw (eds.), *Beyond Structural Adjustment in Africa: The Political Economy of Sustainable and Democratic Development* (New York: Praeger, 1992).

4. Jakkie Cilliers and Greg Mills (eds.), *Peacekeeping in Africa*, Vol. 2 (South Africa: IDP and SAIIA); Mark Shaw, "The Future of Peacekeeping in Africa," *African Security Review*, 4(1), 1995, pp. 28–30; and Timothy M. Shaw, "Beyond Post-Conflict Peacebuilding: What Links to Sustainable Development and Human Security?" *International Peacekeeping*, 3(2), Summer 1996, pp. 36–48.

5. David A. Baldwin, "The Concept of Security," *Review of International Studies*, 23(1), January 1997, pp. 5–26.

6. UNDP, *Human Development Report 1994* (New York: Oxford University Press, 1994).

7. Timothy M. Shaw and Clement Adibe, "Africa and Global Development in the Twenty-First Century," *International Journal*, 45(1), Winter 1995–1996, pp. 1–26; see also David R. Smock (ed.), *Making War and Waging Peace: Foreign Intervention in Africa* (Washington, D.C.: U.S. Institute of Peace Press, 1993).

8. Jeffrey Herbst, "Responding to State Failure in Africa," *International Security*, 21(3), Winter 1996–1997, pp. 120–144, and I. William Zartman (ed.), *Collapsed States: The Disintegration and Restoration of Legitimate Authority* (Boulder: Lynne Rienner, 1995).

9. See the miniseries on "new regionalism" ex-UNU/WIDER (United Nations University/World Institute for Development Economics Research) coedited by Bjorn Hettne, Osvaldo Sunkel, and Andras Inotai (London: Macmillan, 1998–); see also Larry A. Swatuk and David R. Black (eds.), *Bridging the Rift: The New South Africa in Africa* (Boulder: Westview Press, 1997).

10. Timothy M. Shaw, "Africa in the Global Political Economy at the End of the Millennium: What Implications for Politics and Policies?" *Africa Today*, 42(4), Fourth Quarter, pp. 7–30.

11. James H. Mittelman (ed.), *Globalization: Critical Reflections* (Boulder: Lynne Rienner, 1997), chap. 9.

12. Michael T. Klare, "The New Arms Race: Light Weapons and International Security," *Current History*, 96(609), April 1997, pp. 173–179; Ivelaw L. Griffith, "From Cold War Geopolitics to Post–Cold War Geonarcotics," *International Journal*, 49(1), Winter 1993–1994, pp. 1–36; and Andrew Latham, "Light Weapons and International Security: A Canadian Perspective," YCISS Occasional Paper, York University, Toronto, August 1996, chap. 41.

13. Michael Barratt Brown, *Africa's Choices: After Thirty Years of the World Bank* (Harmondsworth, England: Penguin, 1995), and UNRISD, *States of Disarray: The Social Effects of Globalization* (Geneva: United Nations, 1995).

14. Timothy M. Shaw and E. John Inegbedion, "The Marginalization of Africa in the New World (Dis)Order," in Richard Stubbs and Geoffrey R.D. Underhill (eds.), *Political Economy and the Changing Global Order* (Toronto: McClelland and Stewart, 1994), pp. 390–403.

15. Robert D. Kaplan, "The Coming Anarchy," *Atlantic Monthly*, 273(2), February 1994, pp. 44–75.

16. Stubbs and Underhill, *Political Economy and the Changing Global Order*; and Phyllis Bennis and Michael Moushabeck (eds.), *Altered States: A Reader in the New World Order* (New York: Olive Branch Press, 1993).

17. Acharya and Swatuk, *Reordering the Periphery*, and Swatuk and Shaw (eds.), *The South at the End of the Twentieth Century*.

18. Bjorn Hettne, Osvaldo Sunkel, and Andras Inotai (eds.), *Globalism and the New Regionalism* (London: Macmillan, 1998, for UNU/WIDER).

19. Stephen John Stedman, "The New Interventionists," *Foreign Affairs*, 72(1), January-February 1993, pp. 1–16, and "Alchemy for a New World Order: Overselling 'Preventive' Diplomacy," *Foreign Affairs*, 74(3), May-June 1995, pp. 14–20.

20. David R. Black and Susan J. Rolston (eds.), *Peacemaking and Preventive Diplomacy in the New World (Dis)Order* (Halifax: Centre for Foreign Policy Studies, 1995), and Jeremy Ginifer (ed.), *Beyond the Emergency: Development Within UN Peace Missions* (London: Frank Cass, 1997); see also Smock (ed.), *Making War and Waging Peace*.

21. See UNRISD, *States of Disarray*.

22. Nat J. Colletta et al., *The Transition from War to Peace in Sub-Saharan Africa* (Washington, D.C.: World Bank, 1996), p. 72.

23. Baldwin, "The Concept of Security;" Klare, "The New Arms Race."

24. UNDP, *African Futures: National Long-Term Perspective Studies* (Abidjan: UNDP, 1993).

25. *The Economist*, Special Survey on sub-Saharan Africa, 7 September 1996.

About the Editor and Contributors

Olufemi A. Babarinde is assistant professor of international studies at Thunderbird, American Graduate School of International Management, Arizona.

Paul-Henri Bischoff is a senior lecturer in the International Studies Unit of the Department of Political Science at Rhodes University, South Africa.

Christopher Clapham is professor of politics and international relations at Lancaster University, England, and editor of the *Journal of Modern African Studies*.

Nefertiti Gaye is a graduate student in politics at Cheikh Anta Diop University, Senegal.

John R. Heilbrunn is a research fellow at the Center for International Development and Conflict Management at the University of Maryland, College Park, and a consultant to the World Bank.

Assis Malaquias is assistant professor of government at St. Lawrence University in Canton, New York.

Solomon M. Nkiwane is professor of international relations at the University of Zimbabwe.

Julius E. Nyang'oro is associate professor and head of African studies at the University of North Carolina, Chapel Hill.

Maria Nzomo is a lecturer at the Institute of Diplomacy and International Studies at the University of Nairobi, Kenya.

Julius Emeka Okolo is professor of political science and dean of the Post-Graduate School at Usmanu Danfodiyo University, Sokoto, Nigeria.

Jona Rono is a lecturer in government at Moi University, Kenya.

Peter J. Schraeder is associate professor of political science at Loyola University, Chicago.

Timothy M. Shaw is professor of political science at Dalhousie University, Canada.

Roger Southall is professor of political science at Rhodes University, South Africa.

Stephen Wright is professor of political science at Northern Arizona University.

James Zaffiro is professor of political science at Central College, Pella, Iowa.

Index